Acknowledgements

*Tom and I would like to acknowledge the assistance
of the following wonderful people:*

*Fred Harman, Jr. of the Fred Harman Art Museum
for the use of the original
Fred Harman "Bronc Peeler" comic art panels;
John Milliken for the original verse,
"It Is Young Men;"
Jasmine Gnecco and Erna Jenkins for
helping with the transcriptions;
Janise Owens for keeping
Tom organized and on task;
all of the friends and family members who helped
with ideas, editing and the gathering of
photos and other memorabilia;
Justin Fisher for designing the forgottentrails.com web site
and book cover; and Kate Riordan for pulling everything
together with editing, formatting, graphics,
and printing arrangements.*

Thank you all so much.

— Karen D. Fisher

D1603403

Table of Contents

Foreword

Even from a distance his body language told me he was nervous. As I approached the cafe terrace, I wondered just how this meeting was going to unfold. But I knew from the start that this project would be different, that this man was different, that his stories were different, that my approach would have to be different.

He was definitely on edge on this warm August evening in the Sierra foothills of Northern California. This first meeting had been arranged so we could discuss the oral history process and set up a mutually convenient schedule for interviews. After exchanging friendly greetings and a few quick gulps of a cold drink, I told Tom it was evident there was a problem and for him to get it right out on the table.

His speech was halting, hesitant. Tom was sizing me up, too, wanting to explain but not sure if he should, or of how much he should reveal to me — an acquaintance, an unknown entity. My impression was that this man barely trusted anyone or maybe no one at all, and that was the way he wanted to keep it. I could see a conflict taking place, so I patiently let him work through the explanation of his concerns.

"Young lady, you have no idea what you're getting into here."

"Tell me what you mean by that, Tom." My words were soft and clear.

"For fifty years I've kept some things hidden and I'm not sure they should be written down in a book." He stopped. I waited.

"When I was young, I led a harsh life and I did some harsh things to survive. I had to defend my person, and some men lost their lives."

There. He had said it out loud, up front.

"That could be a problem, yes," my voice still calm, gentle. "So, what do you want to do about it?"

"There's some reason I need to get everything down and out. Could be my age, could be to clear out some worries I've kept inside for a long time. Don't really know exactly, but it all needs to come out. The sooner the better."

Keeping most of my thoughts to myself, I said, "It's your call, Tom. I'm here to help you get the story out if that's what you want. We'll do the research, we'll take our time, and we'll work this out as friends. Deal?"

Relieved, he eased back in his chair. The first step had been taken, marking the beginning of a relationship between a master story teller and a trusted listener.

The following pages contain the personal stories of a young Tom Fisk, created from his memories and words. I acted as a facilitator: interviewing, recording, and then gently massaging his words into a written narrative. Every effort was made to stay true to the words, language and expressions of the story teller. Tom's terminology and grammar are indicative of the life experiences he described. Through these stories, Tom has created an early self-portrait colored by his experiences in the Southwestern United States in the 1940s and '50s. To read them is to encounter the depth and drama of a young boy's life in *his* Old West.

As a youngster, Tom was on his own in the tough world of feuding ranchers and abusive ruffians, living among harsh natural elements. Struggling from day to day, he had many remarkable, tragic, and at times comical, experiences. He came of age in a world that had not yet transformed into the highly regulated, fast-paced environment in which we live today.

This is a memory book of personal experiences memorialized by photographs, museum articles, and dusty old artifacts found in barns that had been kept for decades awaiting Tom's reappearance. It tells a story about the formation of a man, his psychological makeup, and the foundation of his value system. This portrayal of a young boy thrust into manhood propels the reader through a thought-provoking, entertaining journey.   Ŧ

— Karen D. Fisher

It is young men

Who light the fuse,

Who follow fate's decree

With everything to lose;

It is young men

Who ride into the night,

To quench the thirst

For purpose and a friendly light.

— John Milliken

Becoming a Young Man at an Early Age

CHAPTER 1

Growin' Up
On My Own

Life in the Depression years wasn't easy for anyone, and havin' a child with asthma made it even more difficult for my parents. I was just a little kid, but I thought my father was just about the smartest man I could ever know. He helped co-found the Sperry Gyroscope Company and created sixteen patented inventions. I wish I could've grown up knowin' him.

When I was around nine years old, the doctors told my parents that if I didn't get to a warmer and drier climate I would die within two weeks. In a desperate act to save my life, my mother left my father in New Jersey where we lived and she and I headed out for Arizona.

My mother left me for the first time two days before my tenth birthday. From that time forward, I was pretty much on my own. I went from odd job to odd job, workin' on different ranches throughout Southern Arizona. This was partly to avoid bein' put in an orphanage. I went on like this for the next ten years.

From time to time my mother would show up and try to establish a relationship with me. I was usually doin' the best I could to make it on my own. One time I really thought she was planning to stay. This was when I was still pretty young. I'd just had my eleventh birthday. She'd been gone for eight or nine months runnin' with the rodeo cowboys, and they moved around quite a bit. There were usually two types of rodeo cowboys. One type was serious about competing and enjoyed what they were doing. Some of them were good at it. They weren't into drugs, but they occasionally dipped into the alcohol during a good dance and a good rodeo. This was their way of life.

There were others who followed the rodeo and entered the competitions if they thought they might have a chance to win somethin'. They never really practiced like the real professionals. They just hauled their horses around and tried to pay their bills with their winnings. I didn't think of them as the real rodeo crowd, but they were certainly a part of it.

My mother ran with those people who hung around the rodeos, mostly drinking. She was an alcoholic. When she'd leave, I never knew if I would ever see her again. Sometimes I was sure that she wouldn't show up again, and then sure enough she would. Somehow she'd find out I'd gotten a job on a ranch, or I'd write to her and she'd come and pick me up.

One time we headed to Tucson. She said we were gonna stay there a little while. Our place was on a street called Indio. There were several cowboys keepin' their horses around there and they'd come and go. They were my mother's friends, and she had lady friends who dated them. I could tell I was in the way, 'cause in order to go someplace she always had to make arrangements for me. Those cowboys didn't care for having me around. I knew they weren't the cream of the crop, and I didn't like them much either! They were standin' in the way between me and my mother.

It was not uncommon, when my mother was gone, for me and those cowboys to get in an argument. One of 'em would pull off his belt and whip me 'til the blood ran. There were times when I'd be whipped with a quirt with my hands tied to the side of a horse trailer. A quirt is a piece of rawhide that's normally used to whip a horse to make him go. In horse racing it's called a racing bat, but the cowboys call it a quirt. It's just a small version of a whip. It can take the hide off of you if it's applied right.

I remember several times in Tucson being beaten bad enough so they had to take me to the hospital. But I'd made up my mind to stick it out there with my mom 'cause it looked like we'd be goin' soon anyway. When my mother said she wanted to go to Wyoming to buy a place up there and maybe settle down, I was ready to go. More'n ready.

About that time my hero was Tom Mix, and he was a heck of a cowboy! I'd seen him in the movies doin' all his own stunts and his horse was real intelligent. Tom Mix could ride and rope and handle a six-shooter. He was one of the old western actors who really was a cowboy! I always admired him, and I thought, "Man! To be like him!"

When I learned that Tom Mix was killed in a car accident in 1947, just outside of Coolidge, Arizona, it hit me kinda hard. They even named the wash where he died after him – Tom Mix Wash.

It was at this point in my early life that I decided I had to have another first name. My legal name was Albert, and that didn't do me right among those rowdy cowboys in Arizona. I admired Tom Mix so much I just took his name. It's been Tom ever since.

I often thought about changing it back to Albert for my dad's sake, but it didn't seem right. The old name just didn't seem comfortable, so I stuck with Tom, and that's how my name came to be.

CHAPTER 2

The Trick to Catching Whitefish

My mother and I went up to Wyoming at the right time of the year after the snows had melted. She rented a little cabin right beside the Snake River. I didn't know it was just rented – I thought this was my permanent home. We set up housekeepin' there and it lasted about a week. My mother bought food and things. But soon a woman and her cowboy friend came by, and then a couple of other cowboys with a couple of other women showed up. Then one day they all left to party and I didn't see my mother again for four months.

Well, I set up to bach it by myself in that little old cabin. I spent some time lookin' around and finding out where I was and who else was around. There were some people across the way by the name of Nethercott. They had a small family farm. I wouldn't call it a ranch.

One day I made my way over there, and asked 'em if they needed any help.

"Where'd you come from?" the father asked me.

"Over at that cabin on the river," I told him.

"Did your mother and father rent that cabin?" he asked.

"Yes," I told him.

"Well, what do they do?" he asked.

"They're just business people," I lied.

"Do you go to school?" he asked.

"Not right now, we're on vacation," I lied again.

"Well, maybe I could find some work for you here," he said. "What can you do?"

"A little bit of everything," I said, but I wasn't feelin' too confident.

"How old are you?" he asked.

I was tall and skinny as a rail so I lied again and told him I was thirteen goin' on fourteen, when I was really eleven goin' on twelve.

"Well, all right," he said. "I need somebody to feed the stock and milk the cows in the morning and in the evening, and I'll pay you for your time."

I told him I didn't want the money, but that I wouldn't mind takin' a good meal around supper time each day. I could see he was poor with his own kids to feed. He said that'd be okay, and I thought I had a pretty good deal.

He had several children and I knew that I shouldn't get too close to 'em. Other kids get restless when someone else comes in and their parents show any favoritism. I'd learned that already. I went ahead and worked there for the next few weeks. They treated me fine and we got along pretty good. They were really nice and I was doin' my job right. But these people were poor and they didn't have a lot of money. I knew life was hard enough for 'em. But for me, gettin' that one meal a day was as good as three meals a day. I was livin' off that one meal just fine.

Soon I started fishin' in that Snake River. I didn't have no bait or anything, but I watched these rich fishermen come to the river from these big guest ranches. They'd come down in a wooden boat and they'd fish along the river. Occasionally they'd walk along the banks fishin'. The first decked out fisherman I ever saw was enough to make me panic and run to the hills! He had them rubber wader things on and a huge fishing creel on him. His hat was all decked out with what I thought was a bunch of brush stuck to it, but that turned out to be fishin' flies. He had things hangin' all over his vest in the front of him, and it looked to me like any man with the right sense wouldn't want all those hooks so close to him. I thought he was bound to get hurt by 'em!

Most of these fishermen would only stay there for a week or so, and then they'd be gone. Then there'd be new ones comin' down. I was friendly and found it easy to make friends. I liked talkin' with them. One asked me what I used for bait and I told him worms, and that I did pretty good with them.

"What've you got for a pole?" he asked me.

"I don't have a pole," I told him, "I use a throw line."

"A throw line?" he laughed.

"Yeah," I told him, "I just curl it up and sling it out there and wait for 'em to bite on that while I just hold on to it."

"I got an older pole," he said. "I wouldn't mind lettin' you try it."

I thought that'd be great, but I didn't realize that an old pole to him was somethin' like I'd never seen before. These fishermen were mostly fly fishermen. Some of them would put on what they called a flat fish, and fish for trout.

"You want to try one of these poles?" he asked me. I said sure, so he started showin' me how to use this fly pole. And I got pretty good with that thing. I could put it out there just where I wanted it. Years later, when I went to see the movie "A River Runs Through It," it just took me back to that river, learning how to cast that line way out there. I could put it out there, let it run down river, and then let it drift back up.

I got pretty good at stockin' my kitchen with those fish. They were easy to catch. Every once in a while I'd hook on somethin' and lose my flat fish. I'd try flies for a while and then go back to worms.

I got to talkin' with the owner of this farm where I was workin', and I told him I'd noticed some fish in a canal nearby. He said they were called whitefish and that they were delicious to eat, but nobody could catch 'em. He said they wouldn't bite on anything.

I thought maybe I could teach a whitefish a thing or two. But when I tried to catch one, I couldn't come even close. That fish'd go right down under there where I couldn't see him. These old canals had been there for years to flood-irrigate across the farms. They looked from four to six feet across, and most of 'em ran from two to six feet deep. The water was clear but the banks had eroded underneath so there was kind of a cove under the sides. These whitefish would come up and down that canal and you could look down in there and not see 'em at all! They would stay back against the bank. The minute I looked in they'd just disappear. But I was determined to figure out how to catch these guys.

I thought about it and thought about it. I laid awake two or three times at night. It's an experience when you're that age, livin' alone. The wind would come up and when somethin' moved I wasn't sure what it was. I did have a .22 rifle that I kept real near 'cause I had seen bear tracks up the river close to the base of the mountain.

So I'd just lay there at night and I'd hear things movin'. I'd always wonder if it was a bear after food in the cabin. I tried to make sure everything was always sealed. I didn't have a refrigerator or an ice box, so whatever I caught that day had to be eaten that day anyway.

Then it came to me one night how I was gonna catch those whitefish. I remembered how the cowboys roped cattle. They'd rope it with a lasso, with the long end tied off to the saddle horn, and the other end on the hondo. A hondo is a circular-shaped thing that the rope slides through. As the rope is thrown, the circle gets smaller as it goes around the calf's throat. When the head pulls up, the rope is dallied to the saddle. I thought if cattle could be caught that way, why not catch fish that way?

The next time I was down at the farm I saw an old piece of chicken wire layin' there. I took that wire and unwound about three or four feet of it. Man! It took me forever to do that. I had to go slowly 'cause I didn't want to break it. I needed to make a loop with that wire.

When I got it done, it was coiled with kinks in it. I thought it wasn't gonna work the way it was. I had to do somethin' more. So I sat there and thought about it for a little bit longer. Then I thought about something I'd seen somebody do – I found a log about twelve inches in diameter, layin' there, stickin' out of the ground. I took that wire, put it over the end of that long log and then started pulling on the wire, back and forth. I worked that wire into the most graceful, beautiful, smooth curve I ever saw! The curve was a one- or two-foot curve, and I knew I was on the right track.

Next I found a nice limb that I could tie the wire on to. I made a loop and decided to set out to see if I couldn't change my luck with the whitefish. I made that loop about four or five inches in circumference, then I bent the wire up straight so it would hold the loop in place. But if I pulled on it and something was in it, the loop would tighten down on whatever was inside!

So I went up to the canal and snuck up beside it. I laid there, looked into the water, and didn't see anything, like usual. But after I laid there for a while, I parted the grass so I could barely see the water, and sure enough, here come a whitefish. It weighed anywhere from five to eight pounds and was about eighteen to twenty-six inches long!

I took my wire and dropped it in there. I let it go down there where I couldn't see a thing. But he saw it and I musta hit him in the nose with it or somethin', 'cause he departed. The water in the canal was goin' so strong the loop wouldn't stand still. I kept practicin' with this thing and finally figured out how to do it. I put it all the way down just before he got there. Then I'd pick it up off the bottom and let it float.

Well, I tell you! The first time I'd grabbed one, I let it go right over his head, pulled up on it, and I knew I had him. He knew I had him, too, but he took off. Me and the pole went right into the canal! It was only about waist deep so I fought him and finally got him out of there. I was so excited I went home that evening with three of those whitefish on a string. When I showed the farmer he was shocked. He said nobody'd been able to do that and he said I had enough to feed the whole family that night! He asked me how I did it but I didn't want to tell him quite yet. I just told him I figured out a way. He sure was appreciative of the fish.   ☥

CHAPTER 3

Fighting Back

While fishing at the river I met this really nice fisherman who'd come up from Cleveland or Detroit. He admired my fishing pole and I explained about the fisherman who gave it to me. He told me I seemed to be pretty good with it and how I was out-fishin' all of them. He said that he'd heard talk about me at the dude ranch where he was vacationing.

I was pretty proud when he asked me to show him how I was doin' it. I was thinkin' that this was a guy who was probably worth a couple of million dollars and I was showin' him how to catch fish. I never did show anyone how I caught whitefish though. That was my secret and I kept it to myself!

Well, after two days of fishin' with this dude, he told me about their Saturday night feed and party. There was gonna be a dance and everything. He invited me to come up and get myself some good food at their big western barbecue. I thought it sounded great to me and I already knew how to get there. It was a well known guest ranch where rich people came to vacation, fish and pretend they were cowboys. He said he'd see me there on Saturday, which was the next day.

I made arrangements at the farm and told 'em that I'd been invited to go up to the guest ranch. On Saturday I went up and it was quite a sight to me! They had a western band playin' and everyone was dressed up like dudes. They had their pant legs tucked into their boots, big loud-colored shirts and some of 'em were wearin' spurs. But I don't think many of 'em had ever been on a horse. They had big hats that kept fallin' down in their faces while they were dancin'. But they were havin' a great time.

I stayed off to the side for the most part but I did manage to get my share of the food! I even asked the cook, who was an old half-Indian feller, to save some of the leftovers in a bag for me. I told him I'd take it home and eat it the next day. So he fixed me up some.

As the night came on, it started to get stormy, which was pretty typical for that country about that time of year. When the rain swept across there it got things pretty muddy. But I stayed on and watched them party and dance. Then it got real late and I started to head home.

This old boy that I knew from fishin' the river asked me if I wanted to stay over at the ranch. He said nobody'd mind if I stayed. They all knew who I was and where I was from. I wasn't lookin' forward to goin' home in the rain, and nobody was waitin' up for me, so I said I'd stay. He showed me the bunkhouse where I could sleep and told me he was stayin' up at the ranch house. This was a dude bunkhouse and there were about three dudes stayin' in there. A dude is just another name for a guest. I didn't know any of 'em. But I found myself some blankets and a place to put up to sleep and bedded down about eleven o'clock. I never had a watch, and I was always pretty alert when I was sleeping 'cause I'd been around a cow camp a little bit. You never know if your horse might step on you when you're bedded down outside.

Around midnight or maybe even later, all of a sudden, I felt somebody on top of me. Someone had his hand over my mouth, and he was tellin' me not to say anything! I first thought that maybe a bear had broken in and someone was tryin' to keep me from hollerin' and spookin' the bear. But I quickly caught on that a bear wasn't the problem.

Now, no one had ever sat down and explained to me what a homo-sexual was. I probably wouldn't have understood anyway. I'd never heard any-thing about that kind of thing. I had no idea that there were people like that. But I knew that what this dude was trying to do to me wasn't normal, and it definitely wasn't right by me. He was holdin' me down, and pullin' at my clothes, 'cause I was sleepin' in my clothes. I got kinda panicky and bit his hand. And then he hit me and bloodied my eye and my nose, and cut me right above my hairline. I haven't thought about that cut for fifty, sixty years. The scar is still in my hairline.

I could feel the blood runnin' down my face. I forced him off some-how, jumped up, and pushed him back. Then I ran out the door. It had quit rainin' but they had taken twelve-inch-wide planks, about eight to ten feet long, and laid them between the buildings so people didn't get their feet all wet and muddy.

I was runnin' on these planks but I didn't know where I was goin', I was just runnin'. There was enough light from the moon so I could see these planks. I just ran from one building to the other, lookin' for an open door. When I found one I went inside and it was pitch black in there. I couldn't see nothin'. Then I turned toward the door and I could see the moonlight stream-ing through the planks. I looked all around me. I could see the door but I couldn't tell where I was. I had no idea. I reached over and felt a barrel, so I ran around to the side of it and hid behind it.

Then I heard him outside, quietly calling me.

"Kid," he whispered, "come here. I wanna talk to you, kid."

By then I couldn't see out of one eye because blood was runnin' in it. I remember it runnin' down into my mouth. I had learned not to cry, and to this day I don't cry. I can be beat but I won't ever cry. When I was younger, in Tucson, fightin' with those cowboys that mother ran with, they would beat me worse if I cried. So I learned not to cry. That left scars on me, not only external but internal, for the rest of my life.

So as I was hidin' behind that barrel, I wasn't crying, but I was so scared that my teeth were chattering. I raised up, looked above the barrel and I saw a shadow go across the door. But he didn't come through the door. As I was lookin' at the door, I felt something in the barrel. I reached in and picked up an ax handle. I thought maybe I could protect myself with it.

Then he came through that door. I'll never forget him standing there and saying, "Kid, where are you?"

He sure as hell filled that doorway with the light makin' him a huge silhouette. He took a step inside, struck a match, and held it up. I was still behind the barrel squeezin' that ax handle tight. He waited, and he looked, and he talked.

"Kid, there's no reason for you to run," he said calmly. "No one's gonna know about this. I'm not tellin' anyone and neither are you."

Then I remember he cursed when the match went out. I could hear him tryin' to get another match. So I raised up and hit him in the head as hard as I could with the ax handle.

Down he went. But he got back up! So I hit him again. I think maybe I hit him three or four times as hard as I could. Then I jumped over him, threw the ax handle down, and ran back to the bunkhouse to get my shoes. One of the guys in there woke up and asked me what was wrong. I told him what happened.

"That son of a bitch!" he said. "He's done it again!"

Apparently they knew him, and knew what he'd done. When they went out, I grabbed my shoes, and ran all the way home to my cabin. I didn't go out of the house for two or three days. Then my farmer neighbor came lookin' for me. He'd been worried about me when I didn't show up to work. I hadn't eaten or done anything since I got back. When he came in, he saw I was startled and had grabbed a board to protect myself.

"You're not gonna hit me with that, are ya?" he asked calmly.

"No," I said, "I just thought maybe it was him comin' back to get me."

"No," he said, "he won't be hittin' ya or hurtin' ya again. But there's some fellas wanna talk to you over at my place."

I had no idea who those fellas were but I put on some clean clothes and went with him.

When we got there, one of the men asked me, "What are you afraid of?"

"There's a man chasin' me," I told him.

"No," he said, "he won't chase you anymore."

I didn't really know enough to ask why. I saw the '39, two-door police car with a big silver star on the door and a spotlight on the side. The man by the car asked me what my name was, and where my parents were.

"How long they been gone?" he asked me.

"I don't know," I answered, "I keep track on the wall of the cabin. Whenever a day goes by, I put a mark on the back of the door, and I know it's been a while."

"A week?" he asked.

"Longer than that," I said, "I haven't seen 'em for about three months, maybe four."

"Well, we're gonna have to take you into town," he said.

"I don't want to do that," I told him firmly.

Then the farmer talked to the man and said he'd take care of it. He told them not to take me into town. I can remember talkin' to the policemen, but I can't remember what else was said. The two men who came in the police car had city slicker hats on with the little crowns in the front. They had pistols on their sides, and badges. I knew they were the law. To this day, I don't remember much of what was said. I do remember just before they left one of 'em came over, gave me a hug, and told me I was gonna be just fine. I told him I'd had a problem a couple of nights before. "Well," he said, "you don't have a problem anymore. Just forget about it."

I know bein' as young as I was, as scared as I was, and alone as I was, it must have had a big impact on how I approached things as I grew up. Like not really trustin' people or dependin' on 'em too much. ⅉ

CHAPTER 4

Hazards of Being
A Powder Monkey

Back in Arizona I got an opportunity to get a job workin' in the mines up in the Dragoon Mountains. These mines had horizontal shafts, not vertical shafts, and they went way back in the mountain. They were usually worked by five to eight men mining scheelite tungsten. Scheelite tungsten is a metallic element used for hardening steel. This one company had two mines with several claims to explore the veins and pull the tungsten out.

Well, I had learned from working with ranchers that in some places the earth was too hard to get through with just a pick and a shovel. I had watched them use a star drill. Now a star drill is a long metal rod with a hole through the center and a star bit on the end. They would hold the star drill in the left hand and a single jack in the right hand. A single jack is a one- to three-pound sledge hammer. A double jack is the one that takes both hands to use, like to pound railroad spikes in the railroad track.

I learned to use the star drill – hit, turn, hit, turn, hit, turn. This would drill into the side of a rock making a deep hole. Then I'd take a stick of dynamite and stick it inside the hole. We usually used a quarter percent nitro stick with a slow burning fuse on it. I'd take the cap and put it in there taped on to the stick. Then I'd take some mud or clay or dirt and fill the hole in behind it. I'd light that fuse and, if it worked right, it would blow that ledge out of the way. Then the men would clean the mess out of the way and move further in through the hole. We didn't have any backhoes or modern machinery like now.

They asked me if I had some dynamite experience, and I told them that I had some on the ranches. I was just a kid about thirteen, going on fourteen years old, when I took this job. When they asked how good I was with the dynamite, I told them I was still walking, wasn't I?

The boss told me they were shooting this one mine twice a day using half sticks, single sticks and sometimes they'd double stick. He asked me to work for a couple of days to see how I'd do.

I was just a cocky kid who thought he knew what he was doing and who didn't really give a damn about the rest of them guys. You'd think they'd be a little worried. I'd stick three or four of those sticks in each pocket and walk around with the caps in my Levi pocket on the left, and the fuse draped around my neck! They called young boys like me who were working the mines Powder Monkeys.

I found out later that they regularly hired young boys who weren't married, didn't have any parents and didn't have any children. At the time I didn't realize they liked me because I was dispensable. If I got blown up there'd be no problem. They didn't have to settle with anybody, and nobody would come lookin'. Whatever they had left of me would go in a box down a hole and that'd be it.

But I was good at the job. I gained the respect of the older men but not their friendship. The old timers taught me to take the cap that fits snug over the fuse and put it in my mouth and crimp it between my teeth. Most of the men at these mines could not handle that. They couldn't figure out why my head hadn't blown off. But I kept crimpin' those caps and carryin' those things around with me. Come lunch time I'd always eat by myself 'cause they wouldn't eat with me. I just thought it was smarter not to leave 'em layin' around where somebody could drop a hammer on 'em or something like that. I guess I was really a walkin' time bomb around there.

I worked up there on and off for about six months. And I did real well and got kind of a reputation for being able to handle dynamite like that. Normally, two or three miners would be turning the core with the hammers, so I didn't have to do any of that. I'd just stand by and they'd tell me to stay back while they would drill the hole! Then they'd let me know when it was my turn to come in. They sure didn't want me in there with them. So I'd go out and sit on the tailing pile and I'd wait for 'em to holler. When I got in there, I would pack in the sticks with the mud and dirt mix. Then I'd set the slow burning fuse.

I never had any close calls, except one instance. There was an older man with a smart mouth, a bad mouth. He had a way of cussin' on me and tellin' me I was gonna get it some day. He thought I took too many chances. Well, one day I found him in the mine sittin' down there eatin' his lunch. So I just casually stuck a fuse in a hole in the wall as he was settin' there.

"Kid, what are you doin' in here?" he asked.

"Just checkin' the hole," I told him.

"There's a couple of 'em started but they're not done," he snarled.

"I'm just lookin' at 'em," I went on. "You enjoying your lunch?"

"Yep," he said.

"Okay," I said.

He was just about two feet away from where they'd been drilling the hole sittin' with his back to the wall, eatin' this sandwich with his head down, not paying much attention. His carbide light was sittin' over by him. A carbide light is a little brass container that you can attach to your cap. You put in some carbide chips with water, and it forms acetylene gas. The gas goes up through a little neck and out a little orifice on the front of the helmet and a reflector puts out the light used by the miners to work the mines.

So he'd taken off his carbide light, and he was sittin' down there with it. I told him it was pretty dark in there and asked to borrow his light. This old boy had been riding me pretty bad and I'd even complained to the foreman one time. The foreman just told me to whip him at something. So I figured somethin' out.

"Do you mind if I borrow your light?" I asked again.

"Kid, I don't want to give you nothin'!" he said. "You ain't worth nothin'! And what do you want to do with the light anyway?"

"I just want to look at these holes," I said.

"Well, look and give the light back – and do it now!" he said.

While I had the light, I slipped about a foot and a half of fast fuse in that hole while he wasn't lookin'. Then I reached over the light, lit the fuse, and said, "This one belongs to you," and out of that mine shaft I went running as fast as I could.

I heard him screamin' and hollerin' and I knew it was pitch black in there 'cause I took his light. He was banging into the walls falling down two or three times, and I don't know where his lunch went. When he finally came out, he tripped over two or three things, and then I lit out! I knew he was gonna kill me. All the guys in camp found out what I'd done and they sat down and laughed so hard.

"If that kid ever comes back, I'm gonna kill him!" he wailed. "Look at me! I'm bleeding in four or five places, and I pert near tore my ear off on the side of the shaft where I hit a rock ledge! Damn that kid! I can't believe he did that to me!"

The guys laughed and laughed. It seemed like they told that story and joked about it all around that country for ten years; how that Powder Monkey kid had taken that old man to task. Later I found out that, in the mine, that old man looked over and saw that fuse burning. He knew there was nothin' left but three inches of fuse on that cuttin'! He just started crawling on his hands and knees 'cause if he stood up he'd have torn his head off. He was down on all fours like a rock cart, followin' the rail as fast as he could.

Well, I didn't go back the next day. But the following day I showed up and I was kind of afraid of the man. The foreman said he wasn't gonna bother me 'cause the guys'd been razzin' him so bad he couldn't see straight. He told me to just stay away from him, and he'd see to it that he didn't dog me. The foreman thought I'd done pretty good and we had a good laugh about it.

CHAPTER 5

Shootout in Pecos

A lot of Arizona country is kinda flat with mesquites and rollin' hills, buildin' up a little higher in the mountains as you go further along the border toward Texas, to towns like Fort Davis, Martha, Alpine, Balmoreah and Pecos. One time I had a chance to go into Pecos, Texas. This was the first time I saw a gunfight battle between two ranchers. A fella at the place where I was workin' in Balmoreah offered to take me in to Pecos for an honest-to-goodness ice cream cone. I couldn't remember ever having one, and he said he'd buy me a big one. He said they had the best ice cream around. He knew I was gettin' ready to move on, and he wanted to help me celebrate pullin' out.

I'll never forget Pecos. It looked about like I imagined it did seventy-five years before I was there. It still had the wooden boardwalks in front of the old false store fronts. The road was still a dirt road and a bunch of old-type cars were parked there. The ranchers would come and go for supplies and feed enough to last them a month or two.

I had just gone in this candy store to get my ice cream cone, and it was the best smellin' place that I'd ever smelled in my life! The aroma just kind of reached out and grabbed me around the nose and ears. It just kind of said, "Tom, come with me. I'm gonna show you somethin' you never knew existed."

I enjoyed myself in there and got this great big chocolate ice cream cone. It was in kind of a funny lookin' holder, and I didn't know whether I was supposed to eat it or not. But I started into the ice cream all right. While I was holdin' and lickin' that ice cream, we went out and started walking down the walkway underneath the overhang of the old-type buildings. There were hitchin' rails on the right-hand side as I walked along, and there was a horse or two tied, but mostly cars.

We got up there a little ways when we heard somebody holler. We stopped and the man that was with me was thinkin' someone was hollerin' at him. But then somebody hollered back from the other way! Then a car pulled up no more than maybe fifty feet from us, and a guy jumped out and walked into the saloon right in front of us. The dirt and dust was followin' this man across the boardwalk.

I remember I didn't want to get my ice cream in that dust, so I stepped off the walkway, started to go around, and the guy walked back out of the saloon carryin' a 30/30 Winchester.

By then I was standin' between that guy's car, with him leanin' over the hood with that Winchester, and somebody behind me, hollerin'. About that time, the guy with me ran and shoved me down. My ice cream hit me just about in the middle of my chest. And there I was layin' in the dirt with my hand in my ice cream and my face in the dirt, and I wasn't sure what was happening 'til the first shot went off.

I heard later that these two had gotten in a fight over a beautiful Mexican girl. I never saw the girl but I did know one of the men. I'd seen him before. His name was Herb Trotter. I'll never forget that name. As I looked up, I saw that Winchester buck up out of his hands, smoke comin' out of the barrel, and then bullets were going right over the top of me. I just laid still 'cause there was nothin' else to do.

There were a couple of shots, and then somebody hollered, "Damn kid! Get the hell out of there!"

That's all I needed to get me out! I remembered half runnin' on all fours, and then boltin' the best I could, out around the front of that car. Herb Trotter was the one that hollered to get me out of there, and when he was lookin' at me, the other guy shot him. Killed him right on the spot.

Well, that was an experience I never forgot. The guy who shot Herb went over to look at him and then the sheriff came. I don't really remember what happened after that. I don't know if anyone got arrested. But while I was standin' there, this woman walked up to me and she remarked on how I'd lost my ice cream cone.

I said, "No, Ma'am, I got most of it still here on my shirt!" I only had two shirts and this one was my best one, 'cause that's what I usually wore goin' into town.

"Would you like me to wash that shirt for you?" she asked me. "And could I get you another cone?"

"I got money to buy another cone, but if you got a place to wash the shirt, I wouldn't mind that," I said. She said she'd get me another cone, and she seemed to know the man who brought me to town. She arranged with him to take me out to her ranch and wash my shirt. She also bought me another cone. I got into the pickup with her and headed out to her ranch.

The Ranching Life

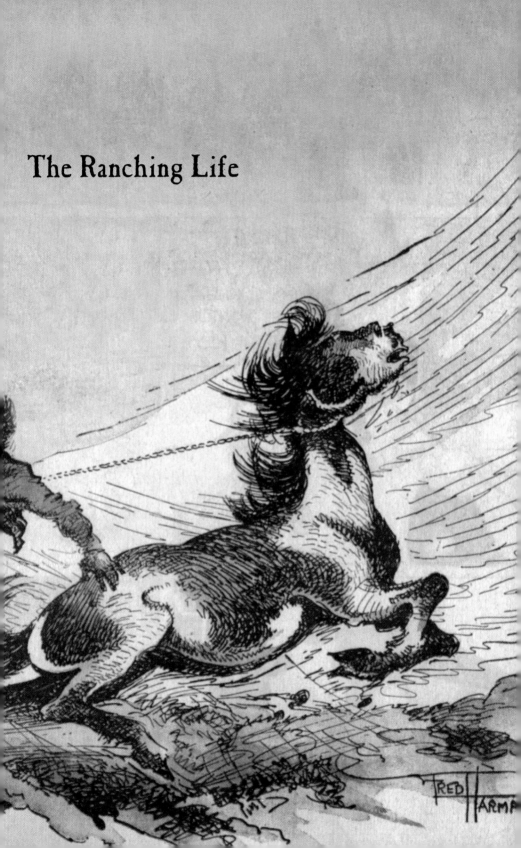

CHAPTER 6

Cowboying on the
Kingston Ranch

I was taken to the Duncan Kingston Ranch out on Cherry Creek. It was nestled right smack in the middle of the Fort Davis Mountains. It was the most beautiful country I'd seen. It had runnin' streams and fresh water pools six to twenty feet deep. Water cascaded down big peaks up there. I could only swim in the summer time 'cause in the winter time it was too cold. I saw bears and lots of deer. It was good ranchin' country down below and they had a summertime ranch high up in the mountains.

I was really impressed the first time I saw their house. It was an old ranch house built in the 1800's and somebody put some good money into it when they built it. The ceilings were eleven feet high. There were carbide lamps on the walls and lots of nice furniture.

Mrs. Kingston was one of the nicest women I'd ever met in my life. Her name was Mary and her husband's name was Duncan. She was somewhere in her forties and was a beautifully sculptured woman. She had a smile that radiated everywhere, and she wore her hair pulled back, tied around with a string. She was the cook and helped manage the ranch.

They had four cowboys working for 'em and they all stayed in the bunkhouse. But they ate in a big room in the ranch house called the downstairs kitchen.

That first day she invited me to stay for supper. I was happy to stay. She said they'd take me back come mornin'. I thought that was fine, too. I had no schedule, and it didn't matter where I slept, as long as I was out of the elements. That first night I was introduced to Texas style homemade preserves. She kept 'em in big fruit jars – peaches, apricots, and apples; you name it, she had it. She opened up a different one every meal and we could have as much as we wanted. She also made the most beautiful biscuits. Of course, they raised beef cattle, so they always had meat at the table. It was a fine place and I kind of liked being there.

Next morning, while we were having breakfast, this beautiful woman asked me where I was headed. I told her I didn't really have a place to go, but I'd been thinkin' about headin' toward New Mexico or back to Arizona. She told me it was about seventeen miles into town from their place. She said if I went back to town, got my gear and came back their way, she'd give me a job. I'd just finished my second plate full of biscuits and gravy, and those preserves, and now an offer of a job!

I told her I'd like a job there. So I went in to town to get my horse, saddle, and my tack, which was my gear, and went back in to the ranch that evenin'. She told me to go down to the bunkhouse where there was plenty of room. I put my horse in the holdin' pen outside so he wouldn't fight with the rest of the horses 'til they got to know one another.

They took me in and I met the rest of the family. They had an older son, about my age, and a young daughter about three years old. She had yeller hair, and wore the prettiest little outfit with an apron. She was a doll and kind of spoiled 'cause they doted over her many an evening.

My job was to keep the livestock up and ride any rank horses that needed toppin' off. There was always a big old cowboy around who would stand and watch for a while, and then come over and tell me a better way of doin' things. I always listened to the old cowboys, but I didn't like listening to the young ones. They seemed to gloat about how long they'd been there and how I'd just hired on.

They usually took a chuck wagon out to where we gathered a big bunch of cattle. It was a big ranch so these rides lasted two or three days. I remember being out workin' the cattle and I had my first chance to see "fast water." I thought that was goin' to be a pretty good experience. I'd never seen it before, and the cowboys'd been tellin' me about it.

When I told one of 'em I was kind of thirsty out there, he asked me if I wanted to go all the way back to the chuck wagon to get a drink. I told him, no, but I didn't see any water around where we were. We were out of the flats and chaparral, down to where the feed was.

Well, he took me to one of these tanks that set in the bottom of an arroyo where a fresno and a team of horses had done up the sides across an inlet so the water would catch and go into the tank. I had seen and worked a fresno before. It's like a large coal shovel with a long, upraised handle on it with about four feet of rope dangling from it. It scoops out dirt and rocks, like a bulldozer today, but it took a team of horses to do it back then. It wasn't easy 'cause if you grabbed that rope wrong, you'd likely end up in the middle of the team of horses – between 'em or under 'em!

So when the rain water would come through that draw, the water would be saved up above. I got off, stretched out, knocked the dirt off of me, took my hat and kind of cleaned it up. That's another thing about a cowboy. He has to look after his hat. You can do just about anything to him, but don't ever mess with his hat! I always made sure my hat was in reasonably good shape.

I was real thirsty but I didn't think this water looked too clean. There was a bunch of little live things floatin' around on top. When I'd get near 'em, they'd scurry off, and when I'd go back, they'd just come back again.

"Is this fast water?" I asked. I had visioned fast water comin' out of a canyon, runnin' low to the rocks, splashin' down and rippling clear and glistening in the sunlight. "That's where I'm gonna get a drink?" I asked him.

"Yep," he says, "come 'ere, waddy, I'll show you where the fast water is." A waddy is what they called a young cowboy.

He got down, took his hat off, laid one elbow down right beside the tank, and leaned over. Then he blew real fast and drank real fast! "That's fast water!" he said while he laughed at me.

That's the way all the sheep and cow manure and those little bugs got blown out of the way. I had to blow and drink before it got back to where I was drinking from. I was really thirsty so I drank fast and then I'd blow, drink and blow again. That was my introduction to fast water.

I wasn't too thrilled with this method of quenchin' my thirst, so to keep my mouth from bein' so dry I reached over and got a pebble as I left and put it in my mouth. That was probably the best way to keep the top part of my mouth from stickin' to the bottom part.

As that day ended, they decided they would have enough time to go back about half way to the ranch. Then they'd finish up at the line shack camp and we'd all go in the next day. When we were ready to head to the line shack, this old cowboy came over to me, complaining about riding this particular horse all day. He said he just made him sore. He was wonderin' if we could trade saddles, or maybe we could just trade horses! I told him I'd be glad to trade horses with him. He sure had a fine lookin' horse! So, he just swung over, smiled, and handed me the reins. I wasn't thinkin' much about it. Everybody was gettin' ready to go, and had their last cup of coffee. The fire was kicked out and covered up, and everybody kind of swung aboard. I was a little late gettin' my gear ready, and I started lookin' around. I noticed there were four or five cowboys just kind of settin' there, fiddlin' with the straps on their saddles, and lookin' at me.

Well, I'd been workin' there for maybe two months and I was being introduced to a horse they called Lettuce. He was a dun goin' down on a grulla. Dun is a kind of a gray color and grulla is a darkish color with a little bit of yellow and orange with brown in it. This horse was these two colors.

The dun was pretty common on a horse, but the grulla was not that common.

The biggest problem they'd been having with Lettuce was ridin' him back home after a day's work. They'd go out and work him, and he was a great cow horse. You'd cut with him, go out and heel with him, and bring calves to fire. But every time, goin' home, somebody'd get on and start ridin' him home and he'd buck 'em off. Nobody bothered to tell me about this problem.

I thought, "Why're they waitin' on me?" I didn't realize exactly what that meant 'til a little later. I climbed up on that cowboy's horse and went about a hundred yards when I noticed him actin' a little different. He just started to balk a little bit. I thought somethin' got underneath his cinch or somethin' like that. So I turned to look down under his cinch and kind of reached back to check, and about the time I reached back, I could see that I could put my hand between him and the saddle! Which ain't normal!

This horse'd been ridden all day, but from that point on, the rodeo was on! He didn't want to be ridden anymore! Well, I stayed on him for the first five or six jumps, and he was sun fishin' and really doin' a pretty good job of buckin'. I was tryin' to stay in time with him by spurrin' up to the shoulders and then goin' back. I knew that was the only way I was gonna stay on. But finally, he broke the rhythm, kind of stopped, and then sun fished back to the left. When he did that, I just rolled off of there and used my nose for an opening wedge across that Texas countryside! I slid to a stop up beside a big rock, and I was sure thinkin' that there had to be a better life than this cowboyin'.

I pulled myself up out of the dirt, and them old boys were just about to die laughin' on their horses.

"Thought you was a bronc rider!" I heard one yell.

"I thought I had a gentle horse!" I told them.

"Nah, he's kind of bad about doin' that on the way home," he said. "We'll give ya a gentle one to ride home."

"No," I said. "I'll ride him again."

So they brought him up to me, I saddled up, and everything went just fine. We rode off, takin' some strays up to the line shack to put in a holdin' pen. But I was watching this horse all the time! That old pony coughed one time, I went back, grabbed that rein, set up there, and put my feet up towards the shoulder! I just knew we were goin' to topple off that canyon somewhere! But he did nothin'! Not a thing! Just kind of snorted, looked back over his shoulder like he was askin' me if I had a problem. I was a nervous wreck the whole evenin'.

Next day, why, when I finished eating, I went out and used the rest room and came back, and wouldn't you know! Everybody was saddled up except Lettuce! Lettuce was still sittin' there!

"This is not my horse!" I said.

"You seemed to get along with 'im real well yesterday afternoon!" one cowboy insisted.

I thought, "That damn thing is gonna buck me off right in the middle of somethin' bad and I'm gonna be hurtin' all day!" But I rode him around anyway. I didn't seem to have much choice. I figured I'd get the knocks out of him this time.

All I could think about was that ground hittin' my face and those reins slappin' me in the face like a black snake whip. So I thought I'd just let him toss around a little bit while those boys were all settin' on their horses watching. One of 'em had his legs swung over the side of the pommel with a smile on his face, just rollin' a cigarette, and lightin' it up.

"Ain't gonna work, cowboy," he said.

"I'm gettin' it out of him if it kills me," I said.

"It ain't gonna work," he insisted.

I reached up, grabbed a hold of the halter, and got a lead rope on him. I figured I didn't want to walk home! If he bucked me off this time I'd try to hold on to that lead rope and pull him in when he came down. Then I reached around and grabbed me a handful of mane with his halter in my left hand. I swung up over there real sweet and snaked into that saddle. I just gradually put my feet forward and leaned back 'cause I knew we were comin' out of there full steam.

I was hopin' I'd make it through the first go and then I'd keep in time with him. Then I'd be all right. If I ever got ahead of him or behind him, timing wise, I'd be lookin' at the saddle while I was hangin' upside down, tied to a horse intent on gettin' rid of me. That's a terrible feeling, and I didn't want to get in that situation. It was too early in the morning. But wouldn't you know, he just rode off just as nice as he could.

All day long I was waitin' for him to do something bad, but by the time I rode in for lunch I was comfortable with him and I just sat around and talked a while. The cook always had the coffee pot on so I plum forgot about old Lettuce. Everybody was talking about everything. Then I got ready to saddle up and go home. I took the saddle off, put him out, rubbed his back down and checked for anything that would cause a problem on him.

Then I saddled him up and climbed on. And I hadn't gone another hundred yards when all hell broke loose again!

Dad gum him! But this time I stayed with him quite a bit! Then he turned and went right into a big mesquite tree and turned us both over. I got down, and this time I was mad!

I was gonna break him of that forever, so I went back on and stayed on him until I bloodied my mouth and nose. A piece of one of them mesquite thorns went through my ear. I remember pullin' that out, but that wasn't my biggest worry. I was worried about that eleven hundred pounds of horse standin' there lookin' at me. He would calm down after buckin' me off, turn around, and walk back up to me. There I was just a pile in the ground trying to get up, checkin' if I had two arms and two legs pointed the right way, and wonderin' how come my head's off to the side so far. My eyes were full of dirt. Couldn't hardly talk 'cause my mouth was full of dirt. And he did this two or three times! He'd stand there, lookin' at me like he was askin' if I was havin' fun yet.

Well, I stayed at this 'til finally me and Lettuce both got worn out. He quit buckin' and they tell me he never bucked again after that episode. It took me about two days to recover from it, and I still don't know which one of us was the most stubborn.

Ŧ

CHAPTER 7

Ŧ

Dodging Hail Storms and Lightning

They took me off the horses for a while so I could recuperate. Winter was comin' on and it looked like it was gonna be a bad one. They said it was gonna set in early with heavy snows up top, so most of the cattle'd been moved down. They had an old pickup, a '37 Ford, and since I was pretty well beat up, they sent me in the pickup to take the salt out to the flats for the cattle by Turkey Creek. These salt bags held about thirty, forty pound blocks and it wasn't much fun puttin' them in the pickup, and the weather was lookin' ugly! The clouds were droppin' down and there was lightnin' flyin'. But I'd always been told if I was ridin' in a pickup, I'd never have any trouble.

So I headed out there with an ol' boy named Slim. I didn't know where he was from, but he looked about twenty-two, twenty-three years old with shaggy brown hair and he never shaved. I know he never brushed his teeth, and he chewed tobacco and smoked all the time. He was friendly and we got along just fine. He was about six-foot-four, quite a bit taller than I was. He said he'd come out of Arkansas when he was a kid and had been workin' the rodeos and hirin' out to ranches.

We'd gotten about half way down to Turkey Creek when it started hailing. When it first started, the hail was about the size of peas. I'd seen hail about that size before and didn't pay too much attention to it. It was just a little larger than hail usually is, which is normally about the size of buckshot.

Well, as we drove on, it started gettin' bigger, so when we got to Turkey Creek, we threw the salt down and started back fast. Then it started hailin' again for maybe two or three minutes, and it came down in huge balls. I told Slim we better get under the truck or we weren't gonna live through this. He agreed, so when the hail was about the size of pullet eggs, then hen eggs, then lemons, we got under the pickup. Even so, the hail bounced and rolled up underneath the truck.

That hail busted every window of that pickup while we watched it dancin' all over the place. After the hail stopped, that pickup looked like it'd been through a war. We came out and there was glass all inside. We had to clean all that glass out so we could drive home, and that was a real cold ride back to that ranch! The wind came in through the truck front winda' and went right out the back winda', takin' part of us with it.

I looked over at Slim, who didn't have a whole lot of meat on him, and asked him if he was all right. He said he was if he didn't move too much. He was afraid somethin' would break off if he did!

Now if cattle get caught in the middle of a hail storm like that, they panic and run. They get themselves into the brush or under a rock ledge, or they'll just run for miles. Luckily, hail storms like that aren't too common, and they usually hit in a spot or two for only a few minutes. But I never saw hail that big again in my whole life and that country was noted for its stormy conditions.

Well, on our way back to the ranch, I asked Slim what we were gonna tell the Kingstons about their pickup.

"We didn't do it!" he said.

"Hell, no!" I said. "But are they gonna believe us?"

"What are they gonna think we done to it?" he asked.

"Maybe they'll think you and I got in a fight and threw rocks at each other," I said.

"No, they won't," he said, "but you tell 'em what happened."

"You're the older; you tell 'em," I said.

So Slim went up there and explained it to 'em while they were settin' there on the porch. Then Duncan came down to me and said, "You boys were a little hard on my pickup, weren't you?"

"Well, did Slim tell you what happened?" I asked.

"Yeah," he said, "he had a real interesting story to tell me. You know, that pickup was new and you've ruined it," he continued. "So I think you'd better have a good explanation."

Well, I knew it wasn't new! That pickup was already old when he was a kid! I explained what happened and what I saw. But he said he'd been in that country for fifty years and never saw hail the size of lemons. Peas, yes, but not lemons.

"Are you sure you didn't get in some kind of avalanche, or run this truck over and roll it down into Turkey Creek?" he asked.

The more I tried to explain, the deeper I got. I couldn't seem to get through to him. Well, all along he knew exactly what'd happened, but he made me tow the line for a while just to make me suffer.

That same winter, about a week later, four of us brought some strays down from Cherry Creek. There were about fifteen, twenty head of cattle in that herd. After we got in, Duncan sent two of us back up there to fix the fence and bring back strays. We rode off up there maybe eight, ten miles in stormy weather to fix the fence and bring them back. Not the kind of weather you normally go out in. The lightnin' was poppin' around us pretty good as we went down, so we stopped off at the old line shack to figure out what we were goin' to do.

This cowboy that was with me, Benny, thought this was pretty hard weather to move cattle in. They were restless and spooky. He thought we could only handle thirty, forty head. If we had more than that it could be trouble. They'd get off runnin' on us and scatter. Then it would take us a month to get 'em.

His plan was to get an old white steer down there (he'd done this before) and the rest of the cattle would follow him. I couldn't figure how the cattle would know to follow that white steer. But bein' a kid, I didn't let it bother me that much.

Well, the reason he put that big ol' white steer in there was so the lightning would hit him and not the rest of the cattle. I heard the ranchers thought some of these white steers were disposable, but I don't know why and I never saw one killed.

We were late tryin' to get the cattle rounded up. It was about sundown and we had another two or three miles to go. The lightning was cracking above us and behind us. I'd slipped into my slicker, and kind of holed up in it by pullin' it over the top of my saddle, saddle bags and me, tryin' to keep as dry as I could. We kept the cattle close and we could see 'em real well. We figured we had just about enough light to get 'em into the stock pens.

I hauled up on the right-hand side of the herd 'cause one of 'em got up a little bit too high up on the side of the hill. I went and ran the old heifer down and in where she belonged. I pulled back in, and then I remember takin' and tyin' my reins around the pommel, puttin' my hands down inside my coat tryin' to warm 'em up a little bit 'cause my gloves had gotten wet. I just had an old pair of leather gloves on.

That's when the lightning hit, just up on the hillside above me, and off to the right. The old pony I was with was a pretty good pony named Shotsy. And old Shotsy jumped, but when he did, I was with him, and he didn't get away from me. I spoke to him to calm him.

Another flash of lightning struck the horn of that big white steer with a ball the size of a large grapefruit. Then that lightning jumped from horn to horn to horn of every cow that was on the perimeter of that herd. It just illuminated the entire area! But it didn't kill any of the cows! It just went from horn to horn with a ziiiip, ziiiip, ziiiip sound.

As Benny and I sat there and watched, we saw a show that we'd never ever seen before or since. I've never seen something like that photographed either. I have heard tell of it from one old cowboy who said he'd seen it happen one time. But that's the reason we usually had a big old white steer with us in stormy weather.

CHAPTER 8

Survivin' the Snowstorm

One of my jobs at the Kingston Ranch was to run some supplies up to a line shack about eight, ten miles up country. I had to take a loaded pack horse in there. It was pretty rough country but I thought that was all right. I was used to it. As I was gettin' ready for one of these trips, the weather was growling and really lookin' mean, but Duncan said it never snowed that time of year. He said his father told him it had snowed once around this time of year, but that was thirty, forty years ago. He said he didn't think it would be too bad, 'cause I could ride up there in a day, spend the night and come back the next day.

I had a pretty good horse and I thought I'd just take the stuff up there and make it just fine. But that day I fooled around some, drinkin' coffee and eatin' biscuits, so I decided I'd wait 'til mornin' to go out. Come mornin' it was just startin' to snow as dawn broke. There was just a little sprinklin' of snow droppin' on the ground. I did notice the wind was picking up pretty heavy, so I saddled up and started out early.

Don't think I'd gone a mile when it just seemed like somebody opened a trap door and everything that was ever white on this earth came out of it. I could not see and I couldn't tell where the trail was. I could just make out a thin line, then it disappeared, and then I'd find it again. The snow was comin' down real hard onto my back, and if I turned around, I'd have to ride into it. I knew I'd never be able to see the trail goin' that way. So I decided to keep goin' on.

I think I'd gone about two miles of the eight mile trip when I knew I couldn't go any further, and there was not much I could do about it. I got off, pulled my saddle off the horse and left it there in the snow. I had a horsehair pad and a big old Navajo blanket on underneath the saddle. I paid seven dollars for the Navajo; it was a good one. It was big and woven tight. I figured the only way I was gonna get out of there was to turn the horse loose. I pulled the bridle off, 'cause I knew if I left it on and my hands got numb, I could drop the reins. With the reins hangin' down, the horse might step on them and cause us both to tumble down one of those ledges or somethin'. Then I climbed aboard, took a piggin' string, laid it around the horse's neck and tied it off with a knot, slipped my hands underneath it up to my elbows, reached up and pulled that Navajo blanket over the top of me. Then I told that horse to go home.

I don't know how long it took, but every once in a while he'd stop. Then he'd choose which way to go. He couldn't see anything of the trail but he knew where that trail was! He'd traveled that trail many, many times durin' his lifetime. The pack horse was followin', and I had that blanket pulled over my head, laying as flat on that horse's neck as I could get.

And we kept goin'. He'd slip a little, and I thought we were goin' over the edge. One time he went plum down on his knees, and I slipped off of him for a minute. He got right back up again, but I was so cold I just about couldn't get back on. I was so stiff I couldn't even bend to jump. The blanket had slipped off and was heavy with snow. I told him whoa, and he waited for me while I took the blanket and kicked the snow off. At one point the snow on the blanket was weighin' me down so bad I couldn't hardly breathe. But I was thankful I had that warm horse under me and that Indian blanket over me.

It seemed like hours and hours went by, and all of a sudden he stopped for good. I tried to nudge him on without even lookin' up, but he wouldn't move. I thought he'd lost the trail or come to a fence and couldn't get through. I knew he was working the trail real good. But this time he wouldn't go on.

I pulled that old blanket off of me, looked around, and he was standing right smack dab in front of the bunk house where the saddles were kept beside the shed. That horse had brought me all the way there! I was so cold I couldn't talk. My hands were so cold I couldn't move 'em hardly. But I opened the corral, turned him in, and threw him some food.

Then I started to the bunk house. Duncan Kingston had seen me come in so he came over and told me to come in the house. I told him I shouldn't 'cause I was all wet with the snow and all. But he insisted I come in and stay for the night. He'd been worried and wonderin' if I'd make it in at all. He thought I made a pretty good move, strippin' that horse and layin' down on him like that. He told me it probably saved my life.

CHAPTER 9

Death on
the Frontier

A ways out from the Kingston Ranch there was a waterin' trough hollowed out of an old pine tree log. It was filled with water so the cattle would water down there. One day that winter there was one little, wild cow at the trough who'd lost her calf. So the Kingstons brought her in to the ranch to milk. But she was really mean, and nobody liked to get near her. She kept off to herself and didn't mix with the others, so they were gonna turn her back out pretty soon.

Well, one morning I went out early, not far from the house, to the holdin' pen. I grabbed up my saddle and brought it out. I was probably a hundred yards from that mean cow standin' there in that pen, when I noticed she put her head down, kind of bellered, and twitched her head a couple of times. I didn't know what she was doing and didn't pay much attention. I didn't think it was important at the time. When you work with cattle all your life, you see odd things like that, and you don't pay any attention to 'em.

Then I heard a scream and I looked over and I seen that three-year-old Kingston girl impaled on the horn of that cow. I grabbed my Winchester out of the saddle boot, ran up about half way there, levered a cartridge in, and shot that cow dead center between the eyes.

That image brings back some pretty bad feelings, and my memory isn't real clear on what happened next. But Duncan heard the shot, and so did Mary. She came running out on the porch, realizin' that her baby had gotten out of the house. Apparently, she had crawled through the corral and was in the pen by herself. When I shot that cow down, the baby was swung off the horn, and the Kingstons didn't know what had happened at first. Mrs. Kingston ran at me, askin' what was wrong and why'd I shoot the cow. I told her the cow had gored the baby. They both jumped over the fence and went in there to where the baby was bleeding pretty bad, but still alive. They grabbed her up, wrapped her in a blanket, ran and got into their pickup, and went into Balmoreah as fast as they could.

The cowboys came runnin' out, askin' me what'd happened, and I didn't know what to do or say. One cowboy walked up and he put his arm around me, and told me he thought I'd done some pretty good thinkin' and that if the cow had gotten her down, she would have gored that baby again. He thought I'd done the right thing. He said maybe some people would say I could've hit the baby, but he knew I was a hell of a shot, and the Kingstons would understand that.

When the Kingstons came back, they didn't have their baby girl with them. I didn't know what to say, so I told them I was sorry about having to shoot the cow. What happened that day was a terrible accident. I heard later that the baby was already dead when they arrived in town.

As the days wore on after that, I knew I couldn't stay there much longer. They'd lost someone precious to 'em, and I reminded 'em of it. I was really someone else's child, and I'd just come for a short stay anyway. So one day I knew I needed to leave and go back down the trail. When I knew it was time to go, I packed up my gear and headed back to Balmoreah. ☥

CHAPTER 10

Ridin' Stirrup to Stirrup with Leonard

While I was in Balmoreah, I got a chance to meet a young man about my same age, or maybe a year older than I was. His father was an alcoholic, and his mother and father had divorced. His mother was working in town cleaning up rooms. I never did know his last name, but his first name was Leonard.

Leonard and I'd been pallin' around there for a week or so, when Duncan Kingston came in to town lookin' for help bringin' some heifers down out of the up-river pasture. He was short of hands and wondered if I'd come back and work for 'em for a couple of weeks.

While Duncan was with me, I ran into Leonard, so Duncan invited him to come along. Leonard had been around a little bit, and he seemed like he knew how to take care of himself pretty good. He'd been on his own a lot, like I had, without much parental guidance, love, security, and all the other fine things that go with a family. Some of us didn't get that when we were young.

So Leonard accepted the invite and came out to where Duncan told him. Duncan also told us there was some fine quail huntin' up in the canyon, and if we got a chance we should go up there, do some hunting, bring 'em back, and have something really good to eat.

On Saturday, after all the cattle had been gathered but a few, and we'd worked the whole day, we saddled up a couple of horses, intendin' to do some huntin'. Most of the cattle had been put out to pasture for the day, and those that were to be sold had been sold.

Things were kind of shuttin' down there. The Kingstons were still in shock from having lost that little girl, and there was no big hurry about anything.

There wasn't much stock around, so Leonard caught a big bay gelding, and I told him that one would probably ride all right. The only other gentle horse there that you could ride without gettin' into a brawl was a dun-colored saddle pony called Onions. The interesting thing about Onions was that he had lost an eye when he was a colt. Now he was seven or eight years old and he managed to get by just fine with just the one eye. A lot of cowboys had rode him in a lot of places and roped a lot of cattle on him. He worked some pretty rough draws and bailed off some pretty tall ridges. Onions seemed to be right there when you needed him. So I chose him 'cause I had confidence in him. And he wasn't too rough a ride — I'd had enough of that with Lettuce.

The canyon was up the road a ways in a place where they'd taken the cattle to lay up from time to time. It was pretty much of a horseback trail all the way up to where they had been gathering the cattle. We had some sandwiches in the saddle bags that Mrs. Kingston fixed for us. I did notice that she didn't talk very much like she used to. I often wondered if it was 'cause I was there remindin' her. I wondered if she thought I should have seen what was happening before it happened and maybe prevented it. But I was told she was just very appreciative that I'd done what I could and that she wasn't upset with me. She was just upset with the world 'cause she'd lost the only daughter she'd ever had.

Well, Leonard and I decided we were goin' huntin', so I slipped a .12 gauge in my rifle boot, and Leonard had this old Iver Johnson 4/10. I don't know how old it was and I'd never seen a gun that old before. It had a big hammer on the back of it and shot a single cartridge. Mine had a double barrel with hammers, and it was real good for goin' after quail and that type of thing.

We rode out and it was a heck of a day. Real pretty. No clouds anywhere and no sign of rain. When we got up into the high country it was pretty cool but I wasn't plannin' to do any swimming. We looked around for a covey of quail and shot three or four on our side of the canyon creek. There seemed to be more on the other side, but I wasn't too keen on going across those wet rocks. I had my boots and spurs on, and jumpin' from rock to rock when they're slippery and slick with that moss on 'em, and fast runnin' water, wasn't too smart in my mind. I just didn't feel like I wanted to climb out of the bottom of one of those pools, soakin' wet in this cold.

But Leonard said he was gonna go across there and get some more quail 'cause they seemed to be flyin' out of the brush on the other side of this creek. I told him I'd wait for him on this side, so we pulled the saddles off and tied the horses up. I started to fix up the quail we'd already shot in a gunny sack so we could tie 'em on the back for the ride home. I knew it wasn't good to get 'em hot, so it wasn't good to keep 'em near the horse. The heat from the horse would have a tendency to spoil them.

While I was fixin' the quail, I looked across the canyon, and I saw

Leonard over on the other side of the creek climbing up the side of a pretty steep bluff. He went up there maybe a hundred, a hundred fifty, two hundred feet, and I thought he was tryin' to get some place where he could get a good shot at some of that quail flyin' up the side of the hill.

He didn't get any shots at 'em though, and decided to come back down. And if he'd come down the way he'd went up, he probably wouldn't of had any trouble. But he angled off to the south a little bit, and found himself on a real steep bluff that he couldn't get off of too easily. He started easing himself down, a little at a time. I looked up at him a time or two and figured we'd probably be going back soon.

I got my horse saddled up and I was gonna saddle up Leonard's horse, when I turned around and saw him crouch down on this rock ledge and use his shot gun as a stick to help him get down this rough spot. His face was pointin' to the right of the ledge, and he was crouchin' over, tryin' to get down one foot at a time. I was thinkin' it didn't look too far to go, just another ten, fifteen feet to the bottom. He took the barrel of his 4/10 and was lettin' it down on the ledge when it dropped from his hand down to another ledge just below him. Well, somethin' hit the hammer, and BAAMMM, he was shot right in the side.

I saw him when it hit. He reached over and grabbed a tree limb and tried to hold on. But it tore loose and he came down. I immediately went across that creek and got over to him as fast as I could. I fell in the water and was up to my waist twice, tryin' to get across.

"Am I gonna die?" he asked me when I finally reached him.

"I don't know," I said. "Let me see how bad you're hit."

"I'm gut shot," he said.

"I need to open up your shirt and see," I told him.

Then I pulled his shirt open, and he was bleeding from ten, fifteen places around little pellet wounds. In the middle there was a pretty big wound. A 4/10 shotgun didn't have a lot of shells like a .12 gauge, but this shot didn't have a chance to spread out much. Most of it went into his Levis and belt and then just up above there it really tore into him.

"What are we gonna do?" he asked, even though he was barely conscious.

"I've got to get you out of here before you bleed to death," I said. "I'm gonna wrap you up in my shirt the best I can to stop the bleedin'. Then I'm gonna tie your hands together and you're gonna put 'em over my head and hang on to me. I'm gonna take you across this creek, but we're not gonna make it without us going in the water, so I want you not to fight it, just hang on to me."

Well, he was a bigger kid than I was. I was tall, but I didn't weigh very much. I remember we made it about half-way across when we went in, and come up, sputterin' and spittin' water. I was standin' almost chest high in the water, but it wasn't rushin' enough to take us down the stream. The extra weight was causing me some problems, and I did go down stream a little bit, but finally we got across to the other side. I untied his hands and got him up, but he couldn't walk. I had to pick him up and carry him over to the horses.

Then I laid him down and asked him how he was doing. There wasn't any blood comin' out of his mouth, and he wasn't coughin', so I figured it hadn't hit a lung, 'cause if it had he would have been wheezin' and foamin' and coughin' blood. I was hoping the rest of it might be repaired, but I didn't really know.

So I cinched the front and back cinch down tight, pulled off my saddle bags and hobbled both of my horse's front feet with my piggin' string. I made sure Onions was standing as close as he could to me so I could get Leonard up in the saddle. Then I took off the hobbles and stepped up behind Leonard.

I guess it was maybe four or five miles to the ranch house, and I knew that he couldn't ride by himself on his horse. So the only thing I could think of was to put him in front of me and try to hold him on the best I could. Well, that horse wasn't too big a horse. But we put on to a high lope, with me stoppin' two or three times to rest. I could feel the blood on my hands, up my arms, and I looked down and saw it was all over me.

Finally, I pulled up at the ranch when Duncan was just goin' in the house. He turned around and asked what'd happened, and I told him Leonard's 4/10 got him in the side. He said to get him in the truck, and I could tell by the look on his face that this was not what he wanted to do just then. He'd just taken his little girl into town with a steer horn through the belly, and now here was another one gut shot.

We got Leonard in the pickup but he couldn't sit up. When we sat him up he started coughin' up some blood. So we put out a blanket in the back, and I jumped up there and held Leonard's head while Duncan drove into town.

We finally got to the hospital – but it wasn't really a hospital like they got now – and Duncan hopped out.

"Got a man that's been gunshot," Duncan told them.

"Bring him on in," they told us, but I'd already picked him up and was takin' him in as fast as I could.

"What am I gonna tell my mother if I die?" Leonard kept askin' me.

"If you die, I'll have to tell her," I told him. "I'd rather you tell her then me! Why don't you just try to live through this so neither one of us will get in trouble."

"She's really gonna be mad at me if I die!" he said.

"Well, I'm gonna be mad at ya if ya die, so don't!" I told him. "Let's just get you in here and get some help."

So we got him in there and these two nurses grabbed him, put him on a stretcher-type thing and I went over to sit down. I was ready to give out and I was breathin' hard. Then one of them nurses grabbed me.

"What are you doin'?" I asked.

"You're bleedin' to death!" she said.

"It's not my blood, it's his," I told her.

"You sure you're not shot?" she insisted.

"No, I ain't," I said, "he's the one that's been shot."

"How'd you get all that blood on ya?" she asked.

I told her how I had to carry him four or five miles on horseback, and that got rid of her.

Well, I remember settin' there, worried about that young boy, and I had my pocket knife out. They'd pulled Leonard's britches off and shirt and stripped him down, tryin' to get at the wound, so they could repair what damage had been done. I sat there with my pocket knife and picked the B.B.'s out of his belt. I got about fifteen or twenty of these little B.B.'s that were in there. I just sat there and pulled 'em out of his belt while I waited to hear how he was doin'.

Finally, they let me go in to see him, and my friend Leonard was tough! He was sittin' there askin' me if I'd gone to tell his mother what happened.

"You're more scared of her than you are of death!" I told him.

"Well, she never wants me to make mistakes, 'cause it could cost her job or somethin'," he said.

"Oh, I'll go tell her what happened," I promised him. So I got Duncan to run me over to pick up Leonard's mother and we brought her back. When I returned to the Kingston Ranch, I remember saddlin' up with all my gear and I told them I was leavin'. Duncan said that'd be fine and he gave me a kind of a bonus along with four jars of apricot preserves. To me, that was just about as good a gift as a man could get in that day. Those preserves were delicious!

I heard later that Leonard lived through all that, but I never did see him again.   ✛

Lessons from a Gunfighter

CHAPTER 11

Chasing After
Brush Poppers

In the fall of 1942 I was roamin' up and down the San Pedro Valley trying to get some schoolin' without bein' identified as an orphan. I knew orphans got sent to orphanages and I wasn't goin' to one of those places. I had a saddle horse and a pack horse, and I'd learned when I was nine to handle rank horses. As I went from ranch to ranch I'd hire on to do rough-string at a dollar a saddle and room and board. I was tall for my age and people called me "Kid." They seldom asked me about my age. Most of the ranchers knew I was a hard worker, honest, and that I did a good job. They didn't ask me too much about my past.

One of the ranches I worked for was the Carlinn Ranch. It was nestled back in a range of mountains on the east side of the San Pedro River. The San Pedro is an interesting river. It dips down through that country runnin' to Arizona from Mexico. The banks are sometimes thirty to forty feet high. Along the banks of that river were stands of mesquite trees dotted with a lot of little cienagas with good, lush, green grass growin' in amongst them. There was always water in that river. Sometimes thirty-five feet higher than you wanted. Other times you could cross over on a horse without any problems. This is the river that was used by the Spaniards to come up from Old Mexico in search of the Seven Cities of Cibola.

I think I was about twelve years old when I started ridin' for the Carlinn, helping to break horses and doin' odd jobs. I had a beat up old bronc saddle fixed up with a set of buckin' rolls. I rode a full-rigged saddle that was made for me by an old saddle maker.

The Carlinn was havin' trouble losing cattle in the brush along the river. When cattle got into the brush like that we called 'em "brush-poppers." The cattle would drift down the river away from the main ranch and get into places where we couldn't take a horse.

They had this old ramrod boss who must have been seventy years old. He was tough as he could be and was hard on the men. He wanted everything done his way and couldn't see anybody else's way at all. After we'd bring some cattle out of that brush he said he wanted those cattle stopped from going back down there. He told us to cut their eyelids off. When I heard that I didn't say anything. I was hoping he didn't mean me. It was one thing to rope a big cow or steer, or brand it, or doctor it for worms or even castration. But I couldn't see cutting their eyelids off. I'd never heard of that before. I stayed out of that one but two other cowboys did it on about fifteen head of cattle.

When I asked one cowboy why, he said it was an old Indian trick. Without their eyelids the cattle wouldn't go through the brush. They knew the brush would blind them if they did. So that was how we kept them from goin' back in the brush after we brought them out.

One day they asked me to pick one of their horses and see if I could find out where some of these brush-poppers were hidin' out. I was agile and I'd spent some time with an Apache tribe. They'd taught me to read signs and tracks. I could tell direction, how many were using the trail, what time of day they used the trail, what kind of cattle they were, and whether it was a cow or a bull. So I agreed to go lookin' for 'em. I picked a horse that had a bosal on, which is a rawhide nose band to keep him from gettin' cold jaw. A cold jaw horse has a habit of changing his mind about whether he wants to obey you or not. Quite often a cold jaw horse ended up a runaway. To me, ridin' a cold jaw horse was a little bit like skiing. There weren't any brakes, and you changed directions all the time, which resulted in the rider landin' hard on the ground now and then.

Anyway, I headed down in the river to work those cattle out. I was ridin' this little old bay with a dark mane, dark tail, two black feet and a snip on his nose. He carried his tail a little bit tight for me, but he seemed like he was willing to meet me half way. When I first put that saddle on him I could put a good-sized cantaloupe between the back of the saddle and his back, which meant he was gettin' ready to buck. He was thinkin' about stickin' my head in the ground somewhere.

There were several other horses to choose from but he was small and I figured I could get into the brush with him. He only weighed about nine to nine hundred fifty pounds, stood about fourteen hands tall, which is not big for a saddle horse. A good saddle horse is about fifteen hands and weighs about eleven to twelve hundred pounds.

Well, I went down into that brush and spent a day or two lookin' the area over. I noticed tracks of a shod horse workin' just outside the mesquite trees. He didn't come into the brush but he was movin' in there doin' somethin'. I saw some sets of elevens that this horse had made in that soft fertile soil. That meant that whoever was on this horse had dallied on something and the horse made two sets of elevens tracks when he braked and came down.

I was wonderin' who else was catchin' Carlinn cattle down here. I knew one of the worst things a man could do around those parts was to steal horses, cattle or water. Many men had been shot and killed over those things. So it never entered my mind that what I was seeing in the tracks was someone other than a Carlinn cattleman. But, I wondered, if they had someone else down there lookin' for cattle, why did they send me?

Back at the camp around the supper fire that night, I asked a couple of the cowboys if they'd been down workin' those river shoals. But none of them had been down there for four or five months. I didn't say anything else about it that night. I just went out to check that little bay, rubbed him down, and made sure his back was good. We'd ridden through a lot of mesquite brush and things can get up under the saddle blanket and wear a hole in a horse's shoulders and cause a fistula. If that happened, that fistula would come up and the horse would be too sore to put a saddle on him. Cowboys knew they had to take good care of their horses 'cause bein' afoot in that kind of country can be big trouble. That night I didn't sleep too well. I was thinkin' about who was workin' the cattle down there by the river.

The next morning I went out and saddled up just before daylight. It was still a little bit cool and I could see my breath. My pony was standin' at the side of the corral snorting, with steam coming out his nose. That little bay had gotten to know me a little bit. We had built up some trust between us. I liked the way he'd go. He had a little shuffle with his walk and we were learnin' to get used to each other. I was able to cover a lot of ground with him and I figured it would take a couple of hours to get to the river bottom.

That morning I took my 45/70 Winchester. I put it in the saddle boot and stuck it up under the saddle. The Straw Boss came out and asked me why I was takin' the Winchester.

I told him I'd seen some deer down there and thought maybe I'd bring one in. He thought it would be fun to hear how I got a deer back to camp on my little green horse. I grabbed a set of hobbles and loaded up to go. But the real reason I was takin' my Winchester was 'cause I knew somebody was down there in that brush, and I didn't know who he was or why he was down there.

When I got down there, I worked around and saw nothin'. The day went by and on the way back to camp that evening, a little forked pronghorn ran out in front of me. I pulled out my Winchester, levered in a cartridge and sited right at the edge of his ear. I whistled real loud and that 'lil buck stopped, stood up and pulled back perfect. I squeezed off a cartridge at him. Baammm! Down went the buck, down went the horse, down went me!

I'd held on to the lead rope, knowin' the pony would get a little upset with the shooting, but I had no idea he was goin' to be that upset. I dropped my rifle and we were in a tug-a-war in the middle of some trees. He was buckin' and pitchin', and I was pullin' on that bosal. Finally, he stopped and calmed down a little bit. I didn't even know if I'd hit the deer or not, but I was pretty badly skinned up and my shirt was torn. In those days, it was hard to find a good shirt I could afford, and I only had two. I figured I'd be patchin' this one. Well, I caught my horse and got him quieted down, picked up my Winchester, put my saddle back in shape, and tightened it all up.

Then we went to look at the deer. I'd gotten him alright, and I was lookin' forward to some fresh meat that wasn't beef. But first I had to get this deer on my horse. After about two hours of fightin' with my horse in the sand dunes and in the water, it was starting to get dark and I didn't want to ride out of there at night. But I'd made up my mind I was gonna ride out of there with that deer no matter what.

I slit the brisket of the deer and put a slot in him big enough to slip over the pommel on the saddle. I was gonna put that deer on the saddle in front of me with the deer's front feet tied to the D-ring on the cinch on one side and the hind feet tied to the saddle on the other side. I took my horse down in the water, thinkin' it would keep him from movin' around so much. But every time I'd get close to gettin' that deer up there on the saddle, my horse'd get so upset he'd start jumpin' around and I'd lose everything. His eyes were blinkin', his ears were goin' back, he was twitchin' and holdin' one foot up.

I ended up hobblin' both his front feet but he still wouldn't cooperate and I was gettin' tired. The deer weighed about one hundred fifty pounds and I was splashin' around fallin' in the water. I finally took my reata off and slipped it over a mesquite branch, pulled it back down, and wrapped it around the deer's head. Then I pulled that horse up underneath the bank and inched that deer up a little bit at a time. I'd get it up close to makin' it and then all hell would break loose. Down we'd go, and my horse would be jumpin' all over. I had sand, water and mud all over me. I was thinkin' that this deer better be mighty good 'cause this sure was causing me a lot of trouble.

Eventually I got the deer loaded on the saddle and tied it down pretty good. I walked the horse for a long ways and made sure everything was workin' right. Then I boarded up on the saddle and that horse just stood still. I knew he was thinkin' that he wasn't happy with the situation. I was thinkin' "please don't do it." About that time he exploded and I flew off about the third time he bucked. This time I lost my lead rope, my deer, my horse, my saddle, my Winchester, and I was afoot with at least six or seven miles to go to camp.

But that horse trailed off a ways, then turned around, and just looked back at me. I was gettin' real sore and tired by then. But I got up and limped over to him, crawled aboard, expectin' the worst. He snorted once or twice but he moved along and didn't do nothin'. Everytime he'd snort, my throat would go plumb dry 'cause I knew he could dump me off on the rocks or onto a tree where I'd lay there and die. But he headed back to camp with me and the deer without a problem.

The next mornin' I went back down to the river bottom again. I brought along some old dodger's biscuits and a handful of jerky. The jerky was good but this cook always put too much pepper in it. I used to get so mad at the cook for doin' that to the jerky, but I had learned you never shoot the cook or the piano player.

Now, since I'd been down there a few days, I'd figured out where the cattle were comin' and goin'. They'd found a brush canyon with some grass in it where they'd go durin' the day and then go down to the river in the evenin'. That brush was so thick the cattle could only go through it by closin' their eyes.

Well, I was sittin' on the ground thinkin' about the situation when I noticed my horse had his right ear cocked up. He straightened up and changed his weight on his foot. Then his head came up, and then dropped down a little lower. He was tellin' me somethin' was close by. I thought maybe it was the cattle movin' back on us. Wouldn't that be fine, if I caught one and tied it up that night? I'd come back the next day, dally it off and take it home. I thought I'd look pretty good to that Straw Boss if I could do that.

So I tightened up my saddle, put my back cinch down tight, took my reata off, built me a half loop, and decided to see what was there. I took a double reins, and had a lead rope all ready so I could control my pony if I had to rope one. I also knew the quickest way to have a finger taken off was by doin' a dallywatta – that's when you dally around the saddle horn real quick and get your finger between the horn and the rope. Dally means winding around. Dallywatta means doin' it in a real hurry.

I heard some noise down there ahead of me. I knew it was a calf, but I thought it sounded odd. I pulled my horse up and listened. Then I kicked off into this little canyon. When I got into the canyon my pony stopped and I knew we had some sort of problem but didn't know what it was. I just eased him along and we were both watchin' close. We went around a corner and there was a man wide-loopin' on Carlinn cattle. I knew it was Carlinn cattle 'cause he had a yearling roped and the mother cow had a Carlinn brand.

Now, if a man is gonna wide loop, which is stealin' cattle, he's gonna take cattle that haven't been branded yet. He usually does this by pickin' young ones that don't seem to have a mother cow around. If you're caught rustlin', the ranchers pick up the mother cow and match it with its calf. That was good enough to get you shot.

Well, I looked at this man who was workin' the cattle, and he looked up at me. I knew I'd never seen him before. He was off his horse and had his horse tied off. He had this yearling calf down with its feet tied up. He also had a runnin' iron with him and I saw it pitched off to the side on the sand. I eased my Winchester out, turned my horse sideways, threw a cartridge in, and sat there watchin' him. He stopped what he was doin'.

He was about six foot four inches tall with a rugged jaw, square and solid. His blue eyes were almost burnin' a hole through me. He got up and started back toward his horse. I knew the only thing he wanted there was his handgun or his Winchester.

"Don't go near your horse," I demanded.

"Where you from, Kid?" he asked me.

"The Carlinn," I told him.

"How long have you been ridin' for them?" he asked.

"About three weeks," I told him.

"You know who I am?" he asked.

"No," I said.

Here was a man about two hundred and twenty pounds, not an ounce of fat on him, shoulders you couldn't fit through a door, a waist you could put your hands around, long bone legs, and a pair of worn out boots with spurs on 'em. And he had a Carlinn yearling down.

This was my first introduction to Sam Gibson of the Buzzard X Ranch.

"I don't know who you are, but I know what you're doin'," I said.

"I know you know," he said. "But what are you gonna do about it?"

"I don't know," I admitted.

"Are you scared?" he asked.

"Yeah," I said.

"You got the hammer back on that Winchester?" he asked.

"No," I said.

"Pull it back," he said.

So I pulled it back and swung my horse a bit to the right and had my gun cradled over on my saddle next to my legs. I knew if I fired my Winchester I was goin' down. I had recent experience on how my pony would react. I didn't know what I was gonna do with this man.

"We could do one of two things," he said. "You could shoot me or I could shoot you if I get to my gun. Or," he continued, "how'd you feel about me turnin' this calf loose and the two of us ridin' off?"

"I'd be willin' to do that last thing," I told him.

"What would you be tellin' them at the Carlinn tonight about what you saw?" he asked.

"You live around here close?" I asked him.

"I got a ranch up that canyon," he answered.

If I told the Carlinn boys about what I saw, several cowboys would saddle up, ride in to that canyon, and have a shoot-out with this man.

"I'm not gonna tell them anything," I told him. "Are you comin' back down here?"

"No," he said.

"Okay," I said.

He turned the calf loose and I watched him as he rode away. Then I took my horse and kept my Winchester loaded as I rode to the trail to watch to see if he was comin' in behind me. I watched behind me several times goin' out of there, but he didn't come back after me.

I didn't say anything about what I'd seen down there, and when the Straw Boss asked me if we could go in there and get some of the cattle back, I told him I thought we could do it. But I stayed out of there for the next two or three days and had no intention of goin' back there by myself again. ⨎

CHAPTER 12

Cattle Ranching at the Buzzard X

I would guess it was thirty days or so after chasing the brush poppers, the Straw Boss asked me to go across the canyon, across the river, and up through another canyon. He said there was a ranch up there and he wanted me to tell the owner that we would be shipping some cattle out in about thirty days. If he wanted to put some in, he'd let him go with us. I asked him how to get to this place, and he said he'd draw me a little map for me to follow. So I took the map, put some stuff in my saddle bags, knowing that I might be gone overnight because it looked like a fair ride, and then I rode out. I followed the directions and went through a couple of gates, up this road, and turned past this pretty good sized barn. I saw some good looking cattle in a catch pen, and I noticed an old wire gate and a big old clamp with long running wire on it. I knew this was used to trap cattle when they come in to water.

I rode up to this adobe house with big thick walls. It must have been double adobe, the windows were set in so deep. The porch was around on three sides, but it wasn't a big place. The porch was made out of cedar and ocotillo cactus for shade. It was held up by big old rough cedar beams, all of them hand hewn out of the local trees hauled down from the cedar breaks. And there, out on the front, was a big dog. In the evening he'd come out, lay down and take off from the day. I knew where I was because I had been told about the Buzzard X and the owner, Sam Gibson.

I hollered the same thing you do every time when you ride into a place, "Hello the house?" Meanin', is anyone home? A man came out and I immediately recognized who he was.

"Step down, Kid, have you had your supper?" he asked me.

"No," I said, "I haven't had no lunch either."

"Come on in." And then he added, "You're the same kid from the canyon, down at the narrows, aren't you?"

"Yeah, but I kind of wanted to forget about that," I answered.

"That's all right," he said, "what do you want to eat, Kid?"

"Whatever you got suits me fine," I told him.

Once inside, I watched him go over and take an old pan that had to be older than he was - I think he was about sixty-five, seventy, and the pan looked rusty but I guess it was clean. It was deep, about five, six inches. I saw him take something out and rub it into something. He poured some fixin's in a big old blue speckly bucket, and it wasn't long to when he had that wood stove going. And about fifteen, twenty minutes later, out of there came some biscuits the likes of which I never saw! Looked like they was raised about five, six inches. I completely forgot about the encounter that we had and that we were really probably supposed to be enemies. Seeing how this man could cook, I almost forgot about why I was down there.

He went inside of his root cellar and come up with some stuff that he had canned. I found out later his mother had done it. Later on I met her. I thought Sam was rough until I met her and learned a whole different idea about what rough meant.

He asked me if I wanted some venison and I said sure. He said he had some beef, too. So he went out to his refrigerator which was framed in the window with water dripping from burlap bags where he kept the food cool. He pulled out this hindquarter of a beef - what was left of it. It was just about the color of black. As a matter of fact, it was black, and just about as hard as the table I was sittin' by.

He took out his pocket knife and asked me how thick I wanted it. I thought if we're going to eat that meat I was gonna die anyway no matter how thick it was, so I figured I might as well die on a full stomach. So, I had him cut me out a thick piece, and he cooked it. And there we sat that evening. Never said a word while he was cooking. I started to say something and he said he didn't like to talk while he was cooking 'cause it took his mind off what he was doing. I didn't say anything at all after that.

I looked around and saw a magazine he'd been reading. I'll never forget the front of it which read, "Rangeland Romances." I picked it up and thumbed through it. I'd never read anything like that before, and I thought, "That's the romantic West?" Well, if that's the romantic West, where was the guy that wrote that book when I was trying to load the deer on my horse down there in the middle of the river when I ended up looking like I'd been in a mud bath somewhere, all beat up and skinned up? That was the West I knew.

"Where'd you get those scabs on your elbows and up the side of your face?" he asked me.

I told him about the deer and what happened to me down at the river.

"Where'd you learn how to rope up that deer?" he asked.

"I learned that down pretty close to the Mexican border in a little town called Fort Huachuca when I was cowboyin' down there a little bit," I told him.

"Why're you here at my place?" he asked.

So I told him why I'd come. He said it sounded good to him and asked me if I wanted to spend the night.

"Yeah," I told him, "I'm riding a green horse and I don't want to take him up through there again. He may step on a stick and I'd be piled into the mud."

He said he had plenty of room. There was no electricity, so he lit up the coal lamp when it started to get dark. We sat around and talked a little bit about everything except what I wanted to talk about. I was dying to know who he was, where he came from, and what had brought him to this part of the country. But he wasn't telling about himself. He asked me what I was going to do with my life and I was wondering what he was after. Everything he said caused me to ponder and wonder what he was really thinking about. Then I'd wonder what I should be thinking about. I knew this man had been wide looping Carlinn cattle and he'd be arrested if they knew. I was a witness to it. If I told the right people, they'd put him in jail or hang him. I didn't know if I should be spendin' the night at his place. I wondered how I was going to get any sleep.

I had my six shooter that I'd carried in my saddle bag, and I had slipped it in when I brought the saddle bags in. I took my war bag in the bedroom with me and late that night, after the coal oil lantern had been turned out and he was in the other room, I slipped that six shooter out, and slipped it under my pillow. There I laid with my hand on it the whole night long. But nothing happened.

Just an hour before daylight, Sam came and woke me up. He told me he wanted me to come back to his ranch sometime. He liked the way I handled myself. He said he saw me set a horse pretty good and that he had seen me in the narrows before I ever saw him. I told him I thought maybe he had.

"Get off work at the Carlinn next weekend," he said. "Ride over to my place and we'll go down to a little old town on the Mexican border."

"Don't know if I can for sure, but it sounds kind of exciting, and I don't have no other place to go and no other person to go see. The others go into town on a Friday night and stay through Sunday night. But I never go."

They'd get drunk and that's something I never did, 'cause my mother was an alcoholic and that's why she'd left me the way she had. I never, ever touch liquor, nor did I ever want to. So I told him I would go with him.

And so, a little friendship got started with a crazy, old, tough, hard man named Sam Gibson and a young cowboy he called "Kid," who was in awe of about everything he saw in that man.

Sam'd be up early in the morning fixin' a fine breakfast of eggs, with me peeling the potatoes, slicin' and cookin' them up. He had some little old paper and a little old bag with the name "Bull Durham" on it, and he rolled his own cigarettes.

Later on, as I got to know him more, I really got respect for how that man could coordinate things on a horse. To me he was like a fine piano player that could do things that no one else could do. But he could do them on a horse! Or afoot, with little or no effort.

So that first morning, as I was sitting there and we'd finished our breakfast, he reached over, took the little lid off of the stove, and messed around with the handle a few minutes. Then he rolled up this cigarette, sticking the wet end of it in his mouth, and he said, "You want one?"

And I said, "Don't smoke. Don't like it. Tried it once, woke up the next morning, and it tasted like a rat slept in my mouth all night. Didn't want to do it, ever again."

Then I saw him get up, wander over and bend that big, old, long, lanky frame down, reach in that stove and grab a coal out of there, take it up in his hand and light his cigarette, and put the coal back down into the stove. At that point, I learned what rawhide really meant! This man's hands, from toiling on that ranch, were impervious to everything - even fire couldn't get through them.

And, later on, a couple of times when he grabbed me with his hands, I knew there was power there that had never been in any other man's hands that I knew. Yet, from this man I learned the tenderness of how to get along with people and how to stand up for my rights.

Later, I heard Sam had killed seven or eight men over a period of years, over water rights, cattle, horses, and beautiful women. He always said to me, "If you have to shoot a man over a woman, make sure she's beautiful." ⨍

CHAPTER 13

Carmella and
All Her Charms

I did go back to Sam's quite a bit on the weekends. I asked the Straw Boss if I could take off on Friday mornings and ride down there to the Buzzard X.

"What do you know about that old man?" he asked.

"I've never seen a man handle a rope as good as he can, and when I rode with him one time I couldn't get near his cattle, but he could talk to them and ride right through them and they don't even move. He'd come up to 'em on horseback and reach out and pet 'em. I couldn't get within a thirty-foot range of one."

"You know, just be careful," he told me. "There's no tougher man in this country than that man."

"I kind of figured that," I said.

"He's killed men," he said.

"I'm getting to wonder if there is anybody that hasn't," I told him.

"Well, he's tough," he said again, "you just watch out."

But I was excited about going down to Mexico, even though I had no idea how we were going to get there. When I got to Sam's that first weekend, I pulled my tack off, took it in, and put it on the saddle rack. I made sure it was secure and got my saddle bags situated. I kept my six shooter with me. I didn't know if we were leaving that night or in the morning.

Sam finally said we'd be leaving come morning and we had a good supper that night. That evenin' we went out and sat. He lit a cigarette up and told me about his mother. She was in the hospital but I eventually met her. She was probably an inch shorter than Sam and weighed about 270 or 280 pounds. The day I saw her she'd taken a rifle and blew the top off of a fence while a sheriff was holding on to it. She was telling him that she didn't want him to come through that gate, and she asked him if he got the message. I remember her real well!

Next morning we got ready, went outside, and Sam opened up the barn and there was a gray, 1937, two-door Ford pickup. Now I don't know if he rolled it off a mountain or he'd been in an accident somewhere with a road grader or something, but this pickup had already had a hard life before I ever saw it.

"Sometimes the road washes out and I have to make a new road," he explained.

Well, we piled in that pickup, he cranked her over, and started up that old flathead V-8 engine. I was excited 'cause we were going to Mexico. I asked Sam what we were going to do down there and he said we were going down to see the whores.

I thought, "uh oh," and told him I was just barely getting ready to turn thirteen years old. And I ain't saying that there hadn't been thoughts in my mind about that subject, because there probably was, but if there had been any thoughts in there, Sam took care of that real quick.

"Kid," he said, "you go down there, mind your manners, and I'll tell you which one of those women is to be yours, and it might be a while, so you can forget rushin' into that!"

"I won't rush it!" I said. "I won't!"

I know my eyes were as big as saucers, because now I was real nervous about going down there. I was going to see this whorehouse and he was going to tell me all about it.

So we got the little pickup running, went down, crossed over, and went on down the road. We traveled down south about sixty miles. We'd get up to about forty-five, fifty miles an hour, and the front of that pickup would just shimmy like heck, but it didn't stop Sam. He'd just slow down a little bit for a while.

When we went across the line I learned that Sam spoke Spanish fluently. The guard asked him about the gringo kid, and Sam told him that I was working for a ranch. He asked if I was any good with horses because the Morales brothers were looking for hired hands.

The guard said they were runnin' the remuda, which is a group of horses that have been caught and confined, but the Federales and the bandidos were taking their horses at night, so they needed some night hawk cowboys to keep the remuda together. The guard said he thought I was too young, but Sam told him I could probably do the job.

When we finally got to the whorehouse a woman opened up the door. She was a beautiful woman in her day. I could just sit there staring and visualize her when she was 18; she could stop coffee pouring from the pot with her beauty. She had gotten up in years now, around 45 or 50, but she still had a lot of grace and a smile that just kind of lit up the room. And she kept herself nicely. She was wearing something that pretty much told me what the rest of her looked like. I remember that real well!

But this first time I met her I remember kind of standing right behind Sam and looking off to the side, embarrassed. And then he reached back, grabbed me and pulled me around in front of him, and he said, "Listen, Kid, this is Carmella."

"Come over here," she said in Spanish, with a big smile on her face. I remember looking around and not being sure what was going to happen to me.

"You Sam's kid?" she asked. Then she reached up and grabbed me and just buried my head right between her breasts! I didn't know whether to breathe or shout, or scream, or gulp. And there I was, I couldn't see anything. I thought I just disappeared into these two large mountains and was never going to come out again. I stayed folded in there, and she just held me and her Mexican perfume rushed through my nostrils. I was in some kind of state and I had no idea what was happening to me.

A tingling sensation went all over me, and I thought, "My word! If this is just the start, what was going to happen next?" But I held on and stayed put. Finally, she turned me loose and I kind of dropped down a little bit on my shaky legs.

Then in Spanish she told me that she was glad to have me there. She spoke a little English and I didn't understand everything she said, but I understood enough. When she turned around Sam slapped her on her rear end, and said he wanted to go in and have some tequila. We sat in this kitchen with a big long table. Sam told me about the room where the gentlemen come to visit the ladies, and that I was not to go in there unless he told me to.

I thought this was a fine place to be so I grabbed myself a seat at that table. And there I sat, not really knowing what I was supposed to do. Carmella poured me some coffee. And when the first girl walked through the kitchen, going out the door into the walled patio, she went by me and just kind of smiled. I immediately looked right back down at that coffee cup. There was no question about it, they were getting prettier all the time. Of course, I'd been working on a ranch for months and hadn't seen that many pretty girls, so I was very appreciative of getting to see any at all.

Well, the evening passed and I could hear the music from the cantina next door, which was also part of the living room. I could also hear the laughter that came from the men's voices. They were boisterous, bawdy laughs, and the girls were giggling. This was a one-story house with rooms out the back and down a long hallway. That evening I saw three or four more girls and I was just dying to ask how old they were, but I knew better, 'cause it was none of my business. I was to keep myself to myself and only do what I was told.

Late that evening when Carmella said it was time for me to go to bed, my ears perked up like a hound dog at a hog yellin'. I was figurin', "Oh, really?" I guessed I'd be sleeping alone, but in the back of my mind I was thinking maybe something else might be occurring.

But being just thirteen, I knew that I was too young. She took me through the room and, as I was looking around, I stumbled over a spittoon that was sitting there in the hallway. I was trying to find out who those guys were in there. I was just all eyes, feet going everywhere, and nothing was coordinated. I had my saddle bags over my shoulder.

Carmella took me in and showed me a place where I could bathe. They had a big tub out in the middle of nowhere, right in the open. She told me to take my clothes off and go in there and bathe. She was talking to Sam in Spanish, and I couldn't quite understand what they were saying. I asked Sam what she was sayin'. He said she wanted me to take a bath and he said to go ahead. She had put clean sheets on the bed and she didn't want dirty cowboys in there. Sam said he only bathed on Saturdays, so I figured I was going to have to go bathe alone.

Carmella gave me a coal oil lantern, and I went out and set it down and looked around. She gave me a towel to dry off and I figured I was going to have to get in this tub and take a bath. But I was worried about somebody coming out there.

I no more than got in that tub when I heard this girl say, "Hey, Gringo!"

"Oh no!" I thought as I sank down as far in that water as I could, without drinking it and breathing it. I kind of looked off the other way, thinking maybe she wasn't talking to me. But she says, "Gringo, you no got no soap."

"Okay. Okay," I said while I put my hand back over behind my head, waiting for that bar of soap to go into my fingers, hoping she wouldn't walk around the other side. Then she just took my head and pushed it under the water, turned around and walked off.

That was the kind of thing that went on for probably a year and a half.

CHAPTER 14

Hired Gun for
the Morales Brothers

I learned most everything that I know about cowboyin' and gun fightin' from Sam Gibson. It was so interesting to watch this man who was all sinew and steel. I was captivated by his very presence. Yet, I knew there was tragedy in his life, despair and hardship.

About the third time we were down by the border together, he told me the Morales brothers were coming to the Gadsden Hotel in Douglas, and they were lookin' for a night hawker. He said they paid good. Sam said he talked to them when he was down there the last time about me workin' for them for a while. He told them that I would ride for them and that I was good with a long rifle. He told them I'd do it for the first month or so for a good horse. They had taken American horses, good breeding ones, into Mexico. The Mexican Federales were trying to get at them, and the Mexican bandidos were trying to steal them. They liked these horses more than anything else because they were really high-blooded, quality horses.

The next weekend we crossed the border in the afternoon and went over to the cantina. We saw Carmella and then went back across into Douglas to the Gadsden Hotel to meet 'em. Now, this place was really special to me. I thought I had just walked into the Royal Palace in England. A spiral staircase went all the way up and around. I can just see it going the full circle. Up on the top were all of the rooms. I heard that this was the place where they had done the deal for the Gadsden purchase of land for the Southern Transcontinental Railroad.

I thought, "This is good," and I asked Sam if the Morales brothers owned that hotel. Sam told me they just lived there when they came up on the weekends. They even brought in women for them. There were three brothers, very rich, who were Castilian Spanish types. When I met them they were very friendly and nice.

And oh, what beautiful outfits! And conchos! Big silver conchos on their belts. And spurs that had to be as big around as a tea saucer that rang when they walked up and down those stairs. They were decked out just fine!

I met with them and made a deal. Sam asked them when they wanted me to start and they said, "Now."

"No," Sam told them. "I hear you have trouble down there, so the kid starts next week, not this week."

I didn't know what to do, so I went back with Sam. He insisted I stay with him for a while so he could teach me how to handle that big rifle of mine. He said the bandidos would come for the horses and they would kill me. So my training, if you want to call it that, started that next week.

I remember saddling up early in the morning and Sam taking me out riding up into the hills when the sun was just starting to come up. It was cold, and I was bundled up with my hands in my chaps, still trying to keep control of my reins.

That first morning Sam rode up to me and said, "They would have killed you an hour ago. I'll show you how they'll come."

So, he told me to sit on my horse right there and stay. Then he rode off. Well, I could hear his horse's feet clacking on the rocks, and I could hear him struggling to pull up a little grade with the horse floundering a little bit, pulling back, and trying to catch his balance. I kept following the echoes in this canyon above me, trying to figure where he would be coming out.

But the echoes were playing jokes on me. I couldn't tell. I thought he was going to come out down here, but yet he was over there. But all the time he was riding back and forth. And just as the sun reached the top of this pass, he came over and out but I couldn't see him.

I could make out his movement, but I couldn't tell where he was. So he came back down at me and he asked if I could hear him.

"Yes," I told him.

"Could you see me?" he asked.

"No," I said.

"You couldn't see me because I came out in the sun. I came out so you couldn't see me down your rifle barrel. You couldn't even make me out because you were looking directly into the sun. When they come, they'll come with the sun behind their backs. They won't show up until they can ride with the sun."

"Get your Winchester out," he said.

I pulled it out and he told me to pull out a kitchen match. I always carried matches for Sam 'cause he could never find them. He smoked and I carried the matches.

Sam reached down with the match and rubbed it on his chaps and struck it up. He turned my rifle over, held the lit match and blackened the rear sight. Then he moved it up the length of that 36-inch barrel and blackened the front sight. So both of those sights were black with smudge from that match.

"Now," he said, "I'm going to ride back up there again. See if you can sight and see me comin'."

This time the smudge took all the glare off the sights and I could make him out coming up at me.

Next he told me how they would come. "There'll be three or four of 'em," he said. "They'll have a gentle horse on a long lead."

"Why the horse?" I asked.

"Once they get the herd horses started, they'll turn their horse loose and their horse will follow the lead rider 'cause he was raised with the rider's horse. The rest of the horses in the herd will go with him. They don't even have to herd them. They're smart on how they steal the horses. But," he continued, "you'll know they're comin' before they get close if you listen to me."

The training went on for a week and I learned and listened well. The next weekend we went down across the border, and there I met one of the Morales' hired hands. They picked me up in an old pickup. I threw my stuff in and we headed for the ranch. The three of them owned a large cattle and horse ranch, as well as a couple of goat and sheep ranches.

They took me to where they kept the remuda in three groups of horses. The biggest one was about seventy-five head, and most of them were broodmares with colts by their sides. I met two of the Mexican Indian vaqueros who had been riding there. They didn't associate with me too much but they talked to me a little bit. I had the chance to put my war bag and my other stuff in the bunkhouse and then I went out with them for a couple of days just to see the place, but there wasn't much to do. I heard some Mexican bandidos had recently caused the loss of about twenty head of horses – very expensive horses. Apparently some vaqueros were not too keen on any kind of gun fightin' and three of them turned and ran when the bandidos came in. I also heard they got fired for it, and whatever else I didn't know for sure. But these two were still there and they were jumpy. They were older men, and I seemed to be the youngest man on the ranch.

I can remember going out for three or four nights to watch the horses. It was cold and it was lonesome. I could hear the coyotes every once in a while. And I wasn't too worried about the bandidos when it was dark. I figured if I couldn't see them, they couldn't see me either. But when the moon was up, that's when I was concerned about them. Sam had said they might come in the full moon but he didn't think so. Too much chance of the horse going down and breaking a leg or something. He said it would depend on how many of them there were.

Well, it just so happened that for three or four nights there were two of us at night until the other guy took sick and left me alone out there. And, I'll never forget that night alone.

It started out reasonably well. I'd taken something to eat. I had the canvas bag with a coffee pot and some coffee grounds, and some Mexican sugar. Mexican sugar is kind of crystalline and shaped like a gold bar. It's hard to chew, hard to cut and hard to do anything with, except stick a chunk down in the coffee which turns the coffee pretty good! It's got honey mixed in with it. That's Mexican sugar.

I had that with me and I was going to get up there and build me a little fire when everything was quiet and nothing was going on. I had some good coffee and got warmed up.

I was bundled up and got to thinking about what Sam had told me. All of the things that he taught me started coming back to me. He had said not to look on the horizon and not to watch the ridge. He said they wouldn't come out of there. If they were there, they'd already know that you were looking. He told me to watch the mares – they'd tell me when someone topped the ridge.

Just a little bit before dawn it was so cold I had my collar pulled up, my hat pulled down and my arms crossed while I was riding this old pony. I thought I'd just go around, make sure everything was okay.

Some of the horses were restless, and as I just kind of topped this little ridge and stood for a minute, several of them perked up. There was one mare with a bell on so you could tell where the herd was if they got moving, and she stopped and looked up on the ridge. Then two or three more of them looked up, and then there was five or six looking up. They kind of stretched and looked up there, but I couldn't see anything. I thought maybe a coyote or wolf had crossed, or maybe a cougar had run across there, or some other animal I didn't see.

I went on ahead and was dreaming or thinking about somethin'. Then I heard a whinny like horses do when they're startled, when something's got their interest. This little mare belched out a couple of times like that, so I stopped and looked up on the ridge again. This time I saw something move, but the sun had started to break right on that ridge and I couldn't tell what I was looking at. Sam had said they would come out of the sun, that they'd come one, two or three, hog style, one behind the other, that they'd never bunch up 'cause that way if you shot one, you might get two. He said there'd always be one or two horse lengths between each of them, making them a harder target.

All of these things were coming back to me that Sam had trained me to do. And there they came, three of them. I could make out the first one on a big black horse, a big Mexican riding in the front. It looked like another two behind him. I didn't know if there were any more. There were about two or three horse lengths between each of 'em.

They rode about a third of the way down the ridge. I had turned my horse by then and I knew what I had. I eased back and pulled my Winchester out of the saddle boot and held it straight down beside me on the other side and moved it up along my horse's legs where the Winchester couldn't be seen by 'em. I wasn't sure what to do. The big one in the front had no rifle, but the two behind did. The one in front had a big pistol and a bandolier across his chest, filled with cartridges. He kept traveling forward and pulled up about a hundred and fifty to two hundred yards from me and sat there with his hands crossed on the pommel, just looking at me. Never said anything, just looked. I eased my horse around real easy so I could gently slide off and pull my Winchester over the side with me.

Sam had told me that when they came, they'd either try me on to see how good I was, or if they recognized me as a kid they might even ride up and try to make a deal with me. But he said if I did make a deal with them and I turned around to ride off, they would shoot me in the back. He said there was no choice in this situation. It was quite a lot to handle for a thirteen-year-old kid.

I'm telling you right now, my knees were knocking so bad that the stirrups underneath them put bruises on both of my knees, and when I was leaning up against the horse my mouth was dry and my eyes kept watering 'cause I was trying to look and not blink. I kept wiping them, trying to clear them so I could see better. I remembered Sam had said not to ever shoot someone as he comes down the ridge, but to wait 'til he crosses and starts comin' up. If you shoot him going down, you're going to overshoot him. If you shoot at him coming up and you miss, you'll hit the horse.

All of this advice from Sam was coming back to me, and I was trying to remember it. What were they going to do?

The first rider started walking his horse, reached down and got his pistol. When he came down over the side he started a long trot. I threw a cartridge into my rifle and laid it across the seat of the saddle. And then I looked through my blackened sights.

The rider came down the ridge, crossed over, topped out on a little ridge and then came down again. He struck a high lope and just as he came up the other side, he was about fifty yards from me. He had a big smile on his face and a big ol' sombrero on his head. I remember taking the squeeze on that Winchester, put it on him and I let 'er go. A big cloud of dust flew from him as that 45/70 hit. He went up, the pistol flew up in the air, his feet went up, he spilled over backwards, and his sombrero just tossed over. The horse went down into the canyon and stopped. The two pistoleros on the hill never moved. I just stayed there. The horse I was riding was gentle and used to rifles. So I levered another cartridge in, and I remember the tears were coming out my eyes so bad that I couldn't see. I sure had tears flowing from somewhere, and I knew that this was all wrong. I didn't know how I was going to live through it.

The other two riders rode down about half way and one of them got off. He led his horse and stayed beside his horse as he was coming all the way up. Sam had told me to shoot the horse if I could. When he was at about forty-five, fifty yards, and got up to where the first man had been, he went up to him. I should have shot then, but I couldn't. I was afraid to. I didn't know what to do. He said something in Spanish to me, but I didn't understand it. By then I was shaking so bad that I didn't know if the Winchester was going to hold still.

He waved the other rider down and rode over to pick up the horse. They never took their eyes off me. At one point, I pulled my rifle back down with the barrel up, and I hoped the whole thing would stop before it went any further.

They loaded the man I shot on his horse with him layin' down on the saddle. They tied his hands to the cinch of the saddle, and tied his feet underneath. Then they just kind of backed off and rode a little ways away. One of them put his rifle up in the air and just kind of looked twice at me, then turned around and rode off.

I couldn't leave the horses and I was standing alone in the middle of this thing waiting for somebody to come and relieve me. My whole life had changed in the last hour and there was no one to talk to. What had I done?

My relief came along a long three hours later.

"Gringo," he said, "you don't look good. You look bad, Gringo. What happened?"

"I shot a man," I told him.

"Where is he?" he asked.

"I shot him over there," I told him. "I hit him pretty good and his friends took him off."

"We gotta go see," he said.

So we went over to where there was a big pool of blood. The blood was foamy and white, which meant I shot him through the lungs.

"He's dead by now," he said. "He won't make it. That's a pretty good shot, Gringo, about fifty, sixty yards. Was he running at you?"

"Yeah," I said.

"It's a good shot, Gringo," he said again. "You'll make a good man. Go on to the ranch house and tell them."

Well, I went to the ranch and told the boss I only wanted one more week and then I didn't want to work for 'em any more. He told me I was pretty young for this job, but if I wanted to I could come back anytime.

"What'd the rider look like?" he asked me.

"He was dressed in black, had a big sombrero, a bandolier, and he carried his pistol on the left side, not the right side."

"Don't know who that was but you probably saved us the herd. It's interesting that they didn't come back. They must of figured you were a pretty good shot."

"Why didn't they shoot back at me?" I asked him.

"Since they knew you were a good rifle shot, they would've had to shoot your horse 'cause it was in front of you. Then they knew you'd probably get one of them, and neither one wanted to be that one, so they just decided it wasn't worth it."

I decided that night hawking wasn't such a good job after all. I also wondered just what kind of friend old Sam was. ꓔ

CHAPTER 15

Showdown with the Federale

I went back to working for Sam anyway. We'd work the cattle throughout the week, and the work was dusty, dirty and tiresome, with long hours. We'd look forward to the weekend when we'd go down to Carmella's place in Naco.

Carmella was Sam's woman. She was kind of rough talking but she treated me mighty fine. The girls there were probably fifteen or sixteen and older, and I was just thirteen or fourteen. Sam made it clear to me the girls were off limits. I really didn't have an interest in them at that time anyway. Sex just didn't appeal to me. I'd come up so rough and tough that havin' a good place to sleep and a good meal meant a lot more to me than anything else at that place. Sam told me he didn't want me breedin' any of the girls and I understood that. He said I wasn't old enough but that he'd tell me when I was. I thought that was fair enough.

Some of the best memories of my childhood are of these girls lookin' after me in that whorehouse. There were about nine girls there and I became their little brother. They wouldn't let me come visit if I didn't bring my laundry with me. When my hair got long they'd cut it. If I didn't want 'em to do it, it wasn't any good to argue with them about it. They were all really pretty. One or two of 'em was a might stout, but that didn't seem to bother anybody. They would come down and see to it that I got fed three times a day, and it was the best food I'd ever eaten. They made sure I liked the taste of it, and I kind a liked that pamperin'. I was appreciative of it, and I always treated them with respect – I never looked at them as being whores. I saw them as my friends. I could talk to them – they spoke in broken English and I spoke in broken Spanish, but we put it together.

Every evening they'd fix me up a room, one of their business offices I suppose, and that's where I would stay. It was kind of embarrassing sometimes when I'd talk the night away with the girls. They would come and go and change. Then someone would say something in Spanish and one would get up and go into the other room. I knew what was goin' on but it didn't bother me none.

Then it would be time to go to bed and I'd go in to make up my bed and always find everything fixed up nice for me. They'd give me a few minutes to pull off my clothes and get into bed. Then two or three of 'em would come in and give me a big ol' kiss on the cheek or on the forehead. Then one of 'em would sit down and tell me a story.

A pretty girl would be sittin' on the side of my bed, tellin' me where she came from, how she came up from out of Mexico, how her parents were so poor that the only thing she could do to keep 'em goin' was to come up and make money and send it back to them. I imagine she wasn't forced into what she was doin', just trying to get something more than a dirt house down south in the interior of Mexico.

Above my bed I could look up and see a statue of the Virgin Mary in a praying mode, kneeling in this little cubicle just over the head of my bed. It had a little place for candles all around it and at least one would be lit. I was afraid that the darn thing was gonna fall off and catch my bed on fire! So every night after they'd leave I'd reach up there and snuff out those candles with my fingers.

I looked forward to that evening ritual when I was down there on the weekends. I learned a lot and talked about this and that, but I mostly enjoyed their companionship.

This went on for some time and every time we'd come down on a trip we'd see about the same people there. We'd cross on the American side and there'd be American guards standing there, reading a book or a paper or something like that. They'd come over, say hello, look in our pickup truck, and then wave us on through. Sometimes they'd just wave us on through. One time we stopped on the Mexican side and somebody said somethin' to Sam about crossin' the border too many times. I understood enough Spanish to understand some of what they were sayin'. They said they wanted to talk to him inside so Sam got out of the truck and left me sittin' in the passenger side of this '37 Ford pickup.

After Sam went in the office I could tell there was some argument goin' on. I knew that one thing you don't ever want to do is get locked up in a Mexican jail or get in trouble with the Mexican government! I was gettin' worried. Anyway, Sam finally came out and I asked him what happened. He told me that the leader of the Federales was upset with him for crossin' the line so often. As I was sittin' there in the pickup I saw this big Mexican Federale come out. He had this pearl-handled .45 automatic. Well, that gun looked to me to be somethin' out of the WWI Pershing era. He stood there in that khaki uniform with a brown strap over his chest, and a belt around his side. He had that .45 right there on his hip, with that pearl handle. My eyes were just kind of attracted to it! I tried to look somewhere else, but I'd end up lookin' back at that pistol with his hand stuck right on it.

Well, he came out there and I knew I'd seen him before. He had a big ol' mustache and to me he looked about the size of a door - the biggest Mexican I'd ever seen! When I asked Sam why this ol' boy didn't seem to take to him, he said it was because they both wanted the same woman.

"I guess that could be a problem," I said.

"Yeah," Sam said. But we went on to Carmella's anyway.

Sam carried a Winchester with him everywhere he went and by this time I was never without my six shooter. It was with me all the time. I kept it stuck down in my boot or in the back or side of my belt, where it wouldn't cramp me. I'd pull the cartridge lever out, and stick it down in the belt. It wouldn't go any further down than the lever and it rode pretty good there! To me it was kind of like gettin' up and puttin' my shoes and socks on. I would just stick that six shooter in my belt or boot when I got dressed.

The next weekend we headed down there again. It was really raining. I told Sam that if he didn't drive that old pickup slower in that rain, we weren't gonna make it down there on that road! The front end was wobblin' all over the place and the roads were slick. He said it'd clear up and not to worry about it.

When we got to the border line that day, that big Mexican came out, just walked around the truck, put his hand on the front of that Ford pickup, reached over and took the water spout off, and looked down in there. Sam was sittin' in the driver's side and I was sittin' there watching.

"What's he doin'?" I asked.

"Just irritatin' me," he said.

"Well, he's doin' a good job of it," I said.

The big Mexican put the spout back on the hood and said to Sam, "Gringo, some day you gonna die in Mexico." Sam didn't say anything to him and just drove off.

Sure enough the weather cleared up and we made it into town. The streets were dirt between the cantinas in this little Mexican village. Big signs advertised the cantinas and the cerveza. Everything was white-washed – they must have bought fifty million gallons of whitewash. The houses were surrounded by walls, making each one like a little fortress. Some were decorated nice with iron gates and things, but most of 'em were very poor.

When we first arrived at Carmella's it was good to get a warm bath in that great big bathtub. Oh, my goodness! That tub sat up on claw legs and it was made of copper! Copper! I don't know where they got that thing! Them girls'd bring hot water from a wood stove where they'd heat up water in big urns and bring it in to pour in the tub. A bath was somethin' we looked forward to.

The next day the weather kind of settled down and around nine or ten in the morning the girls came down to breakfast. The sun was shining outside and a little breeze was comin' up. I was really hungry. The girls said they were gonna have frijoles con huevos, that's beans and eggs, with some tortillas – the food was another wonderful thing about Carmella's!

The girls were dressed for breakfast, and this particular morning one of them showed up with not a whole lot on! I remember Sam gettin' after her and telling her he had a rope on me and he didn't want me stretchin' it out on him. He told her in Spanish to go put somethin' else on. She giggled and laughed about it, came over and sat by me, teased me a little bit, and then went to change.

While we were eating our breakfast I remember hearin' the brakes on a vehicle grind to a stop outside. I was sittin' there at the table, just eatin' my breakfast. I looked up. Sam was settin' at the other end of the table talkin'. Carmella was over gettin' some food and pourin' some coffee. Outside I saw that big Mexican Federale from the border crossing office get out of his pickup. There were drapes on the kitchen windows, and they were kind of red and blue; everything inside was red and blue. It was kind of a velvet red, and some of it was sheer and I could see through it. Anyway, I was lookin' through the kitchen window, through this little entrance way, and I saw the Federale get out and walk around the truck.

From where I was lookin', I was the only one who could see what was goin' on out there.

He reached around over the top of the fence gate, pulled the latch string and opened the gate. You normally couldn't get it open from the outside, but he knew how, and he was big enough to reach across and open it. He came through the gate, slamming it shut.

It happened so fast. When the Federale was only about four or five steps from comin' through the screen door and into the kitchen where we were sitting, I saw him reach in and get that pistol, pull the breach back and load a cartridge. The breach went down and back. And I remember just sayin' to myself, "This is bad."

I turned to Sam and said, "Sam!" But he was talkin' to one of the girls, and they were laughin' about somethin'. Must've been a funny tale 'cause they were really laughin'. Again I said, "Sam!"

"What?" he said.

About that time the Federale reached across to open the door, came in, shut the door behind him, and there he stood. I'll never forget that moment. He had his fingers stuck in this blackish-brown belt with a silver buckle on it, army fashion, with a strap over the chest, his hat on. The hat came up with a big crown, a military hat with a bill on it.

He said somethin' I didn't understand. Sam's hands were up on the table and he was just startin' to eat his food. The Mexican said something else I didn't understand, and then it was just dead silent in that kitchen – not a pan was clinking, no silverware was being put around, just the crackling of the stove. I could hear that stove just poppin' a little bit where they'd put some wood in it. Seemed like an eternity went by with him standin' there. He and Sam said a couple of things and then that Federale went for his .45. He had to pull the hammer back on it – I saw him clear, and I saw the hammer come back. That's when I shot him.

I had gotten my pistol out from my boot and pulled the hammer back. I was holdin' it ready underneath the table. When I shot him, I hit him right where that strap went across his chest. Dust flew up from his body to the ceiling as he stumbled through the screen door and down to the ground. And there he lay.

Sam turned to me and said we had to go. I told him I knew that and asked him what we were going to do with the Federale. Carmella was talkin' to him, and the girls were talkin' to me; everybody was talkin' to somebody! A couple of 'em were screamin' and two or three of 'em were cryin'. They knew that all hell was gonna break loose 'cause the Mexican police were gonna sweep in on them girls. The girls didn't know what they'd do to them, maybe put 'em in jail and everything. Everybody had to get out of there.

Sam told me to go out and get the pickup started.

"Don't you want to stick around to see if he's dead?" I asked him.

"Hell," he said, "you shot him right through the heart! What do you expect? Kid, get the truck started."

I went out and started the pickup and slid over on the passenger side. Sam came out and he told me to act real quiet-like when we crossed the border. He pitched me a gallon jug of mescal, told me to hold it, and to give it to the guard when we got there.

We had about a mile to go from the whorehouse to the crossing and my knees were bouncin' together so hard it sounded like a diesel engine runnin' – clang, clang, clang. I couldn't hardly stop 'em. I just knew we were gonna get caught by the Mexican government, and I knew the Mexican government's policy. They put you in jail, take the key to your cell, tie it around a jack rabbit and then they turn the jack rabbit loose. If for some reason the jack rabbit comes back and gives 'em that key, you get out. Otherwise, you're stayin' in that Mexican jail. I'd heard that story before and believed it. I sure didn't want it to happen to me and I was thinkin' I'd probably be one of the youngest gringos ever put in their jail.

Well, we got across the line all right. I gave the guard the mescal. Sam never said a word all the way back to the ranch. We pulled into the ranch late at night. The headlights were just barely workin' – the generator never did work very well in that truck. Sam still hadn't spoken to me. We got there, I opened up the front gate and he drove in and parked the truck. We went in and set down for a while and made some coffee, but he still hadn't spoken to me.

"How come you were ready to shoot him?" he finally spoke.

"I seen him before you did," I told him.

"What made you figure you had to shoot him?" he asked me.

"I saw he had his gun ready and I figured if he was gonna come in there shootin', he wasn't gonna stop with you – he would probably get me. And you weren't anywhere near your Winchester 'cause I knew it was in the pickup truck. I had my pistol in my boot. There was nothin' else I could do. The scary thing about it was that I shot him from under the table, and I didn't know whether I was gonna hit him or miss him. I thought if I missed him, he'd get us both. But I didn't miss."

Sam told me I had to go to work for another ranch somewhere, just to get out of there. As far as I know, nobody saw anything or knew anything, no names or anything. Sam and I never went back to that whorehouse again. But in those days, with those kind of things, if they found out who it was, they went and took care of the justice. If they didn't, there wasn't much done about it. Mexican troops weren't gonna come over to the U.S. side after anyone and American troops didn't care anyway. They probably didn't like that big Federale anyhow.

This incident left a scar on my life for a long, long time. It's probably okay to take a man's life in self defense. I've learned to live with it.

CHAPTER 16

Trapping Wild Horses

At one point I didn't have any money to buy a horse, so I figured if I could borrow one I'd go chase some wild horses, get one for me, and sell one. I figured I could get a hundred and fifty, two hundred dollars for a pretty good horse. I knew that a lot of wild horses had been domesticated around there. Then there were domesticated horses that jumped a fence and gotten in with some of the wild ones. There were also some of the old, wild Mexican ponies runnin' around, usually mustangs. So I thought I could make a good bit of money doin' that, and have some fun, too. Problem was, I had to figure out how to catch 'em first.

There's one place up in the mountains of Southern Arizona, outside of Tucson, where I knew about a herd that was up there with some pretty good stock. I had seen 'em on several occasions goin' in there to water near this mine shaft, but I could never get close enough to rope 'em. The country was so rough. I'd been in there before, ridin' a saddle mule that loved to run after those wild horses. But I didn't have any plan on how to catch one. That mule would bail off into places that I wouldn't go without a parachute, and it seemed like she just loved to do that just to scare me! I thought she was gonna get us both killed. So, I talked to this old Indian about my problem. His name was Tom White and he was probably the best rough stock handler I had ever met.

We got to talkin' about my horse problem one time out at a ranch where I was staying. I told Tom about the good horses runnin' loose up there and how I couldn't get close enough to rope 'em without gettin' in a place where they would ride me down. He told me there were lots of ways to catch wild horses. He knew how the Indian people had been doin' it for years. So I asked him to teach me how to do it, and he agreed.

Tom told me to get an old rubber inner tube, a cotton rope about five-eighths wide and forty, fifty feet long, a five-gallon bucket, three pieces of cardboard that measured about twenty-four inches by twenty-four inches, a tarp, a shovel and a pick.

"Where am I gonna carry all of that on a horse?" I asked him.

"You'll figure out a way 'cause I know where you been and what you done," he said. "Get all that stuff together and I'll show you how to catch a horse with it."

This was the beginning of a new adventure for me. My previous attempts while ridin' my mule back at that watering hole had gotten me blocked in there and I just about lost my life! I had horse prints right up my chest and on my head. When they came out of there, nothin' was gonna stop 'em and that's how I found out that I didn't know what I was doin'. But I knew they went in there to water, once or twice a day. Then they'd move quickly on out of there when they were done. I knew there had to be a way to catch 'em.

So this Indian explained to me what I was supposed to do. I was to find the roughest part of the horse trail that came down off there, just where they step down into the sand wash. It was just like single stair steps. The horses would come off the ridge, steppin' down a step at a time, and then walk to the bottom.

After hauling all that equipment up there, I spread out that tarp with that old Indian standin' right beside me, and dug a hole right there in that step area where they'd be comin' down. Then I put all the dirt that I took out of that hole on top of the tarp – only on the tarp and nowhere else. It took me a while. It ain't easy diggin' a hole and buryin' a five-gallon bucket. I never realized how big a five-gallon bucket was until I buried one!

That Indian told me to dig down deep and then pull the handle off of the bucket. I noticed he had me do all the diggin'. Then I took the piece of cardboard out and he jerked out his huntin' knife that he carried, and cut a cross in the cardboard. Just a cross. That's all he did to it. The cross didn't go all the way to the ends of the cardboard, just maybe within four, five inches of 'em. Then he took that piece of cardboard and laid it right over the top of that bucket.

We took the dirt that'd been in that hole and pinned the edges of the cardboard down with it. Then he took that cotton rope and spread it out with a loop, right around the edges of that cross. Now, the bucket was in the hole, the cardboard was on top of the bucket, and this cotton rope was on top of the cardboard. Then we buried all of that and kicked the dirt over it so it looked exactly like the rest of the area. We tied the end of the rope on to an inflated tire tube about twenty-five, thirty feet away from the bucket. Then we took the rest of that dirt and covered that rope all the way up to the tire tube. He thought it'd be best if it sat there for a day or two, so the dirt would kind of settle. But I was to be up there every day with a halter and lead rope. He said he'd come with me at the right time to see how it worked.

The first day I noticed some of the horses came in, but they came in another way. The next day while I was sittin' there watchin' 'em with binocu-lars, none of 'em used that trail. They came and they went out, and they never used that trail. The third day, I came down there early in the morning when they came in to water and one of 'em headed down that step area. It was a pretty nice bay mare comin' down and she was leading the bunch. I'd seen her lead that bunch in there before.

She came right down there, and when she stepped in that spot, her foot went down to the bottom of that bucket, and when she pulled her foot back up, the cardboard acted as a cover blocking the rope, and the rope tightened around her leg. And then she had her leg looped, and she was draggin' that inner tube. She dragged the inner tube for three-quarters of a mile 'til it got hung up on some brush, and there she stayed for the day. When I came in the next day I was able to rope her in.

So that's one of the easiest ways that I was taught to catch a wild horse on a trail. But that Indian told me sometimes the horse got hurt that way. So he decided to teach me another way to catch 'em. This other way would take about thirty days, but it worked.

First thing I had to do this time was to find a big gentle mule. Then we went up where there was a good bunch runnin'. We couldn't get close 'cause they'd see us, they'd just wait to see what we were doin' and then they'd run off. But we turned this mule loose and he just trotted off to join 'em. There was a big fight for a while, and a stud tried to run him off, but after a while they calmed down.

After about fifteen days, I went back up there and saw that they were all runnin' together and there wasn't any trouble. The mule was kind of off to the side a little bit, never got up real close, but he was just an old semi-retired saddle mule.

Now that mule had been taught to come to a gunny sack feed bag, cut down the center on both sides – called a morral – so it could be tied around the head of the mule. If it had grain in it you could shake it and the sound would make the mule come in to eat.

So our plan was to go out there the next day with our reatas, halters, and lead ropes, and catch one or two horses apiece. But that Indian still hadn't told me how we were gonna do it. The next morning when I met him there he showed up with a Holstein cowhide – the biggest Holstein cowhide that I had ever seen in my life. It was black on white and was not tanned. It was just a hide that had been draped over the side of a fence. It would crackle and pop, almost like the top of a drum.

Well, Tom said it was time to catch some horses. He took his pocket knife and slit that hide from the top, down about a foot or eighteen inches.

He called the mule in by shakin' that sack, slipped that cowhide over that mule's head, and turned the mule loose to go with the herd again. When he took off down that mountain with that hide on him I'd never seen anything more hilarious in my life. The noise and commotion of that thing hittin' the trees and the cactuses was somethin' to see. But that mule was gonna go back to his friends.

The horses saw that thing comin' and they absolutely panicked. They took off and ran, and our job was to keep track of that mule. He was runnin' at just a nice little pace, and he could do that all day long, which he did! It was five hours later that he was still tryin' to catch up with them. They were tryin' their best to get away from him. Finally, as the herd wore down that mule got closer to 'em. Every time he'd get near the herd with that thing on his back, clunkin' and bangin' and clangin' and comin' at 'em like that, they'd take off. The horses were runnin', their nostrils flared and breathin' hard, with sweat rollin' off their eyes and their bellies. That's when we rode up and caught two of 'em apiece. Thanks to that mule, the horses were so worn out they couldn't run away from us while we roped them in.

CHAPTER 17

Hustlin' at the Pool Hall

Well, I'd just turned fourteen years old and decided the world was mine, only I didn't have any money to enjoy it with. But I was sure at that age where I thought I could conquer it. I'd been having some difficulty supporting myself, and when I wasn't working on a ranch most of my earnings came from hustling in the pool hall. About six months prior, the owner of the pool hall had okayed me to take over running his place in a little old town called Benson, Arizona. It was situated right at the edge of the San Pedro River. This town was supported mostly by ranchers and miners. But it was on the main highway going from Mesa, Phoenix and Tucson towards New Mexico and El Paso, and then on into the Old South.

So there was considerable activity there with probably about twenty-five hundred people in this town. There was no television, so recreation consisted of dances on Saturday nights, sometimes lasting 'til Sunday night.

There was the show. The matinee was thirty-five cents and the evening movie was fifty-five cents for a ticket, but it only showed once a week on Saturday. And then there were several bars – three or four in the town, and a cafe called the Horseshoe Cafe. The pool hall was situated between the show house and Val Kimbro's bar.

Well, you just can't appreciate Val Kimbro's bar unless you've been there. There was a big brass rail that you put your foot on, and the wood looked to me to be maybe a teak or some hardwood with a rosewood trim or something that brought out the beautiful color in it. In the back was a big set of mirrors that ran the whole length of the bar. The ceiling was about twelve, thirteen feet high. It just had the feeling of an old-time bar; and that's what it was.

There were tables on the sides. Didn't have any dancing girls or call girls. They weren't into that. But this is where the people in the town seemed to gather to pass along social thoughts and get drunk once in a while.

You could always tell when Val was around. He was a pretty good sized man – about six-one, six-two and weighed a couple hundred pounds. He wore his pants in his boots with mule ear straps on the outside, giving him the look of a bulldogger or a cowboy. But I think the most exciting thing about Val's bar was that he had a complete stage coach from Wells Fargo, a Winchester collection, and lots of memorabilia going back to the 1800's.

And he knew about it all. Val was in his 60's when I knew him. He was also a barber. For the eight to ten years that I knew Val, I never saw him without his sidekick. When you'd walk up to Val in the street to talk to him you could look down, and there looking at you with his head turned sideways, was a fifty or sixty pound javelina boar, with teeth on him about three and half, four inches long. Well, this pig'd go with Val everywhere he went. Val claimed he was better than a dog for companionship. But when Val would stand, that pig would always get between Val and whoever Val was talking with, and if you so much as reached over and happened to push Val or something, you'd hear the snap of his teeth going together, telling you, "Hands off or no hands at all." And I'd seen him defend Val on several occasions. So if there was anybody figuring on robbing Val, they would have to shoot the hog first. Nobody wanted to mess with that hog!

Val had a habit of taking in an orphan once in a while. He took a liking to me because I had the ability to shoot a game of pool pretty good. And let me tell you, when getting something to eat that night and the next day depends on your winnings, you'd be surprised how well you concentrate on that little ball – and where it goes, and that other little ball, and that little pocket.

I shot pool there for seven years. As matter of fact, I became the youngest billiard champion in Arizona when I was fifteen. I challenged them all. I'd usually go in Friday night and here would come Cactus Jack and he loved to gamble. Nine-ball was his game. And he always seemed to have money. Well, he wasn't that good a shot, but he enjoyed the game immensely. And, there were several other good shots that got in the game, but I managed to support myself pretty well off my winnings.

Well, I found out that shooting pool sure beat riding rough string for a dollar a saddle. The next day I could walk around much easier. I went on to rodeo later and found out that there had to be other ways I could make easier money than that, too. So, from time to time I'd duck back, hone my skills and play pool.

But pool had its dangerous and hard side. When I say hard, I mean not having anyplace to sleep except on that table. Sometimes I would just take a pillow and sleep there 'cause I had nowhere else to go. I want to tell you, there's nothing harder than the top of a pool table. It's a piece of marble that's been honed and polished with its pure intent to be agonizing to anyone who laid on it! But I certainly had my good times there, too. Later on when I got a few bucks, I bought an old Army cot, and that was a lot better than that pool table. But we had some rowdy times in there. Sometimes arguments would break out, but usually the games were pretty peaceful.

I remember one night to the contrary. Somebody accused someone else of not putting their money down – ante up the kitty for nine-ball. Well, a fight broke out, and it's surprising how a pool ball will cut a hole in a wall when thrown with average velocity. It makes a hole about the size of a cannon ball. And believe me, there were lots of holes in some of those walls when the fight was over!

I had the good fortune of not being hit by any of them, and when it was all done, there were a few bloody heads, a hurt arm or two, somebody limping real bad, somebody fussing and cussing over something else, a cut eye and a bloody mouth. But we all got together, talked about it, and decided to just clean the place up and go on with the game.

Val owned this pool hall, but he wasn't there that night. I remember when he came in the next day, he asked if anybody was killed in there last night. I told him no and that I didn't think anybody was seriously hurt. Most of them managed to get to their pickups and there was one that had to be driven home where his wife doctored him up. He didn't go to the doctor, so I thought it all worked out pretty good.

CHAPTER 18

Losin' My Cow Horse

While workin' the pool hall I got to talking to the ranchers, and this one year they had a great year going for beef cattle. The price had never been higher and it was a pretty good year for them to bring in their yearlings and any others to sell. They would gather up their cattle and bring them down from the high country, get them ready for the trucks or get them to the railroad, and then they'd be hauled off to the stockyards for processing.

Well, they were telling me they never had a year where they got so much on the hoof. I got to thinking that maybe there was more money in raising cattle than hitting a little ball around a table lookin' for a hole. I didn't have a ranch, but I might be able to get in on it somehow. I was fourteen years old, and I had a hat, a saddle horse, and a pack horse.

I slept on it for a few nights and talked with more ranchers. I came to find out that up in the Rincons, these ranchers had been losing quite a bit of cattle because they would get into those big rough draws with rocky crags and never come down! Some of them were three, four years old. Big, old, hefty type cattle. Most of them were Herefords with some Santa Gertrudis and Black Angus. There were several different types of cattle, but most of them were Herefords. They weren't mulies, they weren't long horns, they were just regular-horned Herefords. But boy, they were bringing a price that year!

While I was contemplating this idea one day, somebody left the gate open to where I pastured my horse, and it wandered out of the pasture onto the road, where he shouldn't have been. This one night I was winning pretty good – probably won fifteen, twenty dollars – and that was big money then. But I remember the sheriff came in and told me that Midge, my horse, had been killed.

When he said that, why, a chill went through me. 'cause you got to know that Midge was a pure-blooded bay, with black points, black mane and tail, and he was probably one of the best dogging horses the Good Lord ever created. I won some jackpot doggings off of him 'cause he was small and he was fast. He'd get on that steer and I could just get right up on him. Sometimes the steer was so big I could just step up on the steer instead of down on him.

I really, really felt bad. I asked what'd happened and the sheriff said he was dead after being hit by a car. Well, I didn't have any fancy papers on him and he wouldn't have won any English horse shows, but when you called on him, he was there! He would do anything I wanted him to do. He was about ten, eleven years old, and I was only two or three years older than Midge was!

So when he told me he'd been killed I thought I better go see him. But the sheriff said no, and told me to stay right there and keep shooting pool. He didn't want me to come out that door and he didn't want me to say anything to anybody about what he just told me.

I didn't understand, but then he told me Midge had gotten out on the highway and some people had been seriously hurt in their car and they were looking for the owner of the horse. The sheriff said he knew the horse and that it wasn't my fault. He knew who let the gate open. He wanted me to stay there and say nothing to anybody about losing my horse.

So I was pretty sad for several days after that. But later an old cowboy came through and we were talking over a pool game, and he asked why I looked pretty down. I told him I'd lost my saddle horse. And when he asked what happened to him I told him I didn't know, that he was just gone. Then he asked what I was gonna do. Well, I told him I wanted to get in the cattle business.

"You got a ranch?" he asked me.

"No," I said.

"You don't have a horse," he said.

" No," I told him.

"You could catch a cow and put your saddle on it to ride!" he teased me.

"Well, that isn't going to work," I said.

"I'll tell you what," he said.

Then he told me about his spread up there called the Spanish Bell. He said it fronted the federal forest land and it went up above Happy Valley. I knew where that was and told him so. I asked him if he owned that land up there and he said he leased it. He said that if I got myself a horse, I could line camp out at his place. The line shack was about two-thirds of the way up the mountain. He said I could put up there, use his holding corral, and help bring the wild cattle out. He asked if I had a reata and I told him I had the best kind in the country, hand-laced out of rawhide in a pigtail braid.

A reata has four to seven strands of rawhide. The best ones come from elk but this one came off a Mexican steer. And I want to tell you something. I never met that steer but I do feel that someday in the hereafter I'd like to meet him, and shake his horn, and tell him how damn tough I think he really is, because this rope has been with me since I was ten years old.

I can remember when it was first made up for me. I was told by this old half Indian, half cowboy, half Italian, half Swede and half something else, that the way to make this right was to take a calf liver and rub it into this rope the full length of it for a couple of hours. Then you take the hondo – that's where the loop and the rope go together, and tie it to a calf's tail in a small pasture, and let him drag it around for a week or two to break it in.

Well, I kind of felt bad about that because I didn't really feel like my new rope ought to be behind some stupid calf that was dragging it around, knowing what they'd do to it back there, but when I finally got it back, it was so easy to coil.

Now, these reatas, in order to be authentic and be good, have to be exactly forty-four feet long. In today's ropings, they're about twenty-two, twenty-three or twenty-five feet long so the riders get out on their horse, rope the calf, get off the calf, tie the calf up and do it all in some record time. Well, with this long rope, we could get close enough to a speeding wild cow. We didn't want to get too close 'cause that cow could turn and run back at you rather than away from you.

Once you roped a cow, if you got into a brawl with it, you'd get off of your horse, tie it to a tree and if you have a twenty-three-foot rope, it doesn't take long to cover that distance and he's got you. So with this reata I started out roping, and I've roped many wild cattle and trapped wild horses with it. This rope is like a friend to me because it was an important part of my early life. It saved my life several times.

Anyway, this old cowboy said he'd heard tell that I was pretty handy with a rope, and that he knew I'd learned to rope from old Sam down the river.

"That all you learned from him?" he asked.

I recalled the time I first met Sam Gibson when I caught him wide loopin' cattle down by that river and I was scared I might have to shoot him or that he would get to his rifle and shoot me.

"Yeah," I answered, "I don't wide loop."   ⨍

CHAPTER 19

That Renegade Sabino Horse

This cowboy said the cattle up there didn't carry a brand and were on his land. So he'd like to get them out of there, but he didn't have anybody that would ride that country. Most were too smart to get up in there. But if I got myself a good horse he said he would sell everything I brought down. He'd tag their ears and sell them along with his and give me the money. I said I was willing.

Now it came down to how I was goin' to find a horse again, and I didn't have too much time to find one. Well, you don't ever want to buy a flatlander-type horse to go up in the mountains. You've got to have a horse that's been raised in the mountains or he gets up there and he gets to fighting his feet and the next thing you know, the two of you are going down the mountain rolled up like an armadillo, looking for a place to reach over and grab a tree! I didn't know where to go, so I took a ride down the river and went to see Sam.

I hadn't seen him for several weeks so I told him about my idea and how I didn't know how to find a horse. He said Boog Burnett was coming over the next evening. Now I guess Boog was probably one of the best cowboys in the world and I didn't know how old he was – I never did look at his teeth, but I can tell you, he was old. He loved to go to town and have at least one fist fight to clean his system out. And then he could get down to drinking and loving the pretty girls. Sam said Boog used to trap wild horses when he was my age and he suggested I talk to him and find out what he could tell me about it. I asked about staying over, and Sam said he needed a little help in the morning anyway.

Boog showed up carrying a gallon of mescal in a glass jug and riding a green horse. And if you just cleared your throat that green horse'd probably tear up an acre of ground. Every time I saw Boog he was ridin' a green horse that needed to be topped off. It'd have wild eyes, tail tucked down, ears leaning back and fire in his eyes. I wouldn't even get in the same corral with one of his horses. But he always seemed to get where he wanted to go. He came in there to Sam's right up front and jerked that old pony around, whirled him off, stuck his stirrups out in front of him, pulled on that saddle horn and says, "Whoa. You want a ride?"

"No, sir, I don't want to ride that horse!" I said.

"Kid, why don't you go up there and pump some water from the canyon?" he said. "No use you saddling another horse, you can ride this one."

"I really don't care too much to ride this horse," I said, but he insisted. Well, I finally made it up there and pumped the water. I got bucked off three times and I broke a jug once. Never did get the sand out of my hair or my mouth until the next day. I knew if I got that old pony out there in the middle of that sand wash where he had to buck in that heavy sand, it would be harder for him to buck and a little bit easier for me to fall on. I also knew Boog was testing me and after that ordeal he said I'd make a fair hand some day. Not one yet, but some day. I thought that was alright.

Then Boog said that Sam had told him I wanted to go catch some wild cattle. I told him, yeah, but I didn't know how to get them off the top of that mountain. He said the cattle were up there alright and they were big! He said some of them up there weighed twelve hundred pounds. He said I'd have to be riding a heck of a horse.

"You got one like that?" he asked me.

"No, and I don't want one of yours 'cause I'd like to go in and come out alive!" I told him.

Boog turned to Sam and asked him if he thought I could catch that sabino that's running up there. A sabino is a horse with a glass-lookin' eye – one that has no pigment in his eye, and you can see right into it. Some call him a glass-eyed horse, but his real name is what the Indians gave to him: sabino. So I asked where this horse was running and Boog says he's up above the Cox place. Says he's seen him in there several times – he's wild and he's ribbon paint, brown on white. Well, a paint horse like that is white with brown spots on him and then there's a ribbon of different color all around the blotches on the paint. It's a very rare type of paint and a pretty thing to see. Boog described him to me and I asked what a man had to do to catch him.

Boog told me to go up in that country and stake some salt up there. He said to carry up some grain, too. He said the deer were going to eat it for awhile and the cattle would get to it, but after a few days the sabino would find it. Boog said we'd cut his sign every two or three days and see if he'd been in. That meant we'd be lookin' for his tracks. But he wouldn't come in when we were there and I didn't see any way we could catch him without being there. But he said we'd go up together and he thought it would take us three or four days to get him.

I was to come and get him at the ranch, riding one of Sam's horses, and we'd go up there and watch him. Then I was to come up the bottom of this draw, with Boog on top of the ridge above, and then just sit there and we'd do little hand signals. I was not to ever get up on top of the ridge where the horse could see me. If he's coming in, it's a pretty deep corral down there, probably seventy-five to a hundred yards down where he's going in to water. That's where they put the cattle and that's where we'd catch him. If we saw him in there, I was supposed to run and shut the gate on him before he came out. Boog told me he'd run right on top of me if I was in the middle of that gate.

At this point I asked Boog just how big he was. He said about twelve hundred pounds and stood at least fifteen-three hands. He said he looked like he was three, four years old.

Then I asked if he'd ever been roped, and Boog said that shouldn't worry me, and I said it didn't bother me as long as I didn't have to carry a jug of gas at the same time.

So we got up there, and sure enough when I went up the second day, the sabino had come in. I saw his hoof tracks but I didn't see him. I didn't go up close 'cause I didn't want him to smell that me and my horse had been around. I watched his tracks for a little while and could see where he was going to drink. Then I decided I'd ride in there anyway and take a look. I never stepped on the ground or put my boot tracks on the ground. When I was in there I poured him out some grain that I'd taken up there in a burlap sack and figured he'd be coming back.

I rode over to Boog's that night to tell him what I'd seen and done. Then, on my way back to Sam's, what a hell of a rain storm broke out. My gosh, it was terrible! That old pony was good 'cause he took me right back to Sam's place. I thought I was going to get pneumonia. The next day Boog showed up and he was sure that the sabino would come in to eat. He said the day after next he'd come over and we'd go up there before daybreak. It was going to take us about two hours. We were going to be running up these ridges two hundred feet off to one side. Our ponies would pick their way, knowing where they were going in the dark. But it was a scary thing to do before daybreak. Real cowboys didn't take flashlights, so, of course, we didn't.

We went up just at daylight and then I cut off and went down to the bottom of the wash where Boog could see me. He was about two hundred, three hundred yards up on the mountain where he could see, right above the gate to the corral. He couldn't see in there 'cause it wasn't light enough yet. And he just kind of held his hands up like he didn't know. But he had told me that if he was in there I'd better ride the best I ever rode in my life. I was to run in there, drop a loop over that gate, dally it, and pull it right in there behind me. Then I was going to dally around the post and I'd have him. I thought there was no way he wasn't going to see me coming in through that canyon. He'd hear me and he'd see me. Boog just said to take the reins to that little pony, take the rope down, and ride like I never rode before.

I was waiting for Boog to give me the signal that the sabino was in there and I cinched up the saddle and made sure everything was in good shape. Sure enough, here came the signal for me to go. Well, I turned that old pony's head towards the corral and asked for everything that he had. I'll never forget the feeling – them bushes were sniping at the side of my face, popping on the side of my chaps. It was early in the morning, cool, and the wind was starting to blow, kind of blurring my vision a little bit. My horse was really picking it up and laying it down. I was just rounding a corner and I could see that corral gate, just about two, three hundred yards in front of me and I didn't see him come out. But I hadn't seen him go in, neither! I assumed he was still in there 'cause Boog had given me the signal.

As I bore down on that pony to run wide open, POW! A shot went off, and I thought, "Good heavenly days! I'm being shot at! What's going on?"

I just kept on riding for all I was worth. I thought somebody was coming down on me! And then the next shot went off! And then another! And, boy, I'll tell you! I just reached over and I whipped that old pony as fast as I could! So we barreled off into that canyon and rode through and passed that gate about twenty yards worth. Then I seen a big puff of dirt floating up. Then I heard the "clap" of the rifle again. I figured out then what Boog'd been doing. That sabino was trying to come out and Boog was shooting piles of dirt up in front of him to keep him from going through the gate!

No more than fifteen feet from me this horse was coming out of there, and the two of us were on a collision course. Well, that last shot went off and my horse saw it, and buggered off to the side. I pulled him back, and he started to turn to the right. I reached up with my boot heel and kicked him upside the head, made him stay on there; that kept him on his course. I grabbed the lariat, dropped the loop over the gate, dallied on the horn and jerked that gate – almost jerked the whole corral down – ran in there and stopped. I whirled around, got off and did what I was supposed to do.

I had it tied up so I went over, leaned on that post, caught my breath, and thought I just might survive this, when old Boog took another shot. And this one hit a white rock sitting over about three or four feet and it just splattered all to pieces.

Then Boog came off the ridge, and it took him a while. He worked his way down the ridge and still had his rifle with him. He came in there and said he thought that was pretty damn good shooting.

"How come you didn't tell me about it?"

"I figured you'd learn," he said.

"That last bullet wasn't no more than five feet from me!" I said.

"He didn't get out did he?" he said.

"No," I said, "but I didn't know who was shootin' at me!"

"You must have known it was me, 'cause I'm the only one out here and if I'd wanted to hit you, I would," he said. "You know I'm that good a shot, don't you?"

So now we had this horse caught in the corral. And he was just pacing back and forth, with his ears laid back. I put my pony outside the gate and tied him up for a little while. I sat down 'cause my knees were knockin' just a tad. Boog asked me if I was scared, but I said, "No, not too bad."

"I don't think you're too scared. You did some pretty good riding up that wash. Let's go in and rope him. We'll dally him up and put a Running W on him."

"All right, let's do it," I said.

So that day and all into the evening, we took our two horses in there, roped that big horse, and got him between the two of us. We put a saddle and a halter on him. I had to reach around, hook that saddle on him, and ear him down. When I finally tied him down, we put a Running W on him, which is when you put a hobble on each front foot. You run a rope down through the stirrup and through the hobble, back up to the other stirrup on the other side, and down to the hobble and tie it off.

Now, the first thing you want to do when you got a big horse like that, one that powerful, that doesn't have any manners, nor does he care what he does to you, is teach him who's who.

The next thing to teach is the difference between "whoa!" and "go!" He already knows how to go but he doesn't know how to whoa.

Well, when we got out there in the sand wash, the sand was deep and it was pretty soft. Now Boog would just let that horse run and then jerk that rope up, taking both front feet out from underneath him. He used his nose to open a wedge in that sand dune.

Well, after about three times that ribbon paint learned what "whoa!" meant.

I rode that horse for many years after that day. And all I had to say was, "whoa," and he could be jumping into a mountain pass or anything and he'd freeze in the middle of the air!

Now I had me a horse. I broke him out and spent a week riding him. I kind of kept back, and didn't give him any grain. I did give him some pretty good food and water. I made sure that he didn't get sore, but I worked with him until I was getting sore.

He did throw me off two or three times. Then it got to where I could figure out which way he was going to buck and spin and that type of thing. Pretty soon he kind of gave up, and then he went to working.

And gosh, he was good! We'd work in the circular corral, which was a little bit easier way to work the cattle than in an old square one. In a square one, the cattle get in the corner and you had to fight to get them to come out. I learned a long time ago that in order to get a horse to spin on his hind feet and work real well, you need to build the top of the corral out about a foot leaning out from the bottom so that he could ride with his feet along the bottom and his stirrups wouldn't catch on the fence.

Then when I'd turn the horse's head back in there, the horse had no choice but to come back on his feet and work off his back feet. So if I was going to work cattle, the horse's back feet were where his support was to carry him 'cause if he tried to stop and pull on his front ones, he got jerked over. Sam taught me how to use this pony in that arena. He taught me how to get him to where I could pull him back and do whatever I wanted with him.

Sam reminded me that my horse would be the only way I was gettin' back. If I broke a leg, Sam didn't want to come up there and get me 'cause it was too much trouble and too much work. And he said I'd gripe all the way down 'cause every bounce'd hurt and he just wasn't going to do it! So he said I needed to know how to conduct myself and how to take care of myself.

Well, I got this pony going really good and after about three weeks went by, I was ready to get in the cattle business. I got my pack horse and took off with maybe eighteen miles of rough country to cover to get to the line shack on the Spanish Bell. I was ready.   Ŧ

CHAPTER 20

Outsmarting Wild Cattle

Before I left Sam's we had supper that night and I was happy. I had it all whipped now. I was going to go up there and catch me some cattle. Boog was setting across there, smoking one of his hand-rolls, and he asked me how I was gonna get 'em out. And I told him I'd just rope 'em and lead 'em out. He told me my saddle wouldn't hold up, and I wouldn't hold up, either. Then he brought me something to help me out and threw it out on the table. I'd never seen nothin' like it before.

It was a leather strap about sixteen inches, with a big buckle on it and a D-ring right in the center. It looked to me like you could pull a train with it, hand sewn for stoutness, and off the side of the buckle was this D-ring fastened to a universal slip, which is something you can turn over and over and over.

Well, on the other side there was a space in there between that had a kind of a chain-looking type of thing. I didn't know what it was. It was braided rawhide. Then he pulled out another one just exactly like the first one! Around sixteen inches and a buckle on the end. So altogether, we had a ring to one side, and we had a space in there about maybe twelve, fourteen inches where it was tied to this other ring that was just like it!

"Kind of like you, boy," he said, "you're a pretty good kid. I've never loaned this to anybody else, and I want you to bring it back."

"I will," I said. But he didn't say no more! And I thought he thought I knew how to use this, so I wasn't gonna be stupid and ask him what it was. I figured he'd tell me pretty quick. But he didn't say a word about how to use it all that night. It just laid there. So when it came to bed time, why, everybody got bundled up, me in my bed roll, with my tarp pulled over me. I was laying there thinking about what that thing could be and what I was supposed to do with it. But I didn't know whether to ask him or not. About that time, I felt something hit my tarp and lay right on top of where I was laying.

"Dream about it, Tom. Dream about it," Boog said, and he never said another word about it and he went to bed.

Come morning, I was tired, wore out. The smell of coffee was drifting in and bacon was frying. I got a couple of wisps of that and I knew it was time to get up. They were already up and it was just starting to break daylight. I pulled my tarp back, and that thing fell off onto the ground 'cause it'd been layin' there all night. So I brought that thing in there with me and hung it over the back of the chair.

"When you going up?" Boog asked.

I told him I'd like to cut out of there maybe come sunup the next morning.

"All right," he says, "and I brought you another gift."

"Okay," I said, "But Boog, I'm not sure what the hell to do with the first one."

"I thought you'd get around to askin'," he said.

"It's about like that rifle shooting thing up there and this thing's probably gonna get me in the same trouble that did. I don't think I want this. Every time you give me a gift, it just about kills me!"

"No," he says, "this one you're gonna have some fun out of. But come on out to the corral and I'll show you what else I got for you."

Well, I walked out to the corral with him, and there standing in the corral, with a halter and lead rope on, had to be the biggest jack burro I'd ever seen in my life! Now, there's a difference between a mule and a burro. A burro is a breed of its own and a big one can get up to nine hundred, a thousand pounds, but you rarely see one that big. They're more like five to six hundred pounds. But a big one, they are the stoutest things in the world. Now a mule is a cross between a jack burro and a mare horse. But this animal of Boog's was not a mule, it was a mammoth jack.

So here on the end of a lead rope we were standing there looking at each other, and I swear to goodness this burro had ears on him that had to be twelve inches long. He just worked them around picking up sounds, when I came around the corner he was looking at me, and I was looking at him.

"What am I gonna do with this burro?" I thought. "I got a good pack horse. And now I was takin' the stoutest burro I had ever seen, who knows where." He looked to me just like part of the barn. Big old strong legs on him, and he was in good shape,

"Boog, how old is this burro?" I asked.

"I believe he's twice your age and three times as smart as you are," he said.

"Then why are you giving him to me if I have this problem of him being smarter than I am?" I said.

"He's here to help you."

"Okay, Boog, tell me how," I said.

Then he told me what I was supposed to do up there. He dropped down on all fours and he spread out this big place in the sand with his arms. He pointed out the mountain and down into Happy Valley where it fell off into the Rincon. The Canoa ranch is right there, the little Italian place is over there, and the Spanish Bell is right there up front. He said the draw ran up there in the sycamores and that running water led to the top. He said once I went through that forest fence up there, I'd be just above the line shack where I was gonna run into the wild cattle.

He said if I didn't show up in thirty days, he'd watch and see if the wind currents were picking up the buzzards and he'd come get what was left of me. He wanted his rigging and burro back. And it would be better to bury me there, 'cause I had no parents worrying about me.

By then, I was starting to get a little bit upset, a little bit nervous, and a little bit scared. I was just fourteen years old and I really didn't know what I was getting into. He said I should rope the wild cattle with my reata. I was to reach out there with the whole forty-four feet of it 'cause I'd be lucky if I got within forty feet of one of those cattle. I'd probably need four feet just to put around its horns. The next thing I was supposed to do was start shortening my dally and ride to it, shorten up, and then pull back. Then I had to find a tree. "'cause," he said, "it'll horn your horse if you don't do somethin' quick. The whole bunch'll come right at you."

Well, at this time I had my big paint horse, Sabino, and he knew those mountains 'cause he was raised up in there. He never one time put a bad foot down the whole time I was up there. Boog told me to take the big burro up there with me. I was to take some of the finest oats and grain I could lay money on and he gave me ten dollars to help. I thought ten dollars would buy all the grain in Texas!

I took that burro and every day, twice a day, gave him a gallon of oats. I didn't feed him anything else, no grass or any stuff like that. I gave him that gallon of oats right there in the same place in that corral at the line shack, and I didn't ever change the place.

And I kept within thirty minutes to an hour of the same time giving him his breakfast and giving him his supper. Boog said I had to do that for a week to ten days while I was up there getting ready to bring those cattle in.

And so, for a week, I was up there trying to figure out where the cattle were watering and how to get to them. Sometimes I could hear them go out in front of me and go up the other side. I'd see just a flash of the butt of one going over the hill and I thought it was just going to get better. Finally I learned where I should be. And my pony knew how to get to 'em and he knew how to cut 'em off. He'd been around cattle before, and he knew what he was supposed to do up in that rough country.

When I finally got up there to catch my first cow, down it came, just like Boog said he would. I just spurred my pony out of the way and he jumped clear just as the cow ran back at me. I was looking right at her, thinkin' I had her, and then she jerked the entire tree out of my saddle. The tree is the part that goes underneath the leather. I didn't have nothin' left and I was on the ground!

I looked up and saw that maverick going off with my rope, down through that canyon with what was left of my saddle. I watched that wild cow draggin' it and just just bumpin', going rock to rock as that cow went down out of there. I didn't have my Winchester with me 'cause I left it back at camp. I didn't dare to have something that would get in my way so I didn't carry my six gun with me either. I tried to go as light as possible so I could move around.

Well, I ran off towards the bottom of the draw so I could get a look at that cow and see how far she was going. I didn't know what to do! I didn't have another saddle. But as she went around a corner she caught that saddle tree right between two rocks and it jerked her down! After she was jerked down, she got up, ran back, hit the other end, and that saddle tree was still holding her. I ran back to get another rope. I always carried two or three ropes with me 'cause I knew I was liable to break one. I had a big old grass rope with me, and it was pretty long, but not near as long as my reata.

I ran down there and got to where she saw me. As she turned to start toward me I threw a loop around her head, ran over and snatched it onto a tree. Now I had her between the saddle tree that was hooked in the rocks and the tree. So I went around and tied her off, then I got the saddle tree loose by undallying it away from where it had been caught. Then I cinched her up at the tree.

I originally thought I'd go up there and just rope me some wild cattle. I'd just lead 'em out of there. But I found out that leading out a nine hundred pound cow, with me going one way and her going the other way, something had to part, and it did.

I tied her up and I did just what Boog said. I left her tied there that night. Well, I couldn't ride on my saddle 'cause it was in pretty bad shape. But I reversed the saddle blanket, and rode off down to the line camp. Then I rode to the Spanish Bell and borrowed another saddle.

I rode back up there and figured I had my first cow! Boy! It was gonna bring me a lot of money! The line shack had a holding corral and I had only two, three miles to go through that high rough country with my cow. My cow was still tied up to the tree. I knew this was my test. I had left her that night, the whole next day, the next night, and another day. So it'd been two days and a night up there without water or food. But I still didn't want to get right up next to her and get myself stuck with a horn run right through me. I had her dallied to this tree and I fixed it up so she couldn't choke down by putting a loop through the hondo. There was no way she could choke down on me.

When I first roped her I reached around this scrub oak tree, about fifteen, sixteen inches around, to tie the rope off. She'd come around one side of the tree. Then I'd go around to the other side. It wasn't easy but I finally got her where I had a dally on her where she wouldn't choke down on herself and that's where I'd left her for three days. Now I decided it was time to bring her out of there.

So I brought my burro up from the line shack. He'd already had his breakfast that morning. Now I'd been going up there every day scouting the cattle. I'd taken that burro with me each day and had tied him off to a place beside the trail so I knew where he was and I'd pick him up when I was ready to go home. Boog said I could take the halter off of him and leave him alone and he'd go back down to the line shack and I didn't have to lead him or anything like that. That burro knew what to do.

Me and that burro went up to that cow that was kind of weak by now and not really feeling too up to fighting. She was still snorting and butting at us with her head when she could. When we got up to her she tried to gore us by whipping her horns. I finally got up there and got her tied off between two trees. I put Boog's strange collar on that burro and put the burro up beside the cow, and put the other collar on the cow and then took the rope off the two of them.

I want to tell you, there's never been a fight on the mountain the likes of which I saw between that burro and that cow. But that burro was going home to get his grain. They'd go down and over, and that burro would squeal, that cow would bawl and there'd be nothing but horns and hooves and dust flying everywhere. But everytime that burro came up, he was headed towards the ranch. That fight went on down through that canyon, trees being knocked down, brush being rolled over, but every time, when they were done, that burro got up and he was headed towards the line shack! And he knew his supper would be waiting there for him.

I rode back a good ways. My eyes were in amazement! I could not believe the ruckus! I could hear 'em: Wham! Crash! Bang! Then that burro would bray and pretty soon they'd be back up, heading down through there, back on the trail again.

It took him the rest of the day and he was a little skinned up, but that burro led that cow right to where his grain was, and that's where they stood when I took the collars off.

Well, I hauled cattle out of there like that until the snow came, catching one every two, three, four days. I made more money off those cattle than all the money in Texas. That was my start in the cattle business. I returned the burro and the "catch collar" to Boog and thanked him for the training and the experience. To this day I miss old Boog – the good Lord chiseled him out of a granite boulder just for me to see and enjoy.

CHAPTER 21

F

Range War
Between Brothers

Summer time or winter time, it didn't matter. Whenever Sam needed some work done, he would leave a message at the feed store for me to come down to his ranch. This one time, Sam's message was a little different than usual. He wanted me to come down and bring my big Winchester with me. He'd never said that before.

I found a ride down past the narrows and finally showed up at Sam's place. I had my war bag and my tack with me. When I saw him, he was serious, and told me he was havin' trouble with his brother. He said they'd been arguing over the cabin, the land, and the water. His brother had done some bad things, and Sam needed somebody with him when he rode up to the upper country to check things out. He said we'd saddle up the next morning and go up there. He had a feelin' something was wrong. I told him I'd be glad to go with him, and we left at sunup the next mornin'.

We caught the first ridge when dawn had just broke. It was a little cool ridin' and I had my collar up around my neck and was just listenin' to that old pony pick his way up through those rocks. I was thinkin' it wasn't the most beautiful country right there, but it was Sam's country and my country. I could relate to it and I felt at home. It was far from town, the bright lights and the pool hall. I just settled back and enjoyed the ride as my pony was goin' up the ridge.

When full daylight came, we'd made four or five miles up to a canyon that held a big catch corral. Many times when we gathered cattle out of the timber and high country, we moved 'em into this corral. Then we'd pick 'em up and take 'em on down to the ranch. When we got 'em there, we put 'em in trucks and took 'em off to sell. Most of 'em ultimately went to the butcher.

Well, when we topped out of this rise, I heard Sam curse real bad, which I'd never heard before. He just never was a man to curse. I knew he'd killed several men in gun fights, but he had certain values that he stuck by. I respected him for that and I learned a lot from him. But that mornin' I heard him curse. So I rode up to him and asked him what the matter was. He pointed and told me to look at somethin' he said he'd never, ever seen before in his life!

The cattle would normally come down and go to water in that canyon. They'd go through a gate into a big catch pen that was built around a natural watering hole. The hole would pool up with water from the mountain run off. They watered there regularly, and this was all on Sam's property.

As we looked down there that day we saw about twenty, twenty-five head of cattle, which to a small rancher was a large investment, locked out of their waterin' hole.

The cattle were standin' there with their heads down, some were bellerin', some were down on the ground rollin' over, and some were dead. As we rode down through them, I knew this was a terrible thing for someone to do to a rancher. Someone had purposely barbed wired the gate shut so the cattle couldn't get to the water.

We cut the wire and opened the gate but most of 'em were too far gone. We couldn't drive 'em in or lead 'em. They were too weak from hunger and thirst at that point. So most of 'em ended up dyin' in sight of water but not able to get to it. They could smell it, see it and almost taste it. But they couldn't get to it. It was a terrible thing to do.

This was the start of a range war between Sam and his brother. When we finished in that canyon we rode down the mountain. As we started down the ridge that we'd come up that morning so peacefully, enjoying the country, we were on a dead trot. The pressure was in the bottom of my boots and I was standing, not sittin', in my saddle. I had to negotiate every rock and ditch with my right hand on the pommel and my left on the reins. We were movin' fast and I was watchin' every step as we rode down a ridge where we'd normally walk a horse. It was dangerous but Sam had other things on his mind, and I was just followin' him. Sam kept the pace up all the way to the house. When we got there the withers of my horse were foaming white and he was breathin' hard. Sam told me to walk 'em 'cause he didn't want to kill 'em.

"What are you gonna do?" I asked him.

"Just walk those horses and cool 'em off," he told me.

Then he went inside. When he came out, he said it was time to go.

"Saddle up two new horses," he ordered me.

"You want to take Sugar and one of the others?" I asked.

"Yeah," he said, just wantin' me to take care of it.

"What are you gonna do?" I asked again.

"I'll tell ya when the time comes," he said. "But I want you to take your short-barrelled Winchester and load it up. Put a cartridge in the breach and put the hammer down."

He took up his Winchester and told me we were goin' over to his brother's place 'cause this was not gonna happen again. So at a long trot and a lope, we went from Sam's place down to his brother's place, which was about three miles away. Sam's mother and father had homesteaded a hundred and sixty acres and leased the rest of the area from the government. Sam and his brother were the only kids so they split the land and had adjoining ranches. When they got older, his brother married but Sam didn't. One reason Sam never married was probably 'cause his face looked like a fence that had been weathered and worn by high winds and snow. He wasn't much of a handsome man. Sam never decided to settle down with one woman, but he certainly had his share of them down in Mexico!

While we were ridin' to his brother's place I stayed behind him, and the dust was comin' up so I pulled my bandana up over my face. I got to thinkin' that I was ridin' behind Sam at a long trot, with my bandana over my face, and my Winchester in my hand, and if there ever was an outlaw look, I looked like one of 'em! So I reached up and pulled the bandana down 'cause I was not an outlaw, and didn't ever want to be one!

We pulled up about two hundred yards from the house, and Sam gave me my instructions.

"All right, Kid," he said to me, "when we ride in, they'll come out. Keep your horse turned sideways to the porch. Frankie'll come out, and then Frankie, Jr. will come out. I'm not too worried about Frank, my brother. But that son of his can't be trusted. We gotta watch him. But the worst one is his wife. If she comes out, she'll be carrying a double barreled shotgun. Your job is to watch her and if she pulls the hammer back, and takes her hand back down off the stock, I want you to shoot her. If you don't, she'll get us both with her .12 gauge loaded with buckshot. She's the one we got to watch. So while I'm talkin' to Frank, Kid, your job is to watch her."

"I don't want into this," I said. "There's gotta be another way. I've seen some of this already and I don't want any more of this."

"There's no turnin' back now," he said. "Remember what I said, Kid."

I remember ridin' up and him hollerin', "Hello, the house."

They were in there, alright.

"What do you want?" I heard from inside the house.

"You know why I'm here," Sam yelled back. "You come on outside. We'll talk."

The old man, Frank, Sr., came out and he was carryin' a gun. He was holdin' it down to his side with the barrel down. He stopped on the porch and the screen door slammed behind him. The kid, Frank, Jr., came up to the winda and looked out.

"Kid," said Sam, "put your hands on the sill."

"Frank, you put your hands on the sill like he says," said Frank, Sr.

So the kid put his hands on the sill of the window as he was lookin' out at us.

"Where's your wife?" Sam asked Frank, Sr.

"She's in the house," he said.

"Ask her to come out," Sam told him.

"Why?" Frank, Sr. asked.

"You know why," Sam said. "Ask her to come out now."

So she walked out and slipped past Frank, Sr. And when that screen door slammed shut, it was like drums goin' off to me. The horse I was ridin' jerked his head up, and kinda stepped around. It was like he was anticipatin' what was goin' on. It was eerie quiet with everyone watchin' everybody and everybody armed, and then the danged door slammed shut!

Well, there she stood and she had a double barrel .12 gauge in her hands. She was holdin' it crotched in her left arm with her hand on the stock. She turned her body to me and when she did that, I reined my horse around and cocked that Winchester, and she heard it.

From that moment on, as Sam and Frank, Sr. talked about the cattle bein' shut off from the water and dyin', she never one time took her eyes off me. I can't remember her ever blinking as she looked at me. All I wanted to do was wipe off the sweat coming down into my eyelids. It burned like fire! I wanted to make sure I could see, but I was afraid to move. I was afraid to do anything. Every few seconds I'd hang my head back as far I could to get the sweat to run off. But one eye was burnin' really bad as I was watchin' her.

Sam and his brother were hollerin' at one another, and I don't remember a dang word that was said. Because all I was doin' was watchin' her. It crossed my mind what I was supposed to do if she pulled the hammers back on that old shotgun. And then if she slipped her hand down under the stock, I was supposed to shoot her. I was thinkin' I couldn't shoot this woman!

But the look she gave me told me I might have to if I was plannin' on leavin' that place alive. She knew I had reined my horse around to where my Winchester was two or three feet off being straight at her, on level with her. It was sittin' across my lap, and my hand was down to the right side of my leg. The left side of me was facing her. My pony, every once in a while, would kick a fly, and when he'd do that, the sweat would just roll right off my head. He'd stomp a foot, and the sweat would roll. I tried my best to keep it out of my eyes. And she just watched me with a cold stare.

Finally I laid the reins down real slow on the horn, so I could reach up to wipe my eyes. They were gettin' blurry and I couldn't see her. Well, that's when she reached up and pulled the hammers back on that old greener. When she did that, I wiped my face real good. Then I put my hands back down and got my reins real fast so she didn't know what I was doin'.

Her hand just stayed there restin' right on the top of that gun stock. She was only an inch away from puttin' her fingers down, and if she did that I was ready to shoot her. I watched and waited, and I don't think she even breathed. I guess she knew that the person to watch was the kid on the black horse. And I already knew the one that was gonna do the damage to us, so the two of us faced off and waited.

Then I heard something about paying for the cattle and makin' arrangements for it. Apparently Frank, Jr. had locked the gate off, not the old man. There was an agreement made, and Sam told me to back my horse up to the gate.

"Remember what I said about her," he told me.

Then he turned around and rode off and left me lookin' at her! While I was backin' my horse up to the gate, I was thinkin', "What in the heck is he ridin' off and leavin' me here for?"

Then he rode back up beside me. "Kid," he said calmly, "it's over with."

"How can you tell?" I asked him.

"It's over with," he said again.

"Her hand's right there," I told him.

"It's over with, Kid," he said again, "put your hammer down."

I have never in my life felt a more intense feeling than when I turned my horse to go, knowing that shotgun was pointed at my back all the way out. I kept tellin' that horse that if he ever walked fast without runnin', this was the time to do it! I was nudging him and pushin' him as hard as I could. After we rode a while we reached one point where I just reached down, grabbed those reins and hit him on both flanks and took off back to the ranch house!

Sam rode up a few minutes after I did.

"Kid," he said, "you were scared, weren't ya?"

I told him I'd never been so scared in my life!

"Ya did well," he said. "She didn't take you on. She's heard about you, Kid."

So there was some kind of financial arrangement made about the cattle, but it wasn't over yet. Sam went out to feed the stock one day, and there was a gilamonster in the grain bin. When he reached in to get at the grain, the gilamonster didn't bite him, but Sam was mad again. He was sure Frank, Jr. had somethin' to do with it. Sam saw Frank Sr. in town, and they had a big argument over it and three days later, Sam's barn burned down.

When the barn burned down, Sam'd had enough. He'd lost his horse and all his grain. He said he was gonna settle this problem in the next day or two.

"Kid," he said, "get your rifle."

I grabbed one of Sam's "Rangeland Romance" magazines and tried to ignore him.

"Kid," he demanded, "get your rifle!"

"You're not goin' back down there, and if you do, I'm not goin' with ya!"

"I'm not goin' back," he said, "but hurry up and bring your rifle, and get out here."

I went out through the screen door, onto the porch, and gave him my loaded rifle. I had no idea what was goin' on. Then I saw Frankie Jr. startin' down off the top of Sam's side of the ridge. He was about two hundred twenty-five yards away, which was about the maximum for those rifles at that time.

"Sam, what are you gonna do?" I asked him.

"He's been back up there trappin' those cattle off again," he said.

"We don't know that," I said. "We haven't been up there."

About that time, he raised the rifle up, and pushed his finger under the buckhorn sight and then fired at Frankie as he was comin' across. The pony buckled right at the knees and his nose went straight in the ground. I could see the reins fly right up over the top of Frankie's head, and Frankie went down. I couldn't see a gun with him. But he got up and started runnin'. The horse just rolled over and fell butt first right down this little draw. And there he laid. Frankie went runnin' up toward the top of the ridge.

He was down about thirty, forty yards from the top of the ridge and he couldn't get up over it very fast. He was wearin' batwing chaps and they're hard as hell to run in, and had boots and spurs on. Then I heard the second shot and saw it cut out a bunch of dust right up beside of Frankie's head on the side of the hill. The third shot did the same thing while Frankie struggled toward the top where he could get out of range. He just topped the ridge when, with the fourth shot, Sam got him in the leg. He spun all the way around and his legs went up, his head went down and his hat went off. He laid there for a minute, then staggered up, and then crawled off over to the other side of the ridge.

"I think you hit him in the leg," I told Sam.

"Well, he acted like it hit him, didn't he?" he said. "Let's go up there and see what blood we got. We'll track him out and kill him."

"I don't want no part of that," I said. "He's not carrying a gun and I won't go. But I will go up and help get him to a doctor or hospital. I won't have no part of shootin' an unarmed man. I won't do it!"

He looked at me for a long time.

"All right, Kid," he said, "we'll take him in."

So we went up there and I checked the blood. The blood was clean, splattered, but no big pools. It looked like it splattered every time he took a step.

"He's hit in the leg," Sam said, "but I don't think he's hurt bad."

"He's hurt bad enough if that rifle got him," I said.

When we got up to the top, we could see Frankie still runnin' and fallin' and runnin' and fallin' down. Then I saw Sam reach and put another cartridge in the gun.

"Uh uh," I said, "I know I'm just a kid, but this is your place, your battle and your war. I want no part of you ever again if you shoot that man in the back."

"I'll let him go," he said. Then he headed back to the house.

I went back to the ranch and got my saddle.

"You're leavin', aren't you?" he asked.

"Yeah," I said, "there's too much fightin' and shootin' and I don't want to be a part of it. I'll come back and see ya when it's all done."

So I left and I don't know what happened after that – it was a long time before I saw Sam again.   ⟁

Memories of a
Snake Man

CHAPTER 22

Rattlers and the Silver Dollar Trick

This particular day was runnin' real well. It was a hot, muggy type of day in the summer of '43. I'd been working my way into being the person in charge of taking care of the pool hall in Benson, Arizona. That evening I was playing nine-ball, and everybody put in a dollar each game, which was big stakes back then. The players were Val Kimbro, Cactus Jack and some guy named Slim Watkins. They didn't have a whole lot of money but I managed to learn how to step between them and their money.

I was rackin' up the balls and gettin' ready to shoot 'cause the winner breaks. I looked up, and a guy about five-six, five-seven, with a Hollywood smile on his face that bared all his teeth, came into the pool hall. His expression just seemed to mesmerize everybody. He had his hat cocked back on his head as he stepped through the door and walked over to the side and stood there. He leaned back with his arms crossed, with one leg over the other. I'd never seen him before and he stayed there for quite a while as we shot two or three games. Finally, I just eased back there, leanin' on my cue stick, looking at him, wondering who he was, and he walked over and he said I seemed to be pretty good with that stick. I told him I was still learnin' but tryin' hard. Then he asked me how old I was, and I told him fourteen.

"Are you runnin' this place?" he asked.

"They let me take care of the pool hall in the evening, and eventually maybe I'll get to manage it. I do a lot of things to make money, and this is one of 'em. I enjoy doing this."

"Well, I watched you for a while," he said, "and I'll stake you to get the game higher."

"We never play higher because no one has any more money than what we have right here," I said. "If we win ten to twenty dollars in a night, that's pretty good for us!"

"Okay, I'll just watch for a while," he said.

Around ten or eleven o'clock that night, after he'd gone over and had himself a beer or two, he sat down by me and asked when we closed. I told him about midnight and he asked if I was hungry. I said yeah, and he said he'd go get somethin' from the cafe. He went and bought me a sandwich. He introduced himself as Jack Austin and I asked him what he did for a livin'. He said that he milked venom from live rattlesnakes.

I thought, "Yeah, right!" I knew this old boy was pullin' my leg. Probably some of the ranchers set him up to come in here to get me to bite on somethin' I'd wish I hadn't. He was buyin' me a sandwich and being real friendly and everything but I was kind of watchin' him closer now.

We talked for a while and he asked what was next door. I told him it was Val Kimbro's bar, The Lucky Horseshoe. I told him cowboys and other folks came and stepped up to that big mahogany bar, with the tall ceilings and all kinds of stuff from the Old West in there.

I said, "Go on in. You can go through that door right there. You don't even have to go around to the main street. It's part of the pool hall."

So he was gone for a little while, and when he came back, he asked me how much money I made. And I told him about ten dollars. That was enough for gas and oil to get me where I wanted to go and do what I wanted to do. I told him I'd made as much as fifty dollars in one night!

"Kid, I kinda like your style," he said. "How would you like to make more money than that?"

"This isn't gonna be illegal, is it?" I asked. "I'm tired of people shootin' at me. Everytime I get near something illegal my luck turns bad. I'd surely get shot or caught, and I just never had a hankerin' for that."

"No. It isn't illegal," he said. "But I watched you when you got behind, and everybody was just ready to beat you and you just kind of calmly went in there and wiped all the balls out, and came right back at 'em. You don't seem to let things in a crisis bother you."

"I never noticed that but I've been around," I said. "I've been in a lot worse crises than in this pool hall! But you're beginning to get me a little bit worried. Who in the hell are you?"

"I want to show you how to make some money," he said. "So can you shut this place down for a little bit and come next door with me?"

"Yeah, don't know why not," I said.

Everybody was just kind of settin' around and drinkin' coffee. He said he'd meet me in the bar and I said all right. Then he said, "Take this silver dollar and hang on to it for me."

"I'll do that," I said. "I'll meet you there."

Well, it was about fifteen minutes later when he came walking through the door into the bar holding a box. It was about twelve inches wide, twelve inches deep and about fourteen inches long with a latch on the front, and a handle on the top. It had a little bit of wire screening on one side. And I'd been around long enough to know that it was either a very small wild cat in there or somethin' that we probably shouldn't be opening the lid on! This didn't look good to me. But he stepped up there and set it on the bar, and told the barkeep he was thirsty.

Then he said to everyone around, "This is the first time in your life you're gonna see somethin' you never seen before and will never see again. But it's gonna cost everybody in this saloon the price of admission."

Well, everything just stopped. There were two or three card games goin' on, and music was playin'. The old boy that played the piano over in the corner stopped playin', and he was gettin' himself a beer. It was quiet, and Jack said, "Ladies and Gentlemen." I never did see a lady in there that night but there mighta been one there.

He went on, "I've come to show you something that you will always remember, but if there's anybody here that doesn't have five dollars, why you can come up with whatever you like." Five dollars was gonna cost us, so, nobody said anything. These were all miners and ranchers, and not city slickers or dudes. These boys had been around!

And one of 'em says, "Well, what are you gonna do, dance?"

"No. No, I'm not gonna do that," said Jack.

Then the guy said, "Well, I hope you can sing better than the guy that's playin' the piano. I wouldn't mind payin' five dollars to hear that!" And they kind of joked back and forth while Jack didn't say anything.

"I've got something in this cage that I'm gonna take out here, and I'm gonna set it on this bar right here and I've got my assistant right here who's gonna help me." Then he turned and looked straight at me! I hadn't known him twenty minutes and now I was his assistant!

So they were all askin', "What are we gonna see for five dollars apiece?" Everybody was really gettin' kind of excited about this! This guy had a way of just turning a crowd on to where they just knew somethin' was gonna happen that they'd never seen before.

"Give me the box!" he ordered me. He rolled up his shirt sleeves, took his hat off and gently set it down on the bar. And I was standin' there holdin' that box and I could feel something movin' in it. No noise. Just somethin' movin'. It tilted a little bit and whatever it was in there went from one end of the box to the other end. Well, I figured, this has gotta be something that, when the lid comes open, I'm not lookin' in there after it.

He took the box and said, "I don't want anybody to get scared!" And I thought it would have been pretty hard to scare that bunch.

"You got that silver dollar, kid?" he asked me.

"Yep. Got it right here," I said.

So he opened up that box and just as fast as you could blink an eye, his hand shot through the lid of that box, and then I heard him rattle! And out of there he pulled out about a five-foot, coon-tailed, diamond-backed rattler. Well, I don't think it really surprised anybody that much. I mean, they'd seen probably a hundred of 'em each over the years that they'd ranched and cowboyed and been in the mines and everything. But nobody asked him what he was gonna do with it, and I did see a few of 'em take maybe a step or two back, to give him enough room where he could breathe. Just being polite, of course.

Well, he took that snake, put it up on the bar, got it all coiled up while he's still holdin' on to its head. He turned to me, and told me to take a little bit of chewin' gum and put it on the back of that silver dollar. He'd been chewin' some gum, and he gave me just a little bit. I put that little wad of chewin' gum right there, but I didn't know what was goin' to happen next.

"Come on around this other side," he said to me, "and I'm gonna hold his head down, and I want you to set that silver dollar on his head."

"You ain't gonna turn him loose before I get it on there, are ya?" I asked.

"No," he said, "trust me."

"I ain't sure I like this job!" I said.

"Think of this as bein' like shootin' that nine ball in the pocket and collecting the money 'cause I've decided we're gonna half what we make here tonight, you and me."

"If we both live through this, we'll half it!" I said.

I took that silver dollar, reached over there and put it on the head of that rattler while he was holdin' him right behind the neck. And then he told me to back up a little bit but he didn't have to tell me that, I was already movin' away. Then he just turned, and tilted the head of that snake, and took his hand away from him. The snake just laid in that coil, still just rattlin' a little bit at a time. Then he kind of started buzzin' real good, and here was this snake layin' there, with a silver dollar on his head.

"All right, gentlemen. Put your money on the table. Five dollars a head, 'cause I'm going to push that silver dollar off that snake's head with my nose. And when I'm done a week from now it'll happen again right here, and this kid right here's gonna do it 'cause I'm gonna teach him how."

I never said a word. I was kinda lookin' for a door. I was thinkin' if this thing turns out like I thought, I'd like to be the first one out so I didn't get trampled in the stampede!

Then he started chantin' a little bit, and he had a jew's harp. He put it in his mouth, making a sound like booooing-oooii-oooiii-oooiinnn-oooiinng, booooing-oooii-oooiii-oooiinnn-oooiinng. A rattlesnake can't hear but he can pick up heat and vibrations. So he stuck that thing in his mouth, with his thumb on it, going booooing-oooii-oooiii-oooiinnn-oooiinng. Then he reached over and pulled it out of his mouth. He was goin' through this whole thing, movin' back and forth, and that rattler just kept lookin' at him, and moving its head back and forth with him.

Jack kept flippin' and flippin' and flippin' this thing he had in his mouth, and it was kind of melodious, if you want to call it that. Everybody was absolutely spellbound and they couldn't believe what they were seeing! Puttin' that snake on the bar didn't bother anybody. But after thinkin' about what he was gonna do, everybody said they were in.

"Gentlemen, your word's good," he said, "and you don't have to put the money up here. But while I get this snake in position, my assistant here is gonna go through and take your money." So I went through there collectin' the money, and two or three of 'em asked me if this guy was with me, and I told them I'd never seen him before today!

"Is he really gonna do what he says?" they asked me.

"Hell! I don't know! I never seen this before! It's new to you and new to me!" And I said, "Give me your five dollars!" I must have collected from twenty-five guys, and two or three came over from next door in the cafe. Even the cook was there! I saw him standin' there with his apron still on. He shut the cafe down and came on in.

Jack just had this crowd goin' while he was still booooing on that thing in his mouth. Then he took it out of his mouth with his left hand and started movin' it off to the side. And I noticed that snake, instead of focusin' on his face, started focusin' on where that vibration was comin' from. Well, Jack moved slowly around, and he kind of started up there toward the snake, and then he stopped and said he thought it was worth more than five dollars, and everybody said it wasn't. And Jack argued that it was worth more until he said he was just teasin' 'em. He had everyone all riled up. He was a showman extraordinaire.

Sure enough, he moved around until he finally got that snake to where it turned to the end of the bar, and then he said he wanted everybody to be real quiet. Well, nobody even swollared! I don't think anybody breathed! I know they didn't blink their eyes! Everybody was motionless! I remember one guy cleared his throat and he said he was sorry.

And then I saw him do it. It was the first time I can remember having seen anything like that! With that flickin' goin' on in his hand with the jew's harp, he just moved around and moved around and went down, and went down, and down, and he got closer, and closer, and closer, and pushed that silver dollar off of that rattler's head with his nose! And then the place just erupted, everyone applauding and cheering!

Well, we must've made about a hundred and twenty five dollars, and he halved that with me! Then he asked me where I was staying, and I told him about my place out there on the road. It was an old three-bedroom house that they let me stay in for takin' care of the place.

He asked if there was any land on it and I told him about an acre or two, maybe three. He asked if there were any shade trees on it and I said there were two or three at the back. Then he told me he was stayin' up at this old, broken down hotel. He said we ought to have breakfast together in the morning. We'd meet in the cafe there and eat, and I said that'd be all right. So he grabbed that snake by the back of the head, reached over and put him in that pen and shut 'er down. And, of course, the place was just a-buzzin' and talkin' about it.

Then everyone came up and met Jack and he talked with 'em while he handed me the dang cage to hold! I asked him what he wanted me to do with it and he said to take it home with me. I asked if there was any special place I should put it and he said it was good weather so just set it outside. He said it'd be all right and I wouldn't have to do nothin'. I didn't have to feed him or water him.

I went in back and rummaged around and found myself some balin' wire out behind the building, came back and wired that hatch shut!

And he says, "You don't take a whole lot of chances, do you?"

"No," I said. "I don't know anything about it. I don't want that snake loose out there."

This was the start of a relationship between me and Jack that lasted for three years. I found out that he was one of the leading herpetologists in the United States and I was a young, fourteen-year-old kid who was willin', probably, to do just about anythin' to get by.   Ⅎ

CHAPTER 23

Giant Rattler
on the Loose

Jack and I met for breakfast the next morning and he told me about who he was. He said he'd worked with the Ross Allen Farms in Coral Gables, Florida, for about nine or ten years as their head herpetologist. They'd had a falling out and a big lawsuit. So he just pulled up and left, taking four or five snakes with him. He drove out West and got tired 'cause he wasn't feelin' well and pulled into town. Then he showed me why he wasn't feelin' well. He'd been bit between the elbow and the hand on the inside of his arm by a rattler. He just figured he was gettin' too sick and weak to drive much further, so he stopped at this little town where I was living.

"Would you like to learn how to do that silver dollar trick?" he asked me.

"I'd rather watch you do it than me do it," I told him.

"Well, I could teach you how to do it," he said, "if you will let me bush up with you here at your place." Then he asked me if my mother and father were there.

"No," I told him, "I don't have no mother and father at the house, and no one else is stayin' with me. I don't have a girlfriend. I can't even support myself most of the time."

After breakfast we drove over to my place in his old car, I believe it was an old Pontiac station wagon, if I remember right. Anyway, I looked in the back before I got in, and I was kinda cautious about gettin' in the car with him. I was cautious about goin' anywhere with him! I expected him to pull a snake out of his sleeve or out of his pocket like a magician, anytime or anywhere. I was amazed at how he handled those snakes.

I really got to respect that man! He was in his late 40's when I met him, and he'd been bitten about fourteen times by a collection of rattlesnakes and cobras.

We went up to my place, he looked it over, and said it was just right. He told me how I could help him build some pens and how we'd go in to town every day for a couple of days 'til the word got around about the show. Then we'd go every other day. Then we'd do a show on Fridays. This way we'd build it up so we could take their money just gradually. And he said it wouldn't be long before we'd have some good money in our jeans. I wasn't doin' much of anything else so I was willing to work with him on it. We used part of the money we already had and started buildin' some cages out in the back.

While we were making the cages I noticed he'd go out to his car every once in a while and do something but I never paid much attention to what he was doing out there. He said he had about six or seven rattlers with him. He also had a rustle viper and a couple of corals. When he told me he had a cobra with him in the car, I couldn't believe he slept in there with it. Then he told me we had to find a place for Queenie. I said I'd do what I could to help. I had no idea who or what Queenie was.

We went back to building cages, and that afternoon he went out to his car saying he had to bring Queenie in 'cause she was getting pretty hot out there. He asked if he could put her out on the back porch. Well, the back porch was probably about thirty, forty feet long, about seven or eight feet wide, about six, seven feet tall, and seven foot at the eave. It had screens all the way around it, and every three or four feet was a big old four by four post going up to the roof with screen on the outside. The door from the kitchen led out to the porch and from the porch you went out to the backyard. Jack said it would be fine for Queenie.

Queenie turned out to be fourteen feet long and weighed ninety two pounds. She was a Burmese python. Jack told me he needed some help carryin' her from the car to the porch and I started thinkin' that I didn't know where I was headed with this man. But we pulled her out of the car, and he told me I didn't have to worry about her. He said she was the only one he had that was not goin' to give us any trouble. He said he'd had her since she was a kitten – that's what he called it. I asked him what he fed her, a deer or something? He said just mice and rabbits and stuff like that. He said he'd teach me how to do it.

So we took her out there and put her on the porch. We put her up there on this ledge, all stretched out and around the four by four posts. Then he took out a bottle of olive oil, poured it in his hand and rubbed it over her to keep her moist so she wouldn't dry out in that hot weather there.

She just laid there and every once in a while her tongue would dart out while she was lookin' at him. I was still havin' a little bit of trouble with the whole idea, but he said we had to do this at least once or twice a day.

"What do you mean 'we'?" I said. "I don't know her, and she don't know me, and I'm not sure I want to know her! Why don't you stick to doin' it?"

But the days passed on to a week or two, and we went into town like we planned. We put on a demonstration, just like he said, and there were twice as many people there the second time.

I took care of the pool hall during the day, went to school whenever they'd catch up with me, and I'd go back to town in the evenings to help Jack. He knew how to let the excitement build and let the people know something great was coming.

In the process of Jack teaching me about snakes, we got to know and respect each other. He said we'd do good there, and he said before he got done with me I'd have enough money to buy myself a new car.

He asked me if I went to school. I told him I did when I had to, but I'd been kicked out for fightin'. He said he wanted me to go to my school and talk to the principal about puttin' on a snake demonstration. We'd demonstrate for him how we handled the snakes and then he was to call the other schools about doing demonstrations for them, too.

We'd take half of the profit and the schools could use the other half for football and basketball uniforms.

I remember sittin' in the principal's office and giving my pitch to this big ol' principal, Mr. Benedict. He had a little age on him, probably in his 40's, with a receding hairline. He pretty much ran things by the book, and he didn't care for me at all – I had caused him a lot of grief and misery over the years.

He was tipping his chair back and asking me if I really expected him to believe this stuff about the snakes. Then he admitted that he'd never known me to lie to him on anything. So he told me to bring this man in with me the next day and tell him about the snake demonstration idea.

When Jack and I showed up the next day, Jack had that box with him. We talked a while, and then Mr. Benedict asked how safe this whole thing was. Jack told him that nobody could have any harm from this, and that he and his assistant had an entire show that we could put on a stage – a safe distance from the audience, of course.

Now, again, I was hearing this and I had no idea what we were gonna do! After Jack left, and before I went back to into class, Mr. Benedict asked me how long I'd known Jack and was I really his assistant. I told him that I made pretty good money doin' this. He seemed satisfied and said he'd give the snake show a try.

This started an interesting thing between Jack and me. We went down to an old print shop and got 'em to make us up an announcement type of thing. We scheduled the show at the high school on Friday night and he named off three or four things we were gonna do, like fighting a rattler on the stage, loose, in his bare feet. And every time he would say something like that, he'd mention it wouldn't be long before I would be able to do it. But I didn't think an assistant should do much of that. I'd just rather help him build cages and go down there and help collect the money. I did like the part of goin' and collectin' the money. I did that real well. So for the remainder of that year, 'til school got out, we went around to the different high school stages and put on the Jack Austin Reptile Show.

I learned to really like Jack. He never lied to me and never cheated anybody (that I saw). He always did what he said he would do. He did get bitten once in a while, but he would take anti-venom shots and get through it okay.

Then I got a call from one of the school people to go over to Las Cruces, New Mexico. They had a large stage and a lot of people. Jack thought we could really make a lot of money doing a show there so we decided to go and we planned it for about two weeks later. A couple of days later he showed up at my place pretty excited. I asked him where he'd been and he said he had gone into Tucson to talk to some people. He said that down in Brownsville, Texas, a colored man was out castratin' sheep and paint markin' them, 'cause they don't brand them, they just paint a number on 'em, and that man had caught an exceptionally large rattlesnake. Jack said the man was about three or four miles from home and had his piggin' strings and some other rope with him when he caught this huge snake. Jack said he'd gotten a call from a friend of his down there in Brownsville about this snake.

Jack asked me if I could get loose and help him out. I told him that I was already in trouble, with everyone startin' to call me the "snake man," and when I was old enough to date, nobody would ever want to go with me or do anything with me. Then I reminded him that somebody had to look after Queenie and see to it she got that olive oil on her so she didn't dry out. I knew I didn't have to feed the snakes very often but Queenie needed her oil.

I told him I'd just as soon not go on this adventure. But I asked him how big this snake was supposed to be and he said it was over ten feet.

I knew there was no rattlesnake over ten feet; the biggest one I ever saw was an eight footer. Jack said this one had to be larger than that 'cause this colored man wanted $500 for it. Jack asked me if I wanted to kick into it and I said I'd go half with him. So Jack took off in his car and he musta been gone for the better part of a week.

I didn't hear from him while he was gone. I just went back to doin' what I'd been doin' at the pool hall. But business sure had picked up in the pool hall and the saloon while Jack and I were doing those snake shows. I think people who had never drank before started drinking, and people who had never been out carousin' at night were hanging around thinking maybe that snake man and that kid might show up.

Well, at the high school shows Jack would fight with a rattler on the stage. He'd just throw 'em out there and they'd coil up, and he was quick enough to actually go in, step in front of 'em, and they'd strike at him and miss him. Soon I was doing the same thing.

Then we'd show the audience how we extracted the venom from the snakes. Jack would set up a regular card table with legs shorter on one side than the other so everyone in the audience could see the top of the table better. Then he would take a champagne glass and set it on the table. We had a holder to fasten the champagne glass to the card table because of the tilt. Next he would take a piece of light latex rubber and pull it over the top and fasten it around with a rubber band.

Then he would take out a rattlesnake, the bigger the better, usually one that was five or six feet long. We'd always pick one or two of the dignitaries in the high school (at my school I told Jack to pick Benedict to get even with him for all the misery he'd caused me, having me cleanin' up half the school for things he knew I hadn't done).

So Jack would pick someone, the principal or maybe the sheriff, or somebody big in the community, to help with the snake. We'd all get the snake out of the box with Jack holding the head and the rest of us stretchin' him out. It was all part of the show. Then Jack would force that snake's head open until his fangs had dropped out. He'd press down the teeth until the fangs dropped through the top of the latex. The audience could see the venom drop into that champagne glass and it was all a very tense part of the show.

Well, Jack showed up after about seven days down in Brownsville, Texas. He had a big crate box with him and he said the snake was bigger than he thought it was going to be. I said if he was ten feet, that'd be somethin'. But he said he was closer to twelve and he picked up a tea saucer.

"You can put this tea saucer on this snake's head and you can still see his head all the way around it," he said, "that's how big his head is."

"Boy, that's gonna be a draw, isn't it?" I asked.

"Yeah, but he's very strong, so it's going to take three or four of us to get in there and get him out," he said.

Then Jack told me how this snake was caught. Just about sundown this colored man was goin' home from bein' out on the ranch handling the sheep, when he stopped up on a little ridge, sat down, got his pipe out, and lit it up. He just sat there restin' before he headed the rest of the way home. He looked down about twenty, thirty yards below him, and this snake came out and just laid there in the evening sun. He coiled himself a little bit but the snake hadn't seen him. He knew right off that snake was worth some money. So he got a piece of mesquite wood about two or three feet long, tied that piggin' string in a hard knot around the wood right in the center of his rope, and slowly carried it under his arm 'til he got closer. He had formed a little loop on the other end and eased it down there to where that snake was layin'. He said he had two piggin' strings tied together making it about six or eight feet long to the loop. He decided that he was gonna drop this over that snake's head and let him go.

Well, he said the snake saw him, or heard him, or felt the vibration, and turned around and coiled up. He was afraid to get very close but he didn't run from him and wasn't too scared of him. But the snake was not scared of him at all! He said it took him a while to get the loop around him and the snake struck at the wood once, knocking it out of his hand.

After he looped him, he dropped the wood and ran. When the snake headed back to his hole he couldn't get in because he was tied to that piece of driftwood. He was down about half way in the hole, with the other half out. The colored guy just left him there, went back to get his two grown sons, came back there with a big hand-made box, and the three of them stretched that snake out and put him in that box. They cut the piggin' string off and kept him in the box. Then they got ahold of someone who told him about Jack Austin.

We finally ended up puttin' off the show at the Las Cruces High School stage for about three weeks. We ended up doing it in September when everybody started back at school. By then we'd handled the giant rattler a couple of times but he was very strong. When I had ahold of him it was like having a steel cable in my hands. When he'd constrict and move, it would take two or three grown men to control him. We decided we weren't gonna milk him on stage. So we just fed him and left him alone. We'd just show him as a prize in a special cage we built. But we never intended to take him out.

Well, during the show at Las Cruces one of the promoters of the program said he'd give us an extra five hundred dollars if we'd take that big snake out and milk him on the stage.

Jack said he didn't mind doin' it just one time, just for the hell of it! I wasn't sure if I was gonna live through this or not.

Jack got the sheriff up there, and another big boy 'cause he knew it was gonna take about four of us. He said he'd take the head and I was supposed to hold the tail so the snake couldn't anchor. If the snake anchored on somebody, he could twist his tail around and pull back on us and we didn't want that to happen. Jack knew I knew how to keep the snake stretched out, because I'd worked with him enough. And I was handling the snakes, and doin' almost everything Jack was doin'.

One day Jack was teaching me how to push that silver dollar off the snake's head, and he told me that someday I'd take it off with my teeth – like this – and he did it! I can remember that real well!

Well, we got up there on stage and Jack announced what we were going to do. People were everywhere! They got up out of their chairs and came up closer so they could see more. There was a big wide circle of all these people. The sheriff came up, told everyone not to worry and that if it got loose he'd put a bullet right through its head and stop the show.

Jack was at the head and the next man in line was that big sheriff, thinking he was getting votes off this thing. Then there was this other old big boy behind the sheriff and then me at the end of the snake. I couldn't see a whole lot of what was goin' on at the front end.

This snake was enormous! But Jack had a way of showing confidence to the crowd, like he could do anything with the snake. After Jack got ahold of the snake's head, the rest of us got ahold of him and we got him out of the cage, all stretched out, but he was puttin' up a fuss. Jack was just gettin' ready to milk him at the table and he's doin' his monologue and talkin' to the crowd, and that sheriff reached up, grabbed the back of his shirt collar, and fainted! When he went down his arm fell over the top of that snake and he pulled Jack down backwards! This sheriff was about six-two and Jack was about five-six, so it caused Jack to lose control of the snake. The other big guy sold out, let go, and headed for the end of the stage, and he was gone. So the snake was loose, on the stage, with me still holdin' on to his tail!

People were scatterin' but I kept my hold on the end of the snake. I tried to jerk him back and as I did, he struck out at Jack. The sheriff was out, with this snake actually layin' on top of the sheriff's body, and the snake wasn't payin' any attention to the sheriff at all! But Jack was tryin' to get to him the best he could. There were people going through the windows so fast they weren't even touchin' the sides! Chairs were pushed over and knocked everywhere from people tryin' to get out. The show was over and they were leavin'!

Then Jack yelled, "He's got me!" I pulled him as hard as I could to get him off but one fang had entered in Jack's wrist just above the wrist bone, and the other fang went between the first knuckle on his index finger and the second knuckle. And that span was about five inches across there where his fangs went in.

"I've got to get to a doctor," Jack said. "Take care of him, Kid."

Those words haunted me for years. "Take care of him, Kid."

And I thought, "What in the hell do I do now?" The snake was loose by then but he wasn't coiling. He was goin' toward the side and the front of the stage. So I reached down and got him again by the tail, and jerked him. When I did that, he came back three-quarters of his length right at me. Well, Jack had been teachin' me how to duck these snake flashes, so I knew how to keep out of his way. He struck at me three or four times, and I thought that if I could keep him strikin' at me, at least I could keep him where he wouldn't get down there where the people were in absolute pandemonium!

Finally I backed up and felt something behind me. He really wasn't attackin' me anymore, but everytime he'd start off stage, I'd grab him and pull him back, and then he'd come at me!

I reached up, grabbed the stage curtains and jerked on 'em real hard, and they came down alright, but they were over both me and the snake! I figured that if I got him covered with that drape we could get a handle on him. So, I was fightin' for air and light and whatever I could do to get out from under there 'cause I knew he was in there with me somewhere. And luckily, I got out pretty quick. Then I bunched it all around him, and got him all wrapped up in there.

The next thing we had to do was put a tourniquet on Jack. But he already had one on by the time I got to him. When I asked him how bad it was, he told me it was already startin' to swell, and I could see that it was.

"This is gonna be a bad one," he said.

I told him I had the snake corralled under the drape, and he hadn't come out of it. He was so big I could tell right where he was at under there. Jack asked if there were a lot of people hurt out there and I told him some. I told him I'd seen one rather large woman tryin' to run with a chair on her leg, and I'd never seen anything like that before! Some were scratched up and bruised and we were lucky no one got killed.

Jack had to get to the hospital, so he told me it was up to me to get the snake back in the cage. I told Jack that I didn't know how much longer he was gonna have me as an assistant but I'd give it a try. One cowboy came up on stage, and he'd gotten ahold of a big push broom type thing. He asked me if I needed help and I said yeah. He asked if Jack was bit and I told him he was bit bad.

I told him we had to put the snake back in that cage and he said to try and drag him over to the cage first. Then the best thing I could think of was to get help liftin' him into the cage from there. He wasn't goin' anywhere. He was just sittin' there, coiled underneath that big stage drape.

This cowboy hollered at a couple of guys, and a couple of them old cowboys came up there and offered to help. We told them we had to get the snake out from underneath the drape and get him into the cage. They told me to show 'em what to do.

I figured out where his head was and grabbed it through the drape. Then I told them to get his body out while I kept hold of his head. And it was a handful! I had both hands around his neck like it was a power cable off of something that hoists a car up off the ground.

To find his head I moved the drape around and he kept movin' under it. He couldn't tell where I was by sight but could kind of sense where I was. Once I grabbed him I told those guys I wasn't turnin' him loose, so they weren't to turn him loose either! We still had the drape on him while we lifted him to the top of the cage. Then we held him over and dropped him down in there real quick and put that lid on.

I was never so pleased to see a bunch of friendly old cowboys. They weren't afraid to get in there, even knowing that they might get bit! But they knew there were people who would get hurt if they didn't help stop that snake. One of them asked me if I wanted him to get a pistol and shoot him. I told him not to shoot him 'cause we had him. Then the cowboy said something about the damn sheriff not bein' worth nothin'.

The sheriff was still layin' there on the stage. When he woke up a little bit, he sat there saying he was bit. But we told him he hadn't been bit and that we had caught the snake and put it back in the cage.

Jack was taken to the hospital and they doctored him with some antivenom. He stayed there for several days. They wouldn't turn him loose out of the hospital so I put up there in town waitin' for him. They let us have all the money 'cause this happened during the last part of the show, so they figured we earned all our money. But what a finale it was!

When I'd go to look Jack up in the hospital, I didn't have to even remember what room he was in because I could smell him! The skin on his arm went through a green and yellow stage to a purple stage, and he'd sloughed off many layers of dead skin. I can just close my eyes and see that wound, all swollen up! I couldn't tell where his hand and fingers were. He was swollen plum to the shoulder. I couldn't even tell where the elbow was and he couldn't bend his arm at all. He'd broken out in big seeping sores. And then the skin would peel back and I'd see another color underneath there. He was just goin' through the colors of ugly green, a dirty, rotten yellow, and then purple and black. I could smell the rotten skin all the way down the hallway. They kept trying to carve the flesh back to get the fresh flesh to heal.

About eleven days later we loaded him up and his arm looked more like four baseball bats wrapped under gauze. I took him in the car with the snakes, and we went back home.

Jack checked into the little hospital there and told me that I was gonna have to put up with him a little bit longer. I told him that was all right. He went through a really bad time after that and they thought two or three times they might have to amputate his arm. But Jack was resilient. They'd get ready to take it off, then there'd be a change and he'd improve. They tried all sorts of drugs and he finally got through it, keeping his arm. We went on to build enough cages at my place to stock it with three hundred rattlesnakes.

After Jack taught me about everything he knew about snakes, he told me he was ready to move on. He wanted to go on out to Hollywood 'cause he had some things he wanted to do out there. So he moved west and I had myself a new occupation.

CHAPTER 24

Snakin' Through the Snake Pit

Since I was taught how to extract venom from rattlesnakes, it was customary in the valley if someone ran across a rattlesnake, the first thing they did was put him under a box or a wash tub with a rock over it. Then they'd call me – the crazy young kid who lived down on the river. They'd have me come and get it. I paid them a dollar a foot for any snakes I hauled off.

I used to catch rattlers with an L-shaped stick, about thirty-two inches long. I'd never use the old forked stick thing 'cause that didn't work good. That was good for picking snakes up and getting them out of your way, but I couldn't get in there real close to them. They could pick up where I was with their heat sensors.

If they'd been disturbed when they were denning, they were sluggish and cold. The best time to handle a rattlesnake is when he's cold. The colder he is, the easier he is, because he's not near as quick to take advantage of any mistake you make. I'd just take 'em with my stick and get 'em out of the coil. The stick had to be long enough so they couldn't strike me.

After I took 'em out of the coil, I'd let 'em start to run away and they usually ran from me. Rarely have I seen where they'll come right at me, although I have seen that. Then I would pin the head down, reach down behind the head, grab it, pick up the head, wrap it around one time on my arm and hold it. You'd be surprised how much strength they can put into the constriction of their body and they'll try to turn their head on you. I'd only hold 'em there for a second, keepin' 'em stretched out. Then I'd hold them hanging down. You can actually carry 'em by the tail if you're good enough. The body weight keeps 'em from coming back up and striking you. But if they don't have a base to strike off to the side at you, they won't do it. So I could usually carry them out at arm's length and put them in a bag. But I'm not suggesting that you do that.

Two pharmaceutical companies were buying the venom from me. They were using it for research to fight venereal diseases and they were trying it on cancer and diseases of the mouth, and something with eyes. I didn't know all what they were doing. Everything was research. The anti-venom thing was nothing. That was just considered immaterial and small, so I didn't sell it to them for that.

When people caught a snake they would call me and ask if I'd come over and see if I'd like to have it. I usually said I'd be pleased to get it. First, I'd find it under their tub or wherever it was trapped. Then I'd figure a way to catch it and measure it off for 'em. I'd put it in a burlap sack and take it back where I was bachin' in my little house.

I made some pretty good money in all of my little snake ventures. So, one time when I was in town, I stopped off at the Horseshoe Cafe for some breakfast. I was listening to Eddie Arnold sing "Cattle Call." He could really play and sing for such a young man. Then a fellow came in to the cafe and said he'd been looking all over for me. He asked if I was still taking them rattlesnakes.

I told him, yeah, and I thought I recognized him as one of the men that had been working for years on the highway down in the valley. In those days, if you weren't a miner or a cattleman or a store owner or a farmer, then you probably worked for the county, most likely on the roads. Working for the county was usually road grading work 'cause they didn't have bulldozers then. They just had these old road graders. They used to get one of those road graders and hook it up to their pickup and drive it to wherever they were working. Then when it was time to quit that day, they left the grader off the side of the road and went home in their pickup.

So, I recognized this guy, and told him I paid a dollar a foot. But he said I didn't have to pay them anything and that they had a problem down at the narrows, and maybe I might like to come down and work on it. I told him I'd have to borrow an old car 'cause I wouldn't take a decent car out there on that torn up road or it would tear it apart. I asked him if they ran into a den but he just wanted me to hurry and get going, so I told him I'd hurry.

Well, I got there in this old Model A that belonged to a friend of mine, Jimmy Davis. I asked Jimmy if he wanted to go along with me and he said, yeah, he'd go. So, we jumped in this Model A and down there we went. We followed the man who came for me and drove down there, about fifteen, eighteen miles. When we came around the corner, there was this road grader and a great big water truck that they use to wet the road down, but there wasn't anyone in it. There they were, sittin' on top of that grader, maybe ten, twelve feet up from the ground, just sitting up there, drinking some coffee and eating sandwiches. We pulled up there and I asked the man where he wanted me to go.

"I'm gonna point, but I ain't gettin' out of the car," he said. Then he showed me around the corner where that grader had caught its blade in the corner of a big boulder and loosened it. They could have gone around it, but it was loose and would probably cause others to fall down, so they told me later that they decided they would just try to move the boulder out the best they could.

They worked on it and they'd gotten it to the point where they could shove it off to the side of the road, but when they did that, a big cave-type entrance way broke loose underneath. They thought at first that they'd have to fill that hole up, and then they saw that it was a ball of rattlesnakes maybe six feet across, all kind of rolled up into a ball together. They didn't know how many there were there, but they figured about three hundred of them had come pouring out of that cave.

These guys went as far as they could in the grader 'til they were backed up to the side of the mountain but they couldn't get out with it, so they just sat there on top of it. There were these rattlers underneath the grader and around everywhere else. I took my bags and my L-shaped stick and I went in there, while these guys sat on top of that thing and watched me. But they didn't eat a bite, and they didn't drink their coffee. They didn't do nothin' but stare at me! They just set there with their mouths wide open.

Finally, one of them says, "Kid, if I ever have kids, I hope to hell none of them are like you. I can't believe what you're doing down there!"

"Well, that's the just the way I make my living," I told him.

That day, for two and a half hours, I put about three hundred rattlesnakes into my burlap bags and got them all tied. I never went down into where they were coming out of 'cause it was pretty bad in there. And I knew that I couldn't survive down in there. There were enough of them coming out. I didn't have a flashlight and couldn't see down, but I could hear 'em! Oh, I could hear 'em! The noise was deafening how they were rattling!

After I put 'em in the bags, I opened up the back of the Model A and started putting bags in there. I looked over and here was Jimmy Davis standing there on top of the road grader with his arms folded, saying that he wasn't going to come home with me.

"Jimmy, it's your car," I said.

And he says, "It ain't now! It belongs to you and them snakes. I ain't going any where with you."

I said, "Well, I'll take 'em home and get 'em out of there."

Them old boys wouldn't come down off the grader, even after I caught most of the snakes. I asked them if I could come back the next day and get some more but they said they had to get the road opened up. They had the whole road shut and there were some ranchers backed up and they had to get through to get home. The man who fetched me said, "Tom, if it wasn't for that, you could come back and catch 'em, 'cause we'd just love to sit here and watch you catch some more. We're not going to try it. First thing we're goin' to do is dynamite 'em and if that doesn't do it, we're gettin' fifty-five gallons of gas, pourin' it down in there and lightin' it up."

They tried the dynamite, but that didn't do it. The snakes just kept coming from everywhere. They finally ended up taking gas and pouring it down in there, lighting the whole thing up and making an inferno, and killing them all. Then they pulled the rock back to cover the hole back up.

I took the snakes back to my place and took 'em all out of the bags. I had thrown in about six or eight in each bag 'cause that was all I could carry. In size they would run anywhere from the biggest one about seven feet, and the smallest one about two or three feet long.

I had to build some more cages. I only had about twenty or thirty snakes and was just getting started. This catch put me on the map. I kept busy doin' the venom extracting and that was a bonanza for me. I was able to take the money that I got from milking that bunch, and pay for a car and my place.

$$\mathbb{F}$$

The Trials of Living With Snakes

After Jack left I got to be known as the "Snake Man of the Valley." I had a good deal selling the venom to pharmaceutical companies. They taught me how to get what they needed and they'd send me the vials to put it in. They showed me how to refrigerate it so it wouldn't spoil. My kitchen was turned into a regular lab!

Out of the three hundred snakes out on my back porch, most of 'em were rattlesnakes and something like twelve to fifteen were Sonora coral snakes. Now the interesting thing about corals is that an ounce of venom from them was worth about sixteen thousand dollars. But it took six or seven hundred snakes to get an ounce. They were hard to get any venom out 'cause their mouths were so small. And if they bit you, you had about ninety-two seconds to say good-bye to everybody and make out your will. You might as well kick back, pull your boots off, and wait for the end to come. So I didn't mess with them very much.

I also had a couple of cobras but I only used them for demonstration on the stage. They would rear up two or three feet in the air and make quite a sight. They weren't spittin' cobras but they were strikin' cobras. An interesting thing about them is that when they move, they weren't as fast as some of the other snakes. The most dangerous ones were the pit vipers. I had a rustle viper that was real mean. He was green, and about five or six feet long.

When I was gettin' older and wantin' to date, some problems came up that I hadn't figured on. There were some pretty Mormon girls in town and I thought maybe I could get one to go out on a date with me. But they were really hesitant to go anywhere with me. No one would ride in the car, and I had a brand new car and money to spend.

Well, these two girls that my friend and I invited out, they decided they'd come over in their own car. My friend had moved in with me for a while 'cause he didn't have any place to stay since he just got mustered out of the Army. He didn't really like the Army much, but he didn't like snakes either. He did agree that my place was good enough to keep him out of the elements.

One of the girl's names was Joyce Shrode, and she was about five-eleven, maybe six-foot tall. Pretty gal. Kind of spindly legged and thin. She was a pretty good dancer, too. She and her friend, Katie, were gonna double date with us that night. They borrowed their parents' car 'cause they decided they wouldn't ride in my car. They knew that I used my car to go collect the snakes. They weren't gonna take the chance that some of them snakes got out of the sacks and were probably layin' underneath the seats. It was hard to get anybody to ride in my car.

Another problem at my place was that Queenie had the run of the house. She'd gotten to where she knew me and my friend real well. When it was cold she'd climb right up on the end of the bed and lay right there with me. My friend said he couldn't handle that, even though I told him she wouldn't bother anybody. Another favorite thing Queenie loved to do was to get up on something and bail off on me like she wanted to play a little bit. I don't know if she had a sense of humor but I never did play with her very much, mostly 'cause I was afraid of how big she was. She weighed a lot and she was strong. I thought if she ever got coiled around me that would be the end of it, and she wouldn't even mean to hurt me. But she never showed any aggression in the whole time that I was with her. I kept her out on the porch most of the time, but when it got a little cool, we'd let her in the house 'cause we had a wood stove.

Most of the time Queenie had her special spot over in the corner of the parlor. We had this long couch, stretched diagonal against this corner. That's where we set most of the time. We didn't have television, or anything like that. But when people came over we'd set and talk in the parlor.

So these two girls came over that night for our date. We had supper in the kitchen and I was a pretty good cook. I even made pretty good apple pie and we all had a piece of it. Then we went in to set in the parlor for a while before goin' out. The girls wanted to go to the show or somethin', but while we were talkin' and those girls were sittin' on the couch, Queenie quietly crawled up on the back of that couch behind them. Me and my friend had gone into the kitchen to clean up the dishes and Queenie bailed down on them, flipping right over one of the girls and landing on the other.

Well, we heard the screams and we heard something go down heavy on the floor, and then we heard one of the girls go through the door, not out the door – through the door! She took the screen door right off its hinges! There wasn't a screw left in that screen. She dragged that thing all the way to the front gate, and down the road as she was runnin'! I ran to catch her and she was screamin'. I'm telling you somethin', that big ol' girl could run! It was everything I could do to overtake her! When I finally got down there she kept screamin' and hollerin'! I finally got her quieted down, and she was sobbin', and she wouldn't go back in the house.

She was standin' outside, callin' her friend, Katie. Well, the last time I saw Katie, she was flat out on the floor where she'd fainted! So we got her revived and she was mad! Those girls decided they weren't gonna take us out that evening for sure. I guess they were pretty narrow minded about it, but they got in their car, and they were still so upset, neither one of 'em could drive. So I told them I'd drive 'em home and my friend would follow in my car to bring me back. So we made sure they got home alright.

The next day, I got a call at the pool hall from Joyce, and she told me that her father was gonna kill me. She said that after work that night, he was comin' lookin' for me, and she didn't want me to have a shoot out with him! She said she'd been cryin' for about six hours and her father was really mad. We all knew him as "Rifle Ray."

Well, I thought I'd better get out of town for a while. So I hid out for about five days, didn't go to the pool hall, didn't go to school, nothin'. I did call down and asked Val if that guy'd been at the pool hall lookin' for me. He said that he sure had been there, and that he had a rifle with him.

When I finally talked to him he said he was afraid his daughter was goin' insane! I told him that shootin' me wasn't gonna help her! Val told me to let him cool down, and Val talked to him some. But he still came lookin' for me two or three times. Val, the ol' pioneer dignitary that he was, finally got Joyce's father to calm down and quit threatenin' to kill me.

But I can remember goin' to dances later on, and he'd be on one side of the dance hall and I stayed on the other end of the hall, and always knew where the exit door was. He'd just glare at me, so I never did try to date Joyce any more.

I ran that snake business for some time when I was fourteen to sixteen years old. I had money in the bank and everything was going pretty good, 'til something very, very odd happened. I'd probably still be in the snake business if it hadn't been for a surprise visitor showin' up one day.

I hadn't seen my mother since I was eleven or twelve. Well, I came home one afternoon, went out back to check on the snakes, and there she was, layin' on the floor in amongst the snake pens. I just knew she'd gotten bit. I didn't know what to do to. Should I try to revive her? I thought I could put her in the car and take her to the hospital as soon as I could. It was such a shock to see her there.

I half dragged, half carried her out, put her in the car, and drove her in to the doctor. Apparently she'd just fainted when she saw those snakes, and when she came around, she explained it was a little bit hard for her to accept me living with all those snakes. When we talked later, she told me that if I gave up doin' what I was doin' and got rid of all the snakes, she'd come home and stay for good.

"Do you really mean it?" I asked her.

"Yeah," she said, "and I'll quit drinkin'."

So I got ahold of Jack in California and told him what happened. He told me it sounded like a good deal to him; that tradin' in your wealth for a mother's love was a good trade, and I should take it. He paid me for the snakes, took the business over, and headed back to California.

My mother had made a deal with me and she did come back to town, but she didn't move into the house with me. She stayed in one of the old motels in town. I kept goin' to see her while she was there and she stayed around for maybe two or three weeks. Then she got to drinkin' again and she left. I didn't see her again 'til I was eighteen or nineteen years old.

So I gave up my snake venture, thinking she might come back and stay, and I moved on to other things. But my experience with all those snakes, and Jack, made a big impact on my life. Later on, I used a lot of the things I learned during those years to get me out of some real rough spots.   ⊥

$$\mathbb{E}$$

The Wolfman
Lives On

Around 1946 or 1947 I was in high school, off and on anyway. I didn't get very good grades and I certainly didn't like English. I think history was my favorite subject. I didn't like English 'cause I had to do book reports and I didn't like to read. Probably 'cause I couldn't read very well. But I was creative, so I would make up book reports and turn 'em in with a fictitious name and author on it. I figured with all those books in the library at the school, nobody was gonna go lookin' for these books that I made up.

Well, I had one teacher named Mr. Rylance and he taught English. He called me into his office one day and told me he thought there was a chance I could write for a living. He said my book report was so good he got the real feeling of it. He said he'd never read the book and asked to see it. Well, there was no book to show him so I got expelled from his class for two days for makin' things up. When he brought me back into class, he told me he decided to grade me on my reports anyway. He gave me an "A" on both of 'em. He said he never had anybody do that before and he kinda enjoyed it.

This high school was in a small town called Benson, Arizona. I tried all the athletics and was pretty good in football and basketball. At one time in the school gym there was a bigger-than-life-size, ten-foot-tall painted picture of me with my number 44 jersey that they retired at this school. During my sophomore year I averaged six touchdowns per game over a nine game schedule. When I was a junior and senior I got offers to play for the University of Arizona. But I didn't have any parents and nobody lookin' out for me, backing me up, or encouraging me. I wasn't always consistent in my school attendance.

Well, we had a pretty good basketball team during my sophomore year. The A class schools were the big ones in the cities. Then there were the AA class schools, which consisted of the smaller outlying schools. My school was so small we didn't even get a rating. But when they held the annual invitational basketball tournament my school was invited to compete. I thought it would be pretty great to play in a gym with boards that were all nailed down! We were all so excited about this two-round invitational. About a month before the tournament, I even went into Tucson, just to see where we'd be playin'. I went into the high school gym and met some of the kids that were there. I met this one gal as she was comin' out one door and I was goin' in.

"Where do they play basketball?" I asked her.

"Aren't you a student here?" she asked me.

"Not here," I told her.

"Well, who do you play for?" she asked.

"Benson," I told her.

"Where's that?" she asked.

"It's a little town south of here," I told her.

"What position do you play?" she wanted to know.

"Center and forward," I told her.

"You're not tall enough to play center," she said.

"I'm six foot," I insisted.

"You pretty good?" she asked.

"They've got me playin' center, don't they?" I said.

"Come on, I'll show you where they practice," she said. And she seemed to warm up to me.

Her name was Collette Davis. I told her I'd just driven in to town and she told me a little about herself. Boy, she was easy on the eyes, and had a nice personality, too. I could tell she lived pretty much in the fast lane. She seemed pretty excitin' to be around.

Well, I went back to Tucson two or three times before the invitational and got to meet her again. She gave me her telephone number, and I called her up, and I had a date or two with her. I even met her parents who were very, very wealthy. Her father was a contractor and built homes.

She seemed to be real interested in me, and I was certainly interested in her. I met some of her friends and they all seemed to be very wealthy. My car was an old '41 Ford, and they were all drivin' new cars. With the war just over, they were startin' to make new cars.

Collette had a couple of big football/basketball-type boyfriends. They were big guys! One afternoon Collette and I were goin' out to get something to eat, and one of her big friends walked up to me and told me he didn't want me seein' Collette any more. Well, that kind of threat, at that time in my life, meant little or nothing to me. I couldn't have cared less about what he thought. But I didn't want to start a fight and get into somethin' that could turn out real bad.

"Why don't we let Collette be the judge of that?" I asked smartly.

"No," he said, "I'll be the judge."

"No you won't!" said Collette. "I'll be the judge."

"I'll tell you somethin', mister," he said to me, "I understand you're comin' up here to play in the invitational, and if I were you I wouldn't want to play up against me. I'll see to it that you don't make it through the game."

I did keep datin' Collette, even though I didn't like her friends much, and she had a lot of 'em. They had kind of a clique, and I wasn't part of it. They drank beer and liked to party and smoke. Anyway, they were all pretty wealthy, and they thought they were big stuff. I really didn't fit in but I did like Collette.

Well, when the tournament began, on the first day my team wasn't anywhere near Collette's team. They were ranked very high. We played another team that was a little better than our caliber and we beat 'em! Collette was in the stands cheering me on. She was really a good friend and companion to me during those days. She was important to me 'cause I didn't have a lot of friends.

Anyway, on the second day, I got another warning from one of her boyfriends to stay away from her. While we were playin' our game, a couple of her boyfriends were in the stands, and after the game they shoved me into one of the lockers pretty hard. The coach came in about that time and they backed off.

They just didn't like this hick-type kid gettin' Collette's attention and movin' into their circle. They made fun of me, razzing me, and stuff like that. They wanted to know where my horse was tied, and if I had put money in the meter. I did look different 'cause I wore my western boots, and was what I was. But I thought so much of Collette that I figured I'd put up with it. I wasn't afraid to go at 'em if I had to. I'd learned to fight long before that time. I could easily take care of myself, but I decided I wouldn't do that. I tried to have a sense of humor about it. I'd learned one thing about being a cowboy – you had to have a sense of humor to go with it.

Durin' this tournament my team worked our way up through the rankings and we were matched up to play against Collette's team on the fourth day. After the third day of the tournament, Collette and her friends decided they were gonna have a party up on a mountain called "A" Mountain the next night. This mountain had a big "A" on it for the University of Arizona. I heard 'em plannin' on meetin' up there and I began to get a great idea. Just a few days before the tournament I'd gone to a movie with Collette and her friends. The movie was the original "Werewolf" movie. It was part of a series that was real popular that year. That movie was scary to everybody. We were young, sixteen, seventeen years old and got a kick out of that scary stuff.

During the movie her friends were still treating me rude, and the only reason I didn't do anything about it was because of her. She was keepin' them from goin' too far with me. I knew the party was set for the next night after the tournament, and Collette invited me to come up. I told her I had to go back home that night but I'd be back for the tournament and the party the next day. So I drove back down to Benson and went to see a friend of mine who was a taxidermist. He stuffed animal heads and bodies. He also made saddles and that's how I knew him. He did all kinds of strange stuff.

I told him I was having some trouble with some rich boys up in the city and that I was sick and tired of puttin' up with it.

"Well," he said, "why don't you knock the hell out of 'em like you always do."

"There's usually too many of 'em," I told him. "I don't think I can get 'em all at once. I might get two or three and then the rest of them'd get me."

"What do you want me to do?" he asked.

"I don't need any help," I explained. "I'll tell you what I do need, though. I need some old taxidermist stuff."

Then I asked him if he had javolina boar parts layin' around, especially those big teeth that come out the bottom and the top. He did have a head there, and teeth, so I got pretty excited about that.

"What in the hell are you plannin' on doin'?" he asked me.

I told him I wanted to wear the hide and the teeth. I told him about seein' this werewolf movie and he decided to help me out with my plan. We chiseled out the teeth so they'd fit right over my teeth on the top and the bottom. I slipped them on and he had some denture paste to help hold them in place. I was a little worried they'd be stuck there and wouldn't come out. How was I gonna be able to play basketball with these things on? But he said they'd come out okay and he showed me how to do it.

We got those teeth to come right together, and when I opened my mouth, they'd come open. I knew it was gonna work when I did that. But he wanted to do more. We found some javolina hides that had hair on them with the bristles far apart. They were ugly, not like a deer hide. He made some arm guards out of this hide to go over my arms. He made gloves and all I had to do was slip these things over my hands and arms. I was gonna wear a T-shirt and put those arms things right up under the sleeves.

We worked on it all night long! The gloves had big long claws on them. I practiced slippin' it all on. All the fingers had this big hair all over the top of 'em. He gave me some stuff to rub on my face so it'd have hair on it. I didn't know how I was gonna work it all out, but there was gonna be a full moon, and with the right timin' it was gonna work great.

So the next night we went up on "A" Mountain to party. We drove up there in five cars. I had my car and Collette was with me. She had no idea what I had in mind that night. We got up there and parked, and everybody was there, drinkin' beer, and talkin' about the game, and they pretty much ignored me. Once in a while somebody'd make some little insult, or say somethin' about me. They had a couple of candles lit and they were all standin' around the candles, tellin' stories.

We were four or five hundred yards up from the bottom of the mountain, and it was a nice gradual slope down. There were lots of trees and bushes, and then down at the bottom of the mountain there were some houses. There weren't any buildings up at the top, it was just a place where lovers went to park. Down below we could see the houses with fences and lights.

Well, they were all around those candles, drinkin' and talkin', so I thought it was time to get their attention. I went off a little bit, and told Collette I wasn't feelin' too good, and that the moon was makin' me feel funny. She asked me what was wrong but I just told her the moonlight was botherin' me and I didn't feel good. I told her she better go back with the others, that there was somethin' real wrong. I told her not to stay, and she said she was goin' to get some help.

When she turned around and walked away I reached in and grabbed my stuff and slipped it all on. I put those teeth on, the head, the arms and claws, and the face stuff. Then I started moanin' and carryin' on. I went up to a car and smashed a car window and I knocked that sucker right out of there. I turned around and around and made moaning sounds.

It was perfect! Those two-hundred-pound fullbacks left their screamin' girlfriends and headed straight down the side of the mountain with me right behind! The girls were screaming and headed down the road. I could hear 'em breaking trees, limbs tearin' off, and them hollerin' and screamin' and cursin' as they went down. I chased every damn one 'em right off that mountain. I could hear the boys hittin' fences, knockin' boards off, and the lights were goin' on down there. I heard people yellin', "Who's in my yard?" "You watch it, you crazy jerk kid!" and "Get outta here!" Dogs were barkin'. It was just crazy. Those boys left their cars up there with their keys in 'em!

About three quarters of the way down I stopped and turned around to go back up the mountain. I was feelin' pretty good about how I pulled that off. I went around to the other side of the road and came up to Collette and the other girls. She asked me what'd happened and she said the other girls were scared really bad! She said one of 'em wet her pants so bad she can't even go anywhere! I showed her everything and told the other girls what'd I'd done. Those girls got to laughin' so hard about what I'd done to those boys, they weren't even mad at me. But they assured me that I'd better get out of town 'cause those boys were gonna be mad!

The next day at the tournament my team was supposed to play Collette's team. I sure could tell which ones had been up on that mountain. They had band-aids and patches and scratches all over em! The coach found out what happened, and they had the security people there. They were sure those boys were gonna kill me before the game even started. The story got out to everyone and people were laughin' at those boys. They didn't handle that very well.

Then one of those guys came over to me and said he wasn't gonna fight me. He just wanted to tell me that I was "one dirty, mean son of a bitch!" and that it was the damndest show he'd ever seen. He even said I wasn't too bad after all, and he'd learned his lesson from it. He said he was totally scared, and that he bailed off that mountain believin' he was gonna get ate alive before he got to the bottom of it! He was one of the ones who hit the fence down there. He said he even went through a guy's house – went right through the door, ran by people who were settin' there eatin', and out the front door. He said he even went and called the police. He said it was worse than what was in the movie.

Well, my team didn't beat their big city team, but we gave 'em a good game. Collette and I went together for some time, and then she took up smoking and preferred runnin' with the fast crowd, and I didn't like that. Finally we broke up and went our own ways. ☒

Trying Times

CHAPTER 27

Trouble with the Pachucos

For a while I lived on top of an old windmill. As I moved around I had to find a place to lay my head, and usually someone would let me stay for nothing some place where I wouldn't bother anyone. A woman named Mrs. Cox owned this old windmill and she was a really nice lady. She did a lot of nice things for me and for other people. She took a liking to me and let me stay a while. The water tank had fallen long before I got there and someone had built a little store room up there. So every night I climbed up to the top of this windmill to go to bed. She also helped me find a place to store my saddle and graze my horse. I liked it there and I thought I was in hog heaven.

I often walked in to the town of Benson, which was only about a mile away. Benson was an interesting little old town to me. This town was so small the town hooker was a virgin.

I can remember helpin' out at service stations when we had gasoline rationing and there were very few men around to run things. The men were mostly gone away to help with the war effort. Soldiers would get transferred and they wouldn't have enough gasoline coupons to get where they needed to get. One woman came to the station with this problem.

"I have to meet my husband and I ran out of coupons," she explained. "I don't know what to do to get gas. I have 200 more miles to go from here."

"I'll do anything I have to do for some gas," she continued. "Do you know what that means?"

"Yes, ma'am, I do," I answered.

"Is it a deal?" she said hopefully.

"No, ma'am, it's not," I said. "I would never ever take advantage of you or any lady under those circumstances. But I'll get you some gas anyway. I'll work it out with the manager, myself." I knew I could work a few extra hours to make it up and I was glad to do it. Those were hard times. She was very thankful and said she was pleased to meet a young man that felt that way. I remember being impressed by her willingness to give up part of her soul to get to where her husband was. I knew she couldn't think of anything else she could do. Even though I was pretty young, I saw things and felt things that showed me a glimpse of the tragedy of a war going on and how it affected the people at home.

The town was kind of a melting pot for people travelin' through – service people, miners and cattlemen that came in to do business. The ranchers were a mixed blend of people and there were a lot of Spanish speaking people in and around town.

When I was there a lot of problems were developing and the young Mexicans were forming gangs. We called them "pachucos." They went to school along with the gringos, who were the whites. But there was a lot of resentment and the pachucos started beating up on the gringos. Guess it could have been the other way around, too. Things would heat up and get serious at times.

I ran into a gang of five or six pachucos and they had brass knuckles and switchblade knives. They were fearsome to me. I knew they could really hurt me bad with those things. I got hit several times with those brass knucks. I had to nurse myself with cold water for a week after being hit with 'em.

Well, I got sick and tired of being attacked by the gang, and a lot of other people were tired of it, too. We turned to the law but they weren't much help. They thought catching rustlers was more important and, like I said, there weren't many men around to help anyway.

One hot afternoon one of them threw a beer bottle at me as I was walking down the street. It hit me right in the back of my head and knocked me plum over the hood of a car. I remember that my shirt got hung up on the hood ornament of the car and there I floundered in a daze for a few minutes. It never knocked me completely out, but I was pretty groggy.

After that I decided that something had to be done about those boys. I watched them after school and I got to know their route home. They'd go down and mess around town, talkin' in a group like kids do. I never had that many friends. I watched 'em get bored and start harassing people and cause trouble. Then toward sundown they'd get hungry and drift across the tracks, then across about twelve acres of open ground toward their homes in the Mexican part of town.

Their clothing was something similar to what gangs wear today – oversized pants kind of low down on the hips. Some had chains that went from whatever they had in their back pockets to their belts. They'd usually wear funny looking hats and their shirts were loose.

They seemed like deer to me 'cause they were creatures of habit and I could predict when they would move on and when they would drink. They always took the same route.

When I was ready, I went up to my little room over the top of the windmill and I pulled out my Winchester, model 1886 – my big 45/70 caliber Winchester. I loaded it all the way to the top, got my saddle horse and saddled up, knowing I had a job to do. I went into town and walked around at two or three o'clock in the afternoon.

I hadn't been in school for a week or two because I was still trying to get over that last beating. My face and eyes looked pretty bad and I didn't like to answer questions about it.

As I had carefully planned, I went to the edge of the clearing where I knew they would be coming and sat there waitin'. Then I saw them comin' down across the top there. The sun was going down in the west. I struck up a match and blackened my sight so I wouldn't get a glare. Then I dug my heels into the side of the hill so I'd be real steady. I knew I had a pretty good aim at them and I figured I had plenty of time to wait until they were in the middle of the clearing. Then I lifted the buck horn sight and slid the wedge up just one notch and leveled it out for distance.

My intention was not to shoot and hit the boys. If it had been, I would have done it but I just wanted to send them a message that we were all tired of being beat up.

So across they came. They were kickin' up a little bit of dust as they were walking and talking. They were shovin' one another and hollerin' back and forth. They had some beer cans and they started throwing them out and throwin' their switchblade knives at them.

I was happy to see that they were entertaining themselves 'cause it kept them from looking up on the mountain where I was. I waited until they got in the middle of the clearing so I could have shooting time. It would take them a while to get out of range.

When the moment was just right I drew down on a can with the knife blade sticking right up in it. Then I touched off the first round. It hit that can right in the end and just blew that thing all to pieces. A 45/70 bullet weighs 405 grains as opposed to the modern day bullet, which weighs 150 grains. That 45/70 has tremendous hitting power.

Well, the Mexican who was reaching for his knife was so startled he flipped over backwards and landed on his face right down on the dirt. From that moment on I kept pickin' a spot and then lettin' it go. They were all yellin' and runnin' all over the place. They didn't know where to go. I'd pick one and aim just a foot in front of him and touch her off again. When that bullet hit the dirt it sent up a big clod of dirt with sand particles flyin' right up in their faces. I was havin' a good time and two or three of them were going in different directions. They had no idea where this was coming from. They just knew they had to get out of range, but when I'd dog in front of 'em, they'd turn and go the other way. It reminded me of the shooting gallery game at the bar. When you shot the bear he'd turn and go the other way and then you'd shoot him again and he would turn again. Those boys were doing the same thing. I'd shoot in front of them and then they'd turn and run the other way. I'd shoot again and they'd yell and run back the other way.

One of the bigger boys was doggin' it pretty good until he tripped and fell. When he went down he lost those baggy pants and they got caught up around his feet. He was bending over pullin' them up, and when I pulled a shot right in behind him he bolted right out of them pants. He was runnin' with one leg in and one leg out. I watched him runnin' across this field, enjoying every second of it.

I was laughing so hard I couldn't hardly shoot! He couldn't stop 'cause he thought he'd get shot. He was holding on to his crotch and I figured he was hurtin' from something that wasn't normal. He was hollerin' like I couldn't believe it and I didn't know what he was saying in Spanish.

Another one had taken off and was running just as fast as he could but he was pretty fat and was tiring. So I put one in behind him to see what happened. Well, when that bullet hit behind him he picked up speed. I could see he was headin' for this little arroyo that was comin' up, so I put another one right behind him. He jumped as hard as he could but he didn't make it across to the other side. He hit the bank hard and laid on the other side of that ditch bank about waist high. I knew it knocked him quite a bit.

By then I thought they all knew somebody disliked them. But I pulled off my last four or five shots anyway. They were scattered pretty good across that field. Another one was running pretty hard, lost his direction and tore a whole branch off of a mesquite tree. He just went through it and kept goin' until he disappeared.

So there I sat. I touched my Winchester and the barrel was hot. I could feel the heat in my arm when I laid it down across there. I was still sitting there laughing so hard. I was thinkin' that maybe those boys learned something. They never saw who was shootin' at them 'cause they never had time to stop to look.

The next day I went downtown to see what was going on. Some stories were being told all right. I went in to the cafe to get myself a hamburger and I asked the waiter what the story was about.

"Anything going on?" I asked.

"Going on!" he said. "Some damn fool liked to kill seven or eight of them Mexicans down there. He tried to kill them all. Several of them were shot."

"What?" I exclaimed.

"All of them were shot through the leg," he said. "I heard some sharp-shooter guy was up there on the hill trying to kill them all. It's really bad here. This town is just going bad with gangs and shootings."

"Gee... that's interesting," I said. "You sure they were all shot?"

"That's the way I heard it," he said while shaking his head.

I left there and went down to the drugstore to get me an ice cream cone and see what they were sayin' about the shootings. I asked for a root beer fizz (a root beer soda with a little ice cream in it). While I was in there I listened to what people were saying.

"What happened?" I asked.

"We had a serious shooting here," he said. "These Mexicans were giv-ing some trouble and, apparently, some vigilante decided to take them out."

"Well, how many of 'em were killed?" I asked.

"I don't know," he answered, "but there were a bunch of them shot." I was thinkin' that I must have got the message across. I got those boys' atten-tion alright! But I didn't tell anyone that I'd done it. I hung around and shot some pool, beat ol' Cactus Jack out of some more money, and then headed home. I was feeling pretty good that night and I knew none of them was shot.

The next morning when I crawled out of bed I heard this horn honk. It was just after daylight so I got dressed, opened my door up there and saw a man standing there leaning up on his car. He was looking straight and hard at me. I thought, "Oh-oh, we got a problem here."

I wasn't sure what to do so I closed the door, but I knew he'd seen me.

"I saw you open the door and I know you're in there. Now I want you to come out of there and don't come out shooting, just come out talking," he demanded. "Do you understand me, Tom?"

"What am I going to do now?" I thought.

Standing down there beside that car was this big, grizzly old rancher turned sheriff. His name was Clarence Post. Now Clarence Post had three sons. One of 'em was named Phillip, who I thought was reasonable. One was named Bum, for bum post. And the other was named Wart; I liked him the most. Bum Post and Wart Post. Silly names for his kids but I knew Clarence was pretty serious about doing his sheriffin' work.

So I climbed down, walked up to him, and sat down on his two-door, ragtop car.

"I want to talk to you, Tom," he began. "I got in my office early this morning and I had to face four angry Mexican women standing there. One of them had a boy who looked like he been beat to pieces with a mesquite limb.

"There were other boys hurt like they were scratched and scarred. One boy was so sore he couldn't hardly move. They all stood there with their arms folded over, looking at me. I assumed something terrible had happened. Tom, can you tell me what might have happened to those boys?"

I tried to look innocent, but he wasn't buyin' it.

"Now I didn't come here to accuse you of nothin', Tom," he said as he pointed his finger at me.

"Well, it sounds to me like something really did happen," I replied, looking down at the hood of the car.

Clarence kept pointing his finger right in my face. I was sitting still on the car while he went from one fender to the other as we were talking across the hood of his '39 Ford.

"Something really happened," he said, "and I'm gonna be up for election in four months. Them four women are gonna be at every place I'm gonna talk." He was gettin' mad.

"You got any idea what trouble this is going to cause me? What in the hell do you expect me to do about this?"

"I'm not sure why you're up here talkin' to me," I had the nerve to say to him.

"Well, I think you are the one who is causing me these problems," he continued. "I went over to where they were shot at and I listened to what they said. We got one boy who's been at Doctor Hester's office for hours. He had to have bits of gravel pulled out of his testicles. And that damned doctor did it without any novocaine or anything just to hear that Mexican boy holler."

"They were really upset over this, Tom. One mother said her son got hit in his leg and that he has two broken ribs from a fall."

I knew he wasn't hit with a bullet. He was just too fat to get across that ditch but I couldn't tell Clarence that.

"Tom, I also went over there on that hillside and I tracked out where the shooter sat. He dug his boot heels in there. I could tell he'd been sitting there for a while. I also saw where his rifle was resting. The boots would have been like the pair you're wearin' right now."

"Well, there's a lot of people who wear boots like this," I kept it up.

"Yep, I reckon there are," he admitted. "But where were you yesterday around sundown?"

"Shootin' pool," I said.

"What time?" he asked.

"I ain't got a watch," I said. "I don't even know how to tell time."

"Well, I also went and looked at some of those tracks where those boys were runnin'. They got pretty confused. Somebody was shootin' at them. But I don't think he was trying to hit them."

"It's kinda interesting how this happened," I said, but Clarence was getting impatient with me.

"When I tracked this boy's boots, I came around and saw where he'd tied his horse in the brush. That somebody knew what to do, where to go, and how to keep that saddle horse out of sight. You got a horse, don't you Tom?" he asked. "Is your horse here?"

"Ol' Sabino is up there in Parson's pasture," I said.

"What size shoe does he wear?" he asked.

"Well, there's a lot of horses that wear that size shoe."

"Okay. This has to stop right now. Those women are really upset. Their children can't go to school 'cause they're afraid to walk home. I told them I didn't think anyone was trying to kill them but it didn't do no good. Now I ain't sayin' it was you," he said while he kept pointing at me. "I ain't sayin' it was you, but it's got to stop! Now I ain't gonna take this no further. There ain't gonna be no arrest. I ain't gonna go up there to check your rifle."

"There's a lot of them rifles around, for hell's sake," I kept it up.

"Have you shot it lately?" he continued to grill me.

"Man needs to shoot his gun once in a while to clean the barrel out," I said. "I probably did that recently, myself. That's normal, ain't it?"

By now Clarence moved around to the front of the car and was leaning at me right on the hood. He was looking right at me and he said, "Don't ever let me catch you doing something like this again. It's wrong. I ain't saying you did it, but don't let me catch you doing it again."

"Okay, Clarence. I understand," I said.

I knew the word would get out who did it.

"I don't know what's gonna come out of this," Clarence said sadly, and he got back into his Ford.

Well sir, I'll tell you this. For a while a person could walk down through town with dollar bills sticking all out of him and he'd be totally safe. And each day around four or five o'clock, them boys went home, going around that field and not through it. The peace didn't last forever, but it lasted a while.   ⅂

CHAPTER 28

Going Too Far

Travelin' through Southern Arizona, north of old Mexico, Western New Mexico, and Western Texas, most of my time was spent ridin' hundreds of miles on horseback meetin' all kinds of people. But I don't think any were more interesting than the Warren brothers, Bobby and Deedle. They seem to have some type of chemistry that attracted my more adventurous nature.

It must have been in '43 when I met these boys. I remember the war was goin' on then and both of these guys had a deferment called "IY". I was too young and I had a messed up elbow anyway. Of course, now that I think back, the Warrens may have been exempt 'cause of mental problems, especially Deedle. Bobby was tall and lean, about 6'2", very muscular, with blond hair, probably of Nordic or Swedish ancestry. He carried himself really erect and I thought he was very, very intelligent and clever. His ingenuity and engineering skills could have been great had he had the opportunity to go to college. But they had no money or much parental backing.

Only a mother could have loved Deedle, though. His face was as ugly as seven miles of muddy road. He didn't really ever agree with anything and the looks he gave me scared me off at first. He didn't seem to like me much and I learned to feel the same way about him. But I really liked Bobby, and a lot of my engineering skills that I used throughout my life go back to many adventures with him.

But in spite of Deedle's personality, we all had a lot in common, even though I was only about fourteen and they were nineteen and twenty. Both those boys were strong and they usually worked in the mines or at the Apache Powder Company. As a kind of hobby they would go prospecting for gold when they could. That was our common interest. We formed kind of a bond when it came to looking for gold up in those mountains. Another thing we had in common was experience with explosives. And, all of us also had to hunt to put food on the table.

One time while I'd been up in the mountains with Bobby and Deedle, I left my car parked in town. I returned to find that the pachucos had slashed my tires and broke all the windows out. That gang was out loose again and I was beyond being mad. I got Bobby to help me with my car and we talked about what we were going to do about getting back at those guys.

I was ready to lay hands on them, and I came up with a plan. I explained to Bobby and Deedle about an old place with a catch corral at the end of town that belonged to Iva Hibbs. I wanted to really teach those boys a lesson this time. They'd cost me a lot of money, damaging my car and everything. So I sent Bobby and Deedle to Haverty's to get some cane poles that grew like crazy around an artesian well there. I told them I wanted strong ones. But I didn't tell them exactly what I had planned on doin' with 'em.

My plan called for darkness, a hole and a barbed wire fence. We got something to dig out the post hole and went to Iva's at night and dug this hole. We only dug while the trains came through so nobody could hear us. We dug the hole about eight inches in diameter and about two to two-and-a-half feet deep, and about twelve to fifteen feet from the corner of the corral. Then we put a post in it.

Next we went to the Warrens' place and made up a barbed wire fence with ten strands of barbed wired laced every six inches with ocotilla branches. Those ocotilla branches were really hard with a lot of thorns in them. We used the branches as stays in the fence. This fence was going to stop these Mexican boys from bothering us ever again.

We picked a Friday night to put our plan into action. We knew they were always gathered together in town on Fridays. So on Thursday night we took our fence over to Iva's and tied it up in back around to the side and left it there. On Friday night we laid the wires out flat on the ground and covered them with dirt. In the dark no one could see it at all.

Years before I had a steer mad at me inside a corral. I ran out of the corral and pulled the fence shut. The steer got tangled up in the wire and it saved my life. That's where I got the idea for this plan.

That Friday night had a quarter to a half moon. There was just about enough light to see a little but not too much. I really planned this out in detail. I figured I'd given them fair warning the last time they bothered me. This time they went too far.

We planned to get things started around nine o'clock with Bobby and Deedle staying at the corral. I told them I would come running down the road with the gang behind me. I would run over where the fence was buried and then they were supposed to pull the fence up and drop the post in the ground. We were gonna to teach those boys a lesson they'd never forget.

Well, I went up to town and there they were, loiterin' behind the Southern Pacific house. The train came through and made a lot of noise. They didn't see me at first but I saw them. They were about fifty yards across the road from me millin' around and talking. One of them was sitting on a car and they were braggin' about taking a Buick medallion off the hood of somebody's car down the street. They were using it as a bracelet or something.

I eased up closer to them over near the movie house, next to the Horseshoe Bar. Then I thought it was time to see just what we could do. I made sure there was no train coming 'cause I had to run down the street and across the tracks, turn right, run about a hundred yards and go around the corner of Iva Hibb's corral.

I moved out into the open and then the big Mexican saw me. "Hey, look who's here, it's the Gringo," he laughed. "Hey, Gringo, how's your car?"

"I got air conditioning now," I said, playin' it low. "It's cool when I drive."

"But can you drive it?" he taunted. "Your tires not too good?"

"Are you the one who used the navaja on my tires?" I asked him.

"No, Gringo," he said, "I used the rocks on the windows. The windows sure go out easy don't they, Gringo? You not gonna shoot at us no more, are you Gringo?"

"No," I said calmly, "I just came to tell you how sorry I am about that. I just wanted to show you my hand."

Then I hit him smack in the face, knocked him down, and the race was on. I could here 'em pantin' hard as they ran behind me. I could almost feel their breath on the back of my neck. I was hopin' and prayin' there wouldn't be any cars gettin' in the way. I didn't want to hit a car and I sure didn't want any of them to hit one – I had somethin' better waitin' for 'em.

I cleared the railroad tracks and the biggest one was kind of moving up on me a little bit, by himself. I backed off a bit to make sure they were all close enough to see me. There was maybe twenty or twenty-five yards between us and we were really moving. Just as I turned the corner I looked back over my shoulder and they were strung out kind of hog fashion. Looked liked two or three yards between four of 'em in front and two others a little slower behind. I was a fast runner and I wanted to make sure they stayed up with me so as I got closer to the corral I backed off a little bit more.

When I went around the corner of that corral them boys were no more than twenty feet behind me. I crossed the buried fence and then Bobby and Deedle dropped that post in the ground and that wire and ocotilla came right up and smacked them boys with the biggest surprise they'd ever had. They were running full tilt. Their arms went right through the barbed wire and down they went. They even broke the post out of the hole. Bobby and Deedle grabbed the post and ran the wire over the top of them. We had the whole bunch except two, and they turned and ran. They didn't know what was going on and they were too scared to find out.

Then we grabbed those cane poles and started whooping on them. We weren't trying to kill anyone but we wanted to put some bruises on those boys that would tell the tale. We did a pretty good job and I beat a little extra on the one who cut my car up.

Then Mrs. Hibbs came out of the house with a coal oil lamp in her hands.

"What's going on out here?" she yelled out.

But we were already out of there. She never even saw us. We headed into town and hung out for a while at the big cottonwood tree by the railroad tracks. We watched the people start to gather and we could hear them talking.

"Somebody did something bad to the Mexican gang," we could here them say. "Looks like they're pinned under a railroad car or something."

The stories were starting to really go. We could hear people hollering about wire cutters and getting them out. They had lanterns and flashlights and we watched them trying to get them boys out. We thought they deserved every bit of the pain.

But about three days later, here came Sheriff Clarence Post again.

"Tom," he said. "We had another problem with the Mexican gang. Several were badly hurt and Doc Hesser spent all night up 'til noon Saturday sewing them up."

"Sounds like they had a terrible accident, Clarence," I said.

"I'm going to take the brunt of this, Tom," he continued, "but I know you're in on this."

"How do you know that?" I asked.

"Tom, it's either you or the Warrens that figured out that trap," he explained. "It was quite a trick to get all of them like that."

"No," I said, "we missed two of 'em."

Clarence just sat there leaning up against the fence.

"You know," he said, "I'm not going to use that against you. But do you realize what you just said?"

"Yeah, I do," I said.

"Tom, we both know they really deserved this," he said, "but what did you beat on them with? There was a long stripe and then a big red welt, then another stripe and another red welt."

"I'd rather not say anything more about it," I said.

"Tom, you need to leave town," he said. "This is going to cause a lot of problems. And I don't think you should come back here for a while."

I obliged the sheriff and left Benson for a while. I really did hope things would settle down for Clarence's sake. But I wasn't sorry about what we'd done.   ∓

CHAPTER 29

Blastin' the Cannon

Months later I was back in Benson, and the Warrens and I were sittin' around a campfire one night. We were talkin' about how I taught those pachucos a lesson that day in the field and how we trapped 'em in the fence. It had been a while since then but we all knew there was still tension in the town.

"D'you think they'll get that gang back together again, Bobby?" I asked.

"They could," he answered.

I always respected Bobby's opinion. I thought he was really smart.

"Well, there's a bunch of them braggin' about how they're comin' up all together with rifles to come after you," he warned.

"Hell, they could form an army if the parents joined in," I said, getting kind of worried at the thought.

"Yeah," Bobby agreed seriously.

"Hey, Tom, look at this," Deedle yelled out. It startled me 'cause was the most words I'd heard from Deedle in two years.

"Gosh, Deedle talks!" I teased him.

"Don't get him mad," Bobby said.

"Tom, lean over here... I wanna show you something," said Deedle seriously.

He took an iron rod and drew a picture with it in the dirt. "What do you think of this?" he asked me excitedly.

"What is it?" I asked him back.

He drew a little bit more of the picture and it looked like a long thing with a wheel on it.

"It looks like a cigar with a wheel attached to it," I said.

"You wanna scare them Mexicans off?" he whispered.

Well, Deedle had an idea all right. He was drawing a cannon, and we all decided we were gonna build us one. We set out the next day to look for a cannon barrel. Bobby knew of a place where there were piles of old stuff near the Apache Mill. He remembered seeing something that looked like it was a big well-sucker pipe. He went to see if he could get it; somehow he usually came back with what he was after. I told him not to be askin' around town for a cannon barrel.

Now you've got to understand that I never did see the Warrens steal anything. But I knew they had a reputation for stealin'. If they needed something, things seemed to show up and I never asked about where they came from. They always had a fresh supply of dynamite and I know they never bought that because the two boys worked in the mines. They also worked at the Apache Powder Company. Bobby worked in the mix house and Deedle worked in the nitrator where they made raw dynamite.

Well, we decided to make this cannon and Bobby and Deedle figured they could find the materials we'd need. Two days later, Bobby sent a message up to the pool hall where I was hangin' out. The message said, "cannon here." I was wonderin' if they went over to the military base and stole a whole dang cannon.

When I got to the Warrens' place they had our cannon barrel all right. It was about eight inches in diameter, with a two inch wall, six inch bore hole and ten feet long. I thought it looked great. But I had no idea how we were going to make a cannon out of it.

We figured all we had to do was to be able to fire and close one end of it. So we rigged up a big old bellows and made a blacksmith hearth out of rocks. Then we put our barrel into the forge. It was Deedle's job to sit and work the bellows. We had plenty of coal that the Warrens had gotten from the railroad yard. They'd borrowed it, I guess. They had a thing called a midnight requisition.

Well, that night while we were working with the bellows, old man Warren came out and asked us what we were up to. When he caught on to our little project he said we were doing it all wrong and he proceeded to show us how to get the bellows going right. At first there was so much smoke it looked like the whole town was burnin' down. Soon we had a great fire. We built a hearth around it with a couple of rocks formin' a U-shaped opening to lay the barrel in. We had a double jack, which is different from a single jack 'cause it has a big long handle on it that weighs up to eight pounds The single jack weighs two and a half pounds with a short handle on it. The double jack is called a sledge hammer now.

Anyway, we all picked up that barrel and it weighed between four hundred and six hundred pounds. We got up to the hearth and slid it across right into the fire. Then we built the fire up around it. We puffed on the bellows and watched it for a spell, pulling it out every once in awhile to take a look. It finally started to get red at the end. We slid it back in the fire and got ready for the hard part. We had to figure out how to get it over to the anvil and back while we pounded the opening shut.

Old man Warren had been watching us for a while. Then he got up and showed us a cradle thing we could use to swing it back and forth. Well, we must of done that trip ten times. We just beat the heck out of that sucker to get it down and closed on the end. When we got it closed we figured we had it made.

"It won't work yet, boys," said old man Warren. "Now you gotta put a big bolt through it."

We knew we didn't have an adequate drill but we did have a wooden brace and bit for drilling holes. The old man was startin' to take an interest in our project. I don't think he cared for them Mexicans that much and he seemed to enjoy teachin' us stuff. He had an old blacksmith shop with all kinds of things in there. I remember seeing tongs, chisels, punches, long things to hold hot metals, horseshoes, hinges and even nails that he'd made. He could make square nails out of metal and stuff. Bobby was the same way. He could make anything.

The old man went over to his shop and brought back a pritchel, a long punch that is tapered and pretty good size.

"All right, Fisk, you hold this," he ordered.

"You want me to hold this and you're gonna hit it with what?" I argued.

And that's the first time I saw that old man had any humor. "Yeah, I'm gonna hit it," he laughed, "and you're gonna hold it."

"How come we can't have Deedle to do this?" I argued.

"He's my son," he said, "and I won't take a chance on hurtin' my son."

"Okay, then." For some reason that seemed to make sense to me and I gave up arguin' with him.

The first time he hit it I just looked off the other way. But I thought I was gonna lose my arm. When he started hitting on it, that old man swung that double jack clean up in the air and came down full speed and hit that three quarter inch surface with me holding on to that pritchel, scared to death. Well, he drove a hole right down to that clamped part of the barrel and kept driving in larger pritchels until he got a hole big enough to put a one-inch bolt in there, and tightened it. I knew we had a quality bolt in there 'cause it was stamped right on top of it, "Southern Pacific."

After that Bobby borrowed a steel bit and a drill from the Powder Company and we drilled a hole to run a tap. In that tap we ran another bolt with another screw with a hole in it. That was where our fuse was gonna go and that was where we were going to touch it off. We were gettin' pretty excited at this point.

Our next problem was figurin' out how to move this thing around.

Well, Deedle had been out to an auto wrecking yard and he brought back an axle off an old Studebaker truck. It had the tires on it and everything. Deedle figured that the old truck was sitting out there not doing anyone any good. I was worried that some guy was going to come out looking for his truck and find the whole front axle missing. I was wondering if I wanted to get involved with this any further. But it was too much fun to miss out on.

We mounted our cannon up on that axle. The barrel was about eight feet out and two feet lapped over and braced all up. We didn't weld anything. We just clamped it all on with bolts and leather straps. Then we mounted it on a trailer hitch with a bar that dropped down from the pickup and we were ready to go. We could take this thing anywhere.

When we needed some black powder, two kegs and some fuse showed up from who knows where. The old man told us how to load it and he even gave us a couple of boxes of stuff to shoot out of it. Inside those boxes were old spark plugs, pieces of chain, steel balls that just fit in the barrel. He said the balls came from a mill that used the balls to crush the rocks to extract the copper ore.

Well, we were anxious to test the cannon. But I didn't think it would be a good idea to drive through town towing a cannon. I knew there'd be trouble if we did that. So we took the back roads and crossed the river to avoid being seen by anyone.

When we found a good place we realized that none of us knew how much charge to put in. One, two or three handfuls, or three double handfuls of black powder? We didn't know so we just guessed. We thought three double handfuls ought to do it. Then we put the nose of the pickup against an old cattle fence and aimed the cannon down into a clear spot with some mesquite trees.

We put the powder in there with our ramrod and packed the black powder down, using dirt for compaction. Then we added old spark plugs and ball bearings. The old man had told us how to do this. We thought all we had to do was just light it off. Bobby and I decided that Deedle would be the one to light it and so we praised him for helping out so much and told him that he deserved the honor.

We learned real quick that we shouldn't stand next to our cannon and light the fuse with a match. When Deedle touched it off I remember seeing black smoke covering the whole canyon. I saw the cannon go up in the air and Deedle got hit broadside. It pushed that truck right through the fence and into a tree. A wheel hit Deedle and knocked him about twenty feet away. He laid there groaning and I figured we had killed someone with our first shot and he wasn't even hit with the stuff from the cannon. Bobby went over to Deedle and said he was okay. Then he went over to check out the damage to the truck.

In time we learned how to take that cannon out, load it with chains and shoot them out of there and it would whoosh, whoosh, whoosh, down that canyon. It would look like a giant lawnmower had taken off the tops of those trees for 50 yards down there. We did all kinds of things with that cannon. We learned how to put the ball in there and shoot at some white rock target down the hill. We got pretty good at aiming it.

The first thing we learned was to take it off the pickup. Then we put two stakes in the ground and put a chain across to hold the top down. We got pretty good at raising and lowering the elevation by using the hitch. At a hundred yards we could hit a five-gallon bucket.

We felt like we were doing pretty good with that cannon so we thought we were ready to protect ourselves from those Mexicans if they came after us.

Then we got curious about what the cannon could do hitting a building. I knew about an old abandoned adobe building in a canyon outside of town, so I suggested we try it out. Bobby and Deedle were always willing to go along with my suggestions and we knew how to use that cannon pretty well by then.

We figured out how to put an old piece of a car body on top of the cannon while we hauled it behind the pickup. We were tired of using the back roads. So we towed that old car body on the back of the pickup and people would wonder why we'd go through town towing that thing and later come back through still towing it. Nobody could figure out why we did that.

Well, we went out there to the site of that adobe building and loaded that cannon with two balls this time. We aimed and touched it off. Those two balls went toward that old building and they went right through the tin roof about four feet apart and cut two beautiful holes in the roof. We were pretty excited and decided to aim a little lower and see what happened. We were having a great time. We touched that sucker off and this time the balls hit the main beam, and a wall and most of that little building started to collapse. Then all of the sudden out of that building came three very scared Mexicans. One was stark, bone naked, one had overalls on and the other was pretty well dressed. Then a woman came running out.

It turned out they were wetbacks from Mexico. Well, they headed down that canyon until they disappeared. I got pretty scared about this and was wondering if we killed somebody there. We had to go and check. Luckily there weren't any dead bodies in there but the house was pretty well demolished.

We knew we had to hide that cannon right away so we put that old car body back over the cannon and took it up to an old abandoned ranch. We doubled-wired the gate shut so nobody could get in to it.

After about three days the word started getting out about a cannon being in the area. Then Sheriff Clarence Post showed up. Apparently the four wetbacks were hiding up at the Tres Alamos Ranch. None of 'em spoke English. They'd run over to the owners of the ranch, who were Mexicans, and told them that the Army had moved in and artillery was shooting at them. They wanted to turn themselves into the sheriff and surrender. They wanted the sheriff to put them in jail and protect them from the Army.

Clarence said he'd called the Army and they said they weren't having any maneuvers down there. He wasn't sure what to do with these people.

"I'm not sure what's going on here," he said seriously. But he was sure I could explain the situation. This time he told me it would be best if I left town for good. ⊥

CHAPTER 30

Kidnapped at Gunpoint

The year was 1946; the place, Tucson, Arizona. I had moved to the city to try to make some money in a job other than what I'd been doing. I'd been driving around town looking for a job in my 1941 Ford, four-door sedan, that I had bought with money earned from extracting venom from live rattle-snakes. I kinda liked the glare of the big lights and everything that went on in the big city but I really went there to find a job. One afternoon I went to one of those drive-ins where you drive up and the waitress comes out to serve you, sometimes on roller skates, but always in a short skirt. A beautiful young lady would come to the car and you'd roll your window down about three-quarters of the way and they'd hook the tray on the window and you'd get a ham-burger or something to drink.

Well, I was parked there at a drive-in in Tucson on a Saturday after-noon. I'd been out hunting for a job all day and decided I wanted a root beer soda and something to eat. After I finished my food she came back and picked up my tray. When I started to start the car the passenger-side door in the front opened up and as I looked up, I saw five young people – three boys and two girls piling into my car. The one who pulled open the front door slid across the seat and stuck a great big .38 service revolver right in my chest.

He told me not to say anything and to keep quiet. Then he told me to drive. This probably would have caused a heart attack in most people, but having been raised the way I was, it was almost as if I was reliving my younger years. So I told him, all right, but I'd appreciate it if he didn't let that thing go off. He just told me to back out of there.

Three of 'em piled in the back seat and two got in the front. We drove a little ways and then they had me stop. The one in the front seat with the gun got out and went in the back behind me and stayed up close to me. He told me to drive up this road and go out to a place called Sabino Canyon.

Along the way we stopped and picked up another girl. They knew where she would be waiting and she knew they were coming. So now we had a pretty good car load, but in those days, a '41 Ford was built to handle a lot of people. Even so, everybody was pretty crowded in. As I drove, they were talking back and forth, and I asked them why they picked me. They said there was no reason.

I was just at the right place at the right time. I told the guy behind me that I didn't have any money and he said they didn't want money. I told him all I had was my car. He said they didn't even want the car. All they wanted was to go up to this canyon to party and swim. Then he would decide what they were gonna do with me 'cause he knew they'd broken the kidnap law.

So they had me drive about twenty miles to this canyon. We pulled up there and parked pretty close to this old swimming hole. There was no one there and it looked like it wasn't that popular of a place. At first I was hoping that we'd see somebody and they'd see what was going on, but there was no one. After we stopped he told me to get out and stand by the car. A guy named Mason took the car keys from me and told me they were goin' down to the water to swim. Another guy, named Sonny Conway, was holding the gun on me. I remember him real well. He later went to prison for kidnapping. Sonny said he was gonna leave Mason there with the gun while he went down swimmin' with the others. He said when he came back he'd decide what to do with me.

They stripped all of their clothes off 'til they were absolutely naked, except for one girl. But I wasn't interested too much in what they were doing. I was trying to figure out how to get out of there and stay alive. I thought they'd probably turn me loose, but what if they didn't? And this Mason was acting funny. Then there was the drinking and the peyote.

If you mixed peyote with alcohol it was quite a hallucinatory drug. Very strong. I didn't know if they were on loco weed, or what. But this guy was acting a little different and he was big, about six-four, weighin' about two hundred and ten pounds. I was about a hundred and forty-five pounds, six-foot, and I knew that time was running out on me.

After the others left I tried to strike up a conversation with Mason, but he said he didn't want to talk to me. He said the others were gonna come back soon, then he was goin' down and somebody else'd watch me. Then he turned mean, and when one of the guys walked up they decided they were going to kill me. Mason was saying this was fine with him. The other guy went back down to get Sonny.

I'm standing there and this guy has the gun under his arm leanin' up against the car. I was leanin' up against the car, on the front fender.

"Doesn't a condemned man have the right for a last request like a last cigarette?" I asked him.

"You're really carrying this one all the way to the end, aren't you?" he answered.

"Yeah! Why not?" I told him.

Well, I didn't smoke. But he gave me a cigarette, and I stepped near him and asked for a light. I took the cigarette, purposely dropped it, and when I reached down to get it I came up with a rock in my hand and I hit him right on the side of his head as hard as I could. That dropped him sure. The gun went on the ground and I figured I'd killed him, but I wasn't sure, and I wasn't checkin'.

I knew my set of keys were somewhere, but I didn't know where, and I didn't know if I had time look around for them. I could hear the rest of them down in the canyon, starting up the trail, hollerin' and screamin', and their voices were gettin' loud. I knew I kept a spare key taped to the front bumper just in case I lost my keys. So I grabbed it and put it in the car ignition. I looked in the mirror and saw them comin'. I could just see the top of one of their heads coming up out of the canyon, and I thought, "I hope this car starts!" If it floods out on me this time, this is it! I did have the pistol, but I didn't know whether they had more down there with them or not.

Well, the car started and out of there I went! Now, you gotta understand their predicament. I had the car, the gun and all of their clothes piled in the back seat! I kept on the main road and had that thing to the floor. That old flathead V-8 had a top speed of eighty-five but I felt like I had it up to a hundred and five. I was headed to the closest police station I could find 'cause I thought they'd hitch a ride or something else, and track me down.

I thought back about takin' that big kid down. I hadn't known whether I could get him down just by myself. I'd thought about just trying to hit him with my fist but what if that didn't work? And he had the gun. I had to somehow incapacitate him instantly. He had to be out before he ever hit the ground. So I used the rock. I knew I had to make a decision and growing up the way I did there were many times when I had to make that kind of decision.

Well, I'd gone about five or six miles in the car when I heard this girl's voice in the back seat.

"What are you doing?" I heard from behind me. I looked over my shoulder and there was this girl that had not gone swimming because she was sick. She'd been drinking and she'd passed out in the back seat.

She raised up behind me and asked, "Where's everybody at?"

I just remember leaning as far to the left of the steering wheel as I could, taking my fist and backhanding her right between the eyes! Down she went in the back seat again. I drove to the closest gas station, pulled up and asked where the police station was. The attendant asked me what the matter was.

"I been kidnapped," I said.

"You're the one driving," he told me.

"I been kidnapped and this girl in the back was one of 'em that did it."

He looked in the back and asked me if she was all right. I told him I didn't know and that I'd just hit her.

"You been kidnapped and you just hit her?" he asked, and we got into this big discussion.

"I just want to know where the police station is," I said. "I never done anything wrong. I'm just trying to survive!"

He finally said okay and started to give me directions. Then he said, "Hell, just follow me!"

So he jumped in this old pickup truck and took off!

Things weren't lookin' good. I was followin' this old pickup, this girl was moaning in the back seat, and I was flying down the road. When we pulled into the police station, I got out and the gas station attendant asked if he could stick around, so I asked him to watch the girl.

"Well, what do I do with her?"

"If she wakes up, hit her!" I said. "Knock her out!"

"I don't even know her!" he said.

"Hit her anyway! If she wakes up she may have a gun in that back seat."

"I'll hit her!" he says. So he stayed put watching her while I went in and told this police guy sitting behind this desk what was happening. He wanted to know if I'd been drinking. I told him no, sir, and then told him my story. I told him I thought one of them was dead 'cause of me hittin' him with a rock. And then he asked about the girl in the back seat. I told him about the service station guy out there looking after her, and that I told him to hit her if she gets up.

He said we had to do something about this and went for some help. Then we went out to the car and the girl got out. I started to explain a little bit about her and they took her in right away. Then they asked me to lead them back to the canyon. I told them there were five people still there and that they didn't have any clothes 'cause their clothes were in the car.

So we got some blankets to kind of cover 'em until they sorted out whose clothes were whose. I asked one of the police to stay close to me. I had no idea what we were going to run into up there. I didn't want to drive up there with the police two blocks back when the shootin' started. But when we got there Mason was laid out on the ground with Sonny kneeling down by him. Mason's shirt was off of him and Sonny was putting it on himself. I was thinkin', "Oh boy, that guy's dead."

The police got out and got a hold of Sonny, askin' him where the rest of 'em were.

He told them they were down below. Well, then it was my word against the six of them. The police took statements from everybody, and, believe it or not, they believed me.

Well, I eventually got a job in town and two months later these guys who had kidnapped me tracked me down and shot the windows out of the house where I was stayin'. One time they set the house on fire. They had a gang try to find me 'cause even though this guy, Mason, did live, he was never the same. The other guy, Sonny, that had the gun, went to prison for kidnapping. We all went through a trial and I had to have a bodyguard for a while.

I never got too excited during this whole ordeal. I knew that if I thought my way through it, I'd figure a way out. You just play it cool and wait until you get your chance to get away. But I was nervous when that guy with the gun was laughin' and jokin' with the others, 'cause if he'd had a pistol like mine, the slightest pressure on the trigger would have shot right through me and killed me.   ☥

CHAPTER 31

Ŧ

The Mystery of the Indian Burial Cave

At times I used to go onto an Indian reservation to hunt, and I would take my Winchester or my bow with me. I was proficient with the bow, having picked it up from the Indian people who I stayed with from time to time.

On this particular huntin' trip I went up on this Indian reservation on a mule that I affectionately called Pinky or Pink Lady. She was probably one of my closest friends. She was a lot like I was – very independent. But as long as I had a rope on her she was mine. If I didn't have a rope on her she belonged to God. There were times when I chased her further than I rode her! But she was a real talented saddle mule.

Pinky and I, and a friend of mine, Ernie, went up to the reservation to hunt and hopefully bring back some deer and turkey. That first day we hunted up there for a while without much luck. We did jump several herds of wild javelina. They're not usually an aggressive animal like a Russian boar, but if you were to find one in a mine shaft, which has happened to me, and he's behind you and you're in his way and he wants out, it's best to give him as much room as you can... which isn't easy in a mine shaft.

We saw several of those boar up in those mountains that first day but we didn't see any deer or turkey. On the second day of the hunt we decided to go up a different set of ridges. Ernie went down in the bottom of the canyon and I rode a little in front up on the ridge. When Ernie kicked the prey out of the bottom brush, I'd be right there at the top where I could get 'em as they came out. This was what we were doing that second day. So with that system under way we spent most of that day into the afternoon hunting. But still not havin' any luck.

While I was ridin' Pinky up there on that ridge I started hearing an echo sound under her feet. Soon Pinky stopped completely. There's one thing you gotta understand about a saddle mule. They won't do anything that's going to hurt 'em. They have much wisdom about that, probably more than human beings. They won't get put in a position where they're goin' to get hurt nor will they go further out into the hunt than from where they can get back to where they started that day. They have a built-in computer system in their minds telling them that if they go a certain distance they have to have enough strength to get back to where they started.

Somebody asked me one time about the difference between a Quarter Horse and a saddle mule. I told them the difference was a quarter of a mile in a race. 'cause when the gun goes off, the Quarter Horse is running as fast as he can and the mule is running as fast as he wants to. The mule has already figured out that he may have to get back and paces himself.

With that mule attitude in mind, up on that ridge that day, Pinky just stopped. I urged her on gently but she shook her head and that was her way of saying no. I knew I had a problem there, but I wasn't sure exactly what it was. I backed her up and I rode out to the right a little bit. Then I started back up the other side toward the top of the ridge again. Once more, I started to hear this hollow sound under her feet. She stamped her feet a couple of times warning me that this was bad. I sure didn't want to fall through some sink hole, but there was no other way I could get up the ridge. I didn't want to go back down around the canyon and lose sight of Ernie.

So, I decided to bail off of her and walk. I had my shotgun chaps on. It was a pretty warm day and I had my Stetson on. I remember wiping the sweat off my face and tellin' Pinky that I'd go in the front. It was not uncommon for a cowboy to talk to his saddle mule. I told her, "Pinky, all right, I'll go first." Then I took the lead rope attached to her halter and went ahead. I couldn't hear much from my feet but I could hear somethin' strange from under her feet. She was barely willing to go at my urging and she wasn't comfortable goin' forward. The look on her face was telling me she thought we were headed for trouble!

We went on about fifty feet and the ground was still giving us an echo. I was thinkin' that I'd better figure a way out of there, maybe turn to the right or something. I knew that it was not uncommon to go across a piece of ground that was hollow. Sometimes an old mine shaft or some kind of tunnel would be under there or the water had run down through the limestone, seeped in and washed out a hole.

Many times I'd ridden across a hollow spot and then it would quit as I went on a ways. I'd never been over a hollow spot that was as wide as this one. I got the feeling that this thing was very large under there. So I turned to the side to try to find a better way out, and without any notice – the ground collapsed and I fell through!

I went all the way down, about seven or eight feet, and landed hard on the bottom. Just by instinct I still had a hold of that eleven-foot lead rope.

Pinky had stopped at the hole I'd made. That hole was about two and a half, three feet in diameter. After I hit the bottom I just stayed absolutely still. I went down hitting my face on the side and I felt pretty scraped up. I had dropped my gun and I couldn't see it 'cause it was pitch black! I couldn't see a thing!

Finally I stood up and stayed still for a few minutes. I got to where I could see Pinky lookin' down at me through this hole. She had both ears pushed up like she was saying, "I told you so." I knew I had a real problem and I didn't need her rubbin' it in.

Luckily, Ernie, riding on the other side, had looked over my way and saw Pinky standing there with a lead rope hangin' straight down to the ground. Later he told me that he couldn't figure out how or why I had tied her like that. It didn't look right to him. So he tied up his saddle mule and came over to see what had happened. As Ernie came up to the hole he spoke to Pinky and I saw her raise her head up 'cause she knew who he was. When Ernie saw the hole he called down to me.

"Tom, you all right?" he asked.

"Yeah, I'm a little bruised and scratched up," I said. "But I can't see anything in here, it's really black. I can't find my gun and I can't tell how big it is down here."

"We got to figure a way to get you out," he said.

"You can get me out with that lariat rope that's on my saddle," I told him. "You'll have to pull me up to the edge. I'll step in it and you pull but you'll have to stop when I say or I'll hurt my hands as I come up over the top of this granite."

So he left to get the rope ready. I felt like I was in a big room. As I began to move around a little bit I heard one or two rattlesnakes down in there with me somewhere. When Ernie came back he could hear them, too. It was too dark for me to tell where they were but one was off on the left and there was one pretty close to the front of me. Ernie said he couldn't see me, but I could see him framed in the light of the hole. We didn't have a flashlight so I told Ernie to get some rawhide from our saddle bags and some bear grass to make a torch.

After he wrapped some bear grass around a mesquite branch and tied it on with the rawhide, he pitched the torch and some matches down to me so I could see what I was doing.

After he dropped this torch down in front of me, I moved over a little to the right to find it and pick it up. Then I took a step back and fell backwards right on my back. At this point I was starting to get a little more concerned and things don't usually scare me much. I didn't know what I'd fallen over and I was afraid of fallin' into another hole.

Ernie had a hold of Pinky and he was tellin' me to look for the matches. There's nothing more exhilarating than bein' on all fours in a dark cave, groping around for some matches while hearing a rattler shakin' his tail four or five feet away. My heart was racin' but I knew I had to be calm. I didn't want to move too fast and fall over again. I soon found the bear grass torch and, luckily, the matches were near it. I lit it up and looked around.

Ernie was now laying down by the hole looking in and askin' what I was seein' down there.

"Ernie, you gotta come down here!" I said.

"Oh no!" he answered down the hole. "I'm not coming down there. I don't care what in the hell you see! I ain't doing it!"

"Ernie," I said. "I'm in an underground burial chamber."

"Burial of what?" asked Ernie.

"Indians!" I yelled up.

"Tom, Indians don't bury their dead underground!" he said. "They bury 'em up top or they burn 'em. There's no Indian underground burial chambers."

"I'm in one," I insisted.

"Well, tell me what you can see down there," he yelled at me.

First I told him about the rattlers and I got one out of the way. I took a mesquite limb, picked the snake up and slung him as far away as I could. There was another one back behind me, but he crawled under a ledge so I didn't think he was much of a problem anymore.

After that I looked around and saw several large earthenware clay pots. I don't know what was in them, but they were decorative with white, black and red paints. They weren't anything really ornate, but they were beautifully painted.

Close to me on the right against the wall, standing on what looked like a little bed or something, was a quiver and arrows made out of real heavy rawhide. The quiver had paint markin's on it, and there beside it was also a bow. Now, I had been dealing with bows and arrows for many years and I'd seen Indian bows from Southern Arizona where the Apache tribes of the Mescaleros and Chiricahuas stayed, and from Northern Arizona where the White River Apache and the San Carlos Apache lived. All of these tribes had bows that the old people used. The bow down in that cave wasn't like any of the ones I'd seen before.

As I looked over the cave I saw three distinct rooms. One was smoothly hollowed out and very large. I estimated the size of the main room was fifty feet on one side and a good forty or fifty feet the other way. It was square going on rectangular, and I counted nine burial mounds in that room alone. Farther back in there were some other things but I wasn't sure what they were. I did see a shroud-type thing on the side of the big room covering something up, but I never made it over to that side of the room to see it up close.

Removing anything that might have to do with the Indian Spirit People is forbidden and surrounded by Indian legend and folklore. These beliefs are real and sacred to the Indians. They won't even kill a bear 'cause if you hang him up and take the hide off of him you can't tell it's not a man. The carcass looks exactly like a man. I knew they were very protective of their burial grounds. I also knew that going into one unknowingly was just as serious as doing it on purpose. I truly believe that if we'd been found in there they would have not arrested us, they would have shot us.

I knew I had to get out of there as soon as I could. But I did look around for something to bring back to show people to prove what I'd seen. I decided to take the bow that was laying over on a carpet of what appeared to be old pine needles or something powdery. I knew there was something un-usual about this bow. It was really different. I picked it up and it had a leather-looking sock on one end. This sock collapsed in my hands and broke into pieces that I let slide off to the ground. Then I handed the bow out to Ernie, telling him to be careful with it 'cause I thought that it might also crumble. Then I managed to get up out of there using the lariat rope with Ernie pull-ing it up with the help of Pinky.

I knew we had to seal up the hole so we took some of the water we had with us and mixed it with a clay-type substance called colici. This stuff be-comes as hard as cement. There was a lot of that type of clay around so we made a lattice work of ocotillo and bear grass laced across the hole. Ocotillo is six- to eight-foot long cactus with inch-thick spines growing out of it. If you're ever tangled with it, it could rip your shirt up or scar up your chaps really bad.

We cut maybe a dozen branches and interlaced them, lapping one on top of the other, like a mat. We laid it over the hole and put the bear grass on top. Then we took the colici mixture and sealed the lid. When we were all done, we put a pretty good size dead mesquite tree over the top of it. Then we headed on home without catchin' anything we could eat.

It was probably a year or so after I found that bow that I finally took it to the University of Arizona. I sat down with the archeology department head and told him what I had stumbled into. He told me there was no such thing as a subterranean Indian burial ground, and he wanted to know where I really got my hands on the bow.

Well, I wasn't about to tell him where I'd found it. Many times when I was a young boy, riding for ranches, old things would be found or dug up – Indian mummies, arrowheads, pottery, and weaponry. I learned from the ranchers that the minute they took something to the University they would call up one of their benefactors and the artifacts would end up in someone's private collection. I also knew that I had been on the Indian reservation legally for hunting but it certainly wasn't legal bein' in that burial ground and takin' that bow.

But I took the bow in for him to see and asked him to check it out. He wanted me to leave it with him, but I refused. So he scheduled me to come back to have his staff analyze it and have it carbon dated. He insisted that it was not a North American Indian bow.

He said he didn't mean to call me a liar, but he knew I hadn't found that bow in an Indian burial chamber anywhere on the North American continent. He said it wasn't the right type of wood or design and that he had never seen the color combinations on any North American Indian stuff.

This bow has the ends curved up with the string goin' back around. Another interesting thing about this bow is that whoever designed it placed the handle grip so that, unlike a typical American Indian bow, the center of gravity is placed specifically for the arrow to fly efficiently past the bow. The American Indian bow string went over the side of the bow, but on this bow when the string is pulled back and the arrow released, it doesn't have to go out around the handle of the bow. It was definitely designed by an artisan of another culture and time period. Modern technology has just discovered some of the design techniques found in this bow.

All this professor could tell me after taking a sample of the wood was that the wood could only be from the area around Jerusalem or today's Turkey. The tests indicated that the wood pre-dated twenty-five-hundred years ago. The painted triangle and dot designs have never been identified with any culture here.

About four years ago I read that in Northern Arizona they uncovered a hidden subterranean Indian burial site. It had earth mounds, pottery, arrows and quivers, and that type of stuff. I have the article on it from an archaeology magazine. So now they're sayin' that some Indians here did have underground burial sites. I knew that fifty years ago, but that still doesn't explain how this strange bow got there.

Scratching Out a Living

CHAPTER 32

Bounty Hunting for German POWs

While the war was goin' on, the U.S. government was bringing German war prisoners into Papago Park near Florence, Arizona. They had a POW camp where they kept them. I came to learn one thing about these German prisoners – that they were a highly intelligent group of people. They sure knew mechanical and technical things. They seemed able to plan out everything they did real well. I was impressed by 'em.

One day I was in town, and I overheard a call that came in from the government to the sheriff at this restaurant where I was. Two German prisoners had escaped from the camp and they were tryin' to apprehend them. They knew which way they thought the prisoners were goin'. Mexico wasn't that far away. If they could get into Mexico, they stood a good chance of actually gettin' away.

So these two had broken out and headed down the San Pedro River, which would lead 'em right past Bisbee, Naco, and right on down into Mexico. That river also branched off and went through another town called Nogales. Well, I just happened to be settin' there while the sheriff was talkin' on the phone in the restaurant. I heard him ask where they'd be comin' from, and they talked back and forth. I could only hear one side of the conversation, but when the sheriff got off, I asked him what they did with 'em when they caught 'em.

He told me there was a two hundred dollar reward for 'em. I was thinkin' that was a lot of money. So I asked him where he figured they'd come out. He told me they'd probably work their way around behind the Rincons and pick up the San Pedro somewhere.

Then they'd head on over toward New Mexico, or they might get down near where we were and try to go into Mexico. I told him I was interested in hearin' about it 'cause I knew that country real well.

That sheriff hadn't disappeared long in his car when I was out of that restaurant, runnin' over to where I was keepin' my horse. I borrowed a pack horse, and told the people that I was stayin' with that I'd be gone three days. I bought some supplies and I got my 45/70, lever action Winchester. Shoots a .405 grain bullet, and it could just about wipe out a tank if I hit it just right. That gun weighed seventeen pounds fully loaded!

I slipped it into the saddle boot, got some biscuits, jerky, some other food, and wrapped me up a half a slab of bacon, put it all in there, and set out to capture some German prisoners.

I sure knew the country 'cause I'd already cowboyed there. I didn't need any maps. I thought there wasn't anybody in that country who knew it better than I did. So I went up that river, following it all the way up to the narrows. I figured if them boys followed the river, they'd probably stay out of the water. The river had banks about thirty, forty feet high in some places. It wound around and some parts didn't have much water in it and I could even walk across.

I thought the only thing that might force 'em down into the river was when they'd pass through the narrows. It was rugged and I knew they'd be hot and thirsty. So they'd stay pretty close to the water.

I rode up that river, takin' my time. When I got to where the narrows were, I tied my pack horse off, and kind of made me a little camp. Then I went back up there a little ways, about four or five hundred yards from the narrows, where I could see the side of that bank. I sat there and watched for the rest of that day, and most of the next day, but nobody was comin'.

I started thinkin' that I was just wastin' time down there, so I left my camp and my pack horse there, and kicked off down in the river on my horse and rode up there a ways to see if I could see any signs. Well, that river had a habit of just goin' one way and then, all of a sudden, it would go jar off to the right, and then back to the left, like a snaky "S." I was watchin' for tracks to see if anyone was cuttin' sign along the edge of the river. I saw that there were lots of wild hogs runnin' there, a deer or two, and some cattle that would stray down to the bottom to drink water. No sign of people, though.

It was along about noon, and I'd been carryin' my Winchester with me all the time in my saddle boot, ridin' with my head down, not payin' a whole lot of attention. Suddenly, my pony stopped real short. I looked up, and as I turned the corner, both of those German guys were right in front of me. So I just peeled off that horse, draggin' my Winchester with me.

I remember one of 'em sayin' something to me in German, and I didn't understand a word he was sayin'. I tried to tell 'em to put their hands up, and that they were under arrest!

And I'm standin' there holdin' this rifle, and this one guy just folded his arms and smiled. I could tell he thought he was just talkin' to a kid. He was thinkin' if they worked this right, they'd have a saddle horse and a rifle. But I had figured them out.

They were both standin' there in front of me, thinkin' about what they were gonna do. I levered a cartridge into the barrel. One of 'em said somethin' else in German and pointed towards the horse, and then off to the side. Then they started to drift apart. I thought I had to do somethin' right quick! And I wasn't any stranger to having to shoot a man if I had to. I could see four hundred dollars startin' to disappear into the sunset.

So I just took my rifle and I pulled the hammer back on it, and shot right under one guy's foot, knockin' his boot heel off his boot. It knocked him off to the side and down on one knee. Then he really said some things in German which I don't think were complimentary at all! He was shakin' his fist at me. And I just told them both to get back together, and I levered another one in there, and drew down on them.

"You're gonna be dead if you don't do what I tell you to do," I told them. So I turned 'em around, and got 'em up where I could watch 'em good. Then I walked 'em over to the side and I tried to communicate with 'em. I had to wave my arms and show them everything. I couldn't understand them and they couldn't understand me. It was kind of a comical thing but yet it was serious. I knew they wanted my gun and horse and I wanted them and the four hundred dollars that went with them.

I finally got 'em to lean up against the bank. I gave them my piggin' string, and told 'em to tie their hands together. I knew if I got 'em tied together, they couldn't break and run and double off on me. They knew that I couldn't shoot both of them at the same time.

After they were tied together, I took my lariat, tied it to their hands that were tied together and had them walk in front of me. I told them to go ahead and get going. This whole thing probably looked kinda crazy to someone watchin' from the bank, seein' this animation going on. Everything had to be pantomimed! I knew they were so smart they knew what I was tryin' to tell them all along, but they made me do it with my hands anyway.

It made me feel like an idiot, tryin to talk to 'em! But I was pretty serious, and a little concerned, 'cause I knew if those boys got my Winchester from me that I would be no more!

We went up a ways and then I tied 'em to a mesquite tree, and there they stood. I'll never forget it. The water had washed out around the roots of this big mesquite tree, and the roots were big there. Once I had 'em tied, I never got up close to 'em. I'd just pitch 'em somethin' and tell 'em to tie it, and then I'd pull on it and see if it was tied. I knew if I got anywhere close to 'em, where they could get a hand on me, it would be the wrong thing to do.

*"Kentucky" flanks successful bounty hunter Tom on the left,
with the captured German prisoner of war on the right.*

They really learned to respect that rifle. I think they knew that I would probably shoot 'em. I left them tied to those roots and went to get my pack horse, and then came back down.

Then I took 'em out of there, with them walkin' all the way back. I'd let 'em rest, set 'em in the shade, while I'd set crossed-legged with that Winchester and just watch 'em. They tried to talk to me in a little broken English. They wanted to know how old I was. But I knew the wrong thing to do was to get a conversation goin' too much with 'em.

When I got into town, I didn't really know what to do with 'em! So I marched 'em right across the railroad tracks and into the main street. Then somebody saw me with this Winchester, marchin' these two guys, who were obviously German prisoners. They went and called the sheriff and the sheriff came down there.

"By golly, Tom!" he said. "Where'd you find these guys?"

"Right where you said they'd be!" I told him.

"I had no idea that you'd gone down there!" he said. "You coulda got killed in there."

"Yeah," I said, "but a man's got to make some money to live on, don't he?"

Well, to my knowledge, they lost eleven prisoners out of that POW camp over the next year, year and a half. I caught seven of 'em! The other four got by me. But, after that first time, the sheriff'd come and find me wherever I was stayin' and tell me about one that escaped.

I remember the sheriff comin' in one day and tellin' me that one had gotten out, maybe two, and he thought they were headed down that same river. I asked him when they got out and he told me it was two days before. Well, I remembered the last time when he told me that, I had to wait two days before I ran into them. This time I waited a day or two before I went down, so I didn't waste my time. He said they were payin' two hundred dollars and if I wanted to get them, that'd be fine with him! So, I went down there, and pulled the same thing off again.

Sometimes I'd have to ride up past the narrows. But I found out the best way to find out if they were in that river bed or in the brush, was not for me to look for them so much as for me to watch my horse. The horse had such good eyesight and keen hearing that he would pick up on any movement ahead of us before I did. So when I was ridin' really slow through there, takin' my time, I'd watch my pony's ears. When they went up, or he stopped, or his head moved different, then I'd just quietly back him up out of sight, get off and wait to see what we had there.

So I was pretty good at doin' this. One time I took one kid down with me from school. He thought it would be exciting. A day and a half later, right after we caught two prisoners, I turned around and saw that my friend had wet his pants. He said he was so scared he never wanted to do that again.

One time a couple of 'em picked up rocks and started throwin' 'em at me. Some started runnin' and I'd have to ride 'em down and rope 'em! Sometimes I had a little trouble with one of 'em on the end of the rope. He'd turn around and go different ways. So what was I gonna do with him? I turned around and dragged him for a while, 'til he'd had enough being drug through the dirt. But I made some good money off those Germans for a while there.   ✠

CHAPTER 33

Working for the Movies

I did a lot of jobs to keep things goin'. I also had restless feet and liked to try anything on, at least once. For a time I worked for the movie production companies on location in Southern Arizona. When I was nine years old, my first job was with Republic Pictures as an extra. That's when I got my social security card. The movie was called "Arizona" with Jean Arthur. If you ever get a chance to see it, look at that blond-headed, really handsome young boy sitting beside Jean Arthur on the lead wagon coming into old Tucson.

From that time on I had an opportunity to work on many movies as the production companies came and went, makin' Western movies in the Avra Valley in Arizona. The movies I worked on were successful and can still be found and watched. I enjoyed working as a wrangler and stunt man on the movie "Red River," which was the first time I met John Wayne, who later became known as "The Duke." I played cards with him when I was fourteen or fifteen years old when I had hired on as an extra.

One time they made me play an Indian and they gave us some horses that weren't too well trained. During the shooting foray we were supposed to charge this group down by the river and these horses had never heard gunfire! None of us "Indians" had saddles, of course.

So the first volley went off as we were chargin' down there. My horse was so startled, he changed direction and headed back where he'd come from. And he went without me, 'cause I flew off into the brush and down the hill. Well, two or three of the others had been bucked off too, so here came a horse runnin' by me and I just ran and jumped on him and kept on down into the battle scene.

I was still carryin' this rifle they'd given me, so I went on through the charge, shootin' and everything. I thought I did pretty well, considerin'. I even got a couple of speaking parts after that. The director thought I did some pretty good thinkin' out there. But it wasn't really good thinkin', I was just tryin' to stay alive! I knew there was a bunch of guys with the same upset horses comin' right in behind me. The best way to survive was not to be afoot, and not to be layin' down, but to get on another horse and ride out of there! I wasn't tryin' to charge anybody! I was just tryin' to get as far from all that mess as I could get, but I ran right into it, and made the best of it. It just happened to work out really good.

Well, I worked on several movies. Some with Glenn Ford, Jimmy Stewart and with Wayne again. I worked on the "Fury" series, which was very popular in the '50s. I worked on "High Noon" with Gary Cooper. Most of the time I was a wrangler or an extra. I really enjoyed that type of work. And once the movie people got to know us we signed on with a wranglers union so they could get in touch with us just about any time.   ⌶

CHAPTER 34

Wild Burro Round-up

One movie I remember real well had a great scene in it with stampeding wild burros. John Wayne was in that one, but I can't remember the name of it. They wanted at least a hundred burros coming down out of the mountains into this little town. They didn't want wild horses, just burros. Well, they could find one burro here and one there, but they needed a lot more than that for this one scene, so they put out a call for twenty dollars a burro to anybody who wanted to rent their burro out for a couple of days.

I got wind of that deal and rounded up a couple of guys to help me with an idea I had. I thought we could go down across the border about twenty, thirty miles west of Nogales to a little town called Sassaby. I thought we'd go down there and make a deal with the Mexicans. I knew they had a lot of burros around there. I'd been there, and I remembered seein' 'em all over the town. I figured if we offered 'em two dollars apiece to borrow 'em for the movie, we'd get a pretty good profit on the deal.

Well, we put the word out and we told them we'd have them back in about a week. We set up the time and place and got a couple of old trucks to haul them in. So all we had to do was to gather 'em up, get them to the trucks, and truck 'em out.

Well, we did have one serious problem to deal with. Hoof and mouth disease restrictions were still in effect, and to bring cattle across was a federal offense! No livestock of any kind was supposed to come across the border. We knew we weren't supposed to do it and that we shouldn't be doin' it, but we were gonna do it anyway. We didn't really see the harm in it. But we couldn't just go in there and truck 'em out that easy. We had a plan, though.

We told the Mexicans if they'd get 'em all together, hold 'em down in a canyon and keep 'em real quiet, we'd come in there just at sundown and sneak 'em out of there at night. I took a couple of boys with me that were pretty handy a-horseback, and told 'em that I'd cut 'em in on the profits.

That night there were about fifty or sixty burros in that canyon. Now, a burro has a mind of his own and it usually has nothin' to do with your plans! I thought if we put one big white one in there at least we could see where they were. It was a moonlight night, and we picked a white one out that we could easily see. The Mexicans were excited about the deal, so they were helpful.

Just up the hill about three-quarters of a mile away, was a Mexican immigration station where we usually crossed the border. We figured about that time of night they'd be gulpin' the cerveza down and not payin' much attention. We thought we could just ride in there and, as long as we kept quiet, we could take them burros out of there, and get 'em to the trucks where we had a little catch corral. The two trucks were hid in the trees, about a mile from the border crossing.

There was no fence on the border there, it was just an imaginary line out there in the dark. We got down to the canyon and got organized. Everybody was creepin' around, talkin' real quiet like. I'd told the boys to bring their Winchesters in their saddle boot 'cause we didn't want to deal with the Mexican police.

"We're not gonna shoot anybody, are we?" one of the guys asked.

"No, I don't plan on it, but I ain't gonna end up in no Mexican jail either!" I told him. "If they come after us they're gonna be a-horseback. A Mexican officer who's a-foot ain't gonna catch a gringo on a horse. So don't shoot him, shoot the horse."

He wasn't too pleased with the idea of what we were doin', but he came anyway.

So we were just bein' real quiet, slippin' around, gettin' them burros all bunched up.

They were actin' pretty good, not bein' too noisy. They'd bray now and then, but then nobody was payin' attention to that, it goes on all the time. One of the riders headed out of the canyon and the burros followed him. He'd gotten a halter on a gentle burro, and was leading this burro out. When you're runnin' livestock some place, you put three riders behind and one in front. If it works right the herd will follow the lead horse, with or without a rider. We figured that'd work and we were doin' great, movin' along good, gettin' close to the trucks, when we heard this loud bell start ringing.

"What in the hell is that?" asked the ol' boy that was workin' the flank with me.

"I don't know, but it's comin' straight at us!" I said.

"It's gonna wake everybody in the whole country up!" he said.

Well, it turned out that these Mexicans had a bell mare that always went with the livestock. Whenever they turn something out, she'd go with 'em, and if they wanted to find 'em, they'd just listen for the bell mare.

She'd been separated from her burro friends and had gotten out of the corral, and was comin' after 'em. We couldn't see her, but we could certainly hear her! She was gettin' louder all the time. I looked up on the side of that ridge where that station was but nothin' was happenin' yet. So I told the guys to just keep 'em movin'.

The next time I looked back up on that ridge I saw a light. It must have been about nine, ten o'clock. I told the boys that we had a problem. I told them to get these things movin' quicker.

"Where's that mare at?" one of the boys asked as he rode up.

"Over there somewhere, in the brush," I said.

"Well, you want me to shoot her?" he asks.

"No! Don't shoot her for cryin' out loud!" I said. "You'll have the whole danged army down on us! They'll come pourin' out of there! Then we'll be in the middle of a gunfight with 'em!"

I told him to get up close to her, take his pocket knife, and cut that bell off of her. Meanwhile, I could see lights goin' on up there, and I could see some people walkin' around the building. I could tell they were watchin' and lookin' down where we were, but they couldn't see nothin'. I knew they could hear that little mare, wanderin' around, and I hoped they'd seen or heard her before and they wouldn't bother about it.

We finally got to where the trucks were parked. I think we started out with sixty head of burro and ended up with about forty. The other twenty of 'em we never did see again. I still have no idea where they went. We rode through thick, heavy mesquite brush, and things were poppin' around us. There's nothin' that hurts worse than mesquite brush scratchin' you up – well, maybe a bullet in the shoulder or an arrow in the leg would hurt more. But in a cool evening like that night, when a mesquite limb hit my ear lobe, or any part of my ear, it was just bloody and hurt so bad. Them things were really snatchin' and grabbin' at us as we went through there.

We got the burros all up to the catch corral by the trucks and we put our lariat rope on 'em, one at a time, and we'd just drag 'em up on the loadin' ramp and on in to the truck! And all the time we were doin' this we're still lookin' over at those lights, wonderin' how long it was gonna take them to find their horses and come down to see what's goin' on. We knew they weren't gonna get in there with a jeep. It was too rough. We stopped a couple of times to listen, but it was too noisy with them burros brayin' and movin' around. We couldn't hear anything. I kept saying that we had to hurry and load and go!

We finally got all loaded up – saddle mules and horses were loaded in the trailer, burros in the trucks. The trucks were parked where they couldn't see the headlights. But we knew any minute the Mexican police might show up and we all knew that you don't mess with Mexican police – meaning you don't get caught by 'em!

Well, we managed to get all them burros out of there that night. We even went back and got another load. We took 'em all in to this movie location the next day. As we unloaded all those burros, they asked us where we got 'em and we told them we just borrowed them.

They got their burro chase using about forty, forty-five of our burros. We lost five on the chase and never did find them. But we charged them fifty dollars a burro for the ones that they lost. By the time we took them back, the Mexicans forgot how many burros they had given us. We had the bell mare with us, too. We'd taken that darned bell off of her.

After the filming we made her up a new collar, put the bell back on, and turned them all loose near the border where we had crossed to get them. That bell mare took 'em all back across the border and into town! By that time we just wanted to get out of there, with our cash, of course.

CHAPTER 35

⅂

A Cattleman's Nightmare

In the fall of one year, in the late '40's, hoof and mouth disease was prevalent in Mexico. The cattle were infected and dying. There was a great fear that the disease would get across the border into the American population of cattle. The ranchers would go broke if it crossed over, and open hostilities were breakin' out between the ranchers along the border.

So the U.S. federal government stepped in and hired people to go down and work with the Mexican government to eradicate, or at least control, the problem.

Now you gotta understand that most of the cattle belonged to big ranches but there was a lot of smaller, little outfits, just families with children, who depended on their livestock for their survival. They usually lived in small, dirt adobe houses. This disease had wrecked the economy for them as well as for the big ranchers.

The Mexican government was not organized, and they didn't have a health department like we did in the U.S. But some type of arrangement was made where people from the U.S. would go down there to help with the diseased cattle. They didn't want to send U.S. federal troops 'cause the people might think they were being invaded. So they hired us gringo cowboys to go down.

I heard about the job, and I thought it might be somethin' I could do. So I hired on and went down. It was an interesting and alarming time down there. The disease was getting closer to the U.S. border and people were becoming really nervous.

They took in bulldozers and dug trenches that were about two bulldozers wide about ten, twelve feet deep, and a hundred feet long. Then they brought cattle up and crowded them up to the trench line. We sat on the other side of the trench with rifles and shot 'em down as fast as we could shoot. Then they bulldozed 'em into the trench, dumped lime over 'em, and buried 'em.

I hadn't really known that I'd signed on for that kind of job. I had no idea what was goin' on 'til we were taken out there. By that time I was all the way down in Mexico and I didn't have a way of gettin' back. The federal government didn't furnish transportation back but they did furnish our food while we were there.

Some of these cattle were diseased and some of 'em were not. But they didn't know which ones were and which ones weren't infected, so they just killed them all. We just shot 'em all. We laid on the banks of those trenches with .30-06 rifles, which were 1906 rifles manufactured by the federal government. We had wet burlap bags on the barrels to keep 'em from burning us. Each shooter, for at least a week to ten days afterwards, had a black and blue area about the size of a fryin' pan from the recoil of the rifle. These bruises were all the way from the middle of our chests to about half-way down our arms, both left and right, 'cause when we got so sore we couldn't shoot on the right, we'd switch to the left to keep going.

We had to put those burlap bags on the barrel 'cause the rifle would get so hot the breach would start to lock up. We were shooting so many cattle I couldn't count how many. At any one time there were about eleven shooters. There was one guy down there that I was workin' with who'd gone down there for the adventure of it. He was a member of one of the richest families in the U.S. I got to know him and like him. He was a pretty nice kid. But he liked to get out of line and do things to try people on and see what they'd do. That type of guy. I told him that in Mexico that's not the smartest thing to do. I told him to keep pretty humble down there, 'cause some of these people were pretty upset about losing their cattle.

So one evening he wanted to go into town and get some beer. I told him I didn't drink, but he wanted me to come along anyway. He also wanted to find a cool well and put some cold water on his shoulders. That was the only thing we could do 'cause there was no ice there. The cold water would help keep the swelling down a little. Boy, it sure hurt the next morning when we started shootin' again.

Well, we went into town that night and I told him I didn't think we should hang around there long. But he wanted his beer so he went to get somethin' to drink in the cantina.

"You're makin' a mistake goin' in there," I told him.

"Why?" he asked.

"These people are losin' too much lately," I explained again. "If you're goin' in there, you'd better take that Winchester with ya."

"Nah," he said, "you stay out here and hold it."

I stayed in the Army jeep holdin' the Winchester. I had a bad feelin' and I wasn't goin' in there.

"You really aren't gonna come in?" he asked. "They got some pretty good lookin' girls in there. I'll find one you like."

"Uh-uh," I said, "I don't want nothin' to do with it. I've been around these people. I was raised around 'em. I speak their language and I respect them. They're goin' through some sad times and I don't want to get involved with this."

He went in there and I could hear him laughin' and carryin' on. So I just kicked back and stuck my hat over my head, my feet over the dash, and rested. I was hurtin' pretty bad! Then I heard a loud noise, but I couldn't tell exactly where it was from. I sat up in the jeep and looked around. I saw maybe eight or ten women comin' and one or two of 'em had pitch forks with 'em. One of 'em had a shovel, and a couple of 'em had machetes. The two or three in the front were pretty large women. They were sayin' that we were killin' their steers and cows.

Even if those ol' Mexican cattle couldn't win a prize anywhere, they gave milk for those women's children. And these women were not gonna let their babies starve to death 'cause of us. We'd been out there killin' their milk cows along with the beef cattle. I tried to get my friend's attention but I couldn't get him to hear me. I didn't want to go up there with my rifle 'cause that woulda started somethin', and I didn't want to leave my rifle in the jeep. So I was blowin' on the horn, and blowin' on the horn, tryin' to get him to come out so we could get out of there. And there's nothin' worse than the sound of an old jeep's horn. It's terrible and it just seemed to stir things up even more.

He finally came out and was headin' for the jeep, when those women were gettin' pretty close. I fired off a warnin' round in the air but they never stopped. This one woman came up there in front of me and accused me of killing their babies' food.

"You, gringo, are not gonna leave here," she yelled. "We're gonna kill you like you're killin' our cattle."

"Then I'll have no choice but to kill you first," I told her. "I don't want to do that but if you force me to I will."

I saw my friend standin' behind 'em, and they hadn't seen him yet. I was tryin' to talk to them and, at the same time, tryin' to tell him to get over away from 'em. But they turned and saw him. Then they went after him with those machetes. I got the jeep started and drove through those women, and I know I hit two or three of 'em. I wasn't goin' really fast but I had to get through to him. When I got to him I threatened 'em with the shotgun again and stood 'em off with it. I shot two or three times right at their feet. Dirt and pebbles went onto their feet, and up their legs. But things weren't lookin' any better for us.

They were at the point where they didn't care if I killed them. They were losing something that was most precious to 'em. I grabbed my friend, threw him up on the hood, and there he laid. Boy, he was bleedin' bad. He'd gotten hit by a machete between the right ear and the jawbone. The skin was laid wide open. I could see his teeth and his jaw. He had another slash across the chest and I could see it had cut through his muscles. Part of his vest was layin' open where they cut through the shirt.

But I threw him up on the hood of the jeep, got back in, and started backin' up. They backed off a little bit this time and gave us room to get out of there. I got him into the nearest town with a doctor, but he never made it.

That was the second time in my life I was confronted with the idea of having to kill a woman. It was a hard spot to be in. But that woman knew, when she looked at me, and we weren't more than ten feet apart, that I'd do it if I had to. And I remember her sayin', "Gringo, you're killin' my children." I knew there was nothin' I could say to change her mind about that.

CHAPTER 36

Los Lobos: The Ways of the Wolf

Lobo. The Spanish word for wolf. To some people in Arizona this word brought instant fear. Bein' so close to Mexico, large wolves would occasionally drift across the border and come after the cattle. I'd heard many times about these wolves being pretty good size, but I'd never seen one 'til I met up with Shorty Hightower. I always thought that was a great name!

He owned the J-6 Land and Cattle Company in Mountain View in Southern Arizona. Shorty had been losing cattle to this wolf that was killin' 'em and not even eatin' 'em. Well, Shorty went after that wolf, tracked him down, shot him, and brought him into town with him. He'd tied that dead wolf on the back of his pickup, and to this day, it was the largest wolf that I ever heard had been taken.

I don't know what he weighed, but Shorty'd taken the dead wolf's front legs at the knees and tied them to the top of the pickup bed. Then he slit the hock in the hind legs and laced the chain from the pickup bed through it and tied it to the top. He had to take a rope and tie his belly up off the ground to the bumper. That wolf stretched clean across the pickup bed and all the way from the top of the pickup back to the ground. I figure he weighed somewhere between 400 and 450 pounds, the most enormous thing that I'd ever seen in my life.

Well, people around there were losing sheep to coyotes, too. But wolves were the worst. Sometimes these wolves would come up the river out of Mexico and they would pull down a full-grown cow. Since this was a big problem, I thought maybe there was a little money to be made in solvin' it. So I approached the Fish and Wildlife Service and they put me on as a government trapper, payin' me a bounty for every one I got.

Settin' out a trap line is kind of interesting, and I was successful at it, but I didn't like doin' that very much. I didn't care for killing a defenseless animal with a trap. I just thought there had to be a better way to get those wolves and coyotes.

Well, this friend of mine had gotten mustered out of the Army and was taking flyin' lessons on the GI Bill. He used to go up in this old L9 Ryan. It was a two-seater with wooden spar wings and a seven cylinder engine. It was fabric-coated, both on the wing and the fuselage.

I got to talkin' with him about huntin' the wolves and coyotes from the air. He'd only started his flyin' lessons about one month earlier, but he asked me if I wanted to learn from him. Now, he'd only been up with an instructor a few times but that didn't seem to bother him.

I told him I'd like to learn how to fly and I was thinkin' I'd take my Browning automatic shotgun up there. We could go up there in that plane and go down in them canyons, even get down in that river bed, and in the valley. I figured we could shoot 'em from that plane! That seemed a lot easier than trappin' them. Sounded like a great plan to me and my friend agreed.

Well, I'll tell you, there's nothin' more interesting than learnin' to fly from someone who had just learned that morning! He'd take it up solo just a bit sooner than you would now with the FAA. He would go up with the instructor and get an hour's lesson in the morning, gas that thing up, and go back up solo. Then he'd come down and pick me up out on this dirt road. What he learned that mornin' he taught me that afternoon! That's how we both learned to fly.

We had some real dip-dee-dos in that plane! Sometimes it wouldn't work right, and he'd say we were goin' down! I'd tell him to pull it up, and he'd say that he hadn't learned that part yet. The engine quit on us once, but he pushed the throttle and the choke and it started up again. I don't know how we lived through it, but I sure learned to fly. And so did he.

So we teamed up to go hunt those wolves and coyotes from the air. He'd be in the front seat and I was in the back seat. He'd spot 'em and then he'd roll that plane up on its wing tip and then circle around, and I'd shoot 'em out of the back of the plane! Then we'd go pick 'em up and turn in the fur for our bounty. I know it sounds kind of gruesome, but there was a good reason to go after those animals. In those days people who had cattle counted on the cattle for food for their families and to keep their farms and ranches goin'. Cattle paid the bills. It was important in that area and the cattle had to be protected.

I'll never forget when we were after one particular wolf. I'd shot at him and missed two or three times. We turned the plane around and went in lower. I couldn't remember if we'd ever gone that low before. But the chase was on. So we stayed down low at the tree level line. We turned and went down, maybe four miles, and turned round the corner and right below us were some cattlemen pullin' cattle out of the brush – brush poppin'.

Well, those cowboys must have had thirty, forty head of cattle between the three of 'em. But when we came around the bend, we weren't no more than fifteen feet above them and their steers. I remember lookin' out past the prop and seein' that the lead cowboy's eyes were about the size of a four-inch wall pipe. When he saw us, he could not believe that propeller was comin' straight at him. He dove off his horse believing his end had come!

The cattle went everywhere! We pulled back up but they were pretty well scattered down there. One of the cowboys ran for his Winchester, tryin' to get it out of his saddle bag, but the horse was buckin' and kickin' him. It was quite a calamity down there!

After we landed, we were told that we ought not to fly for a few days. I knew them boys that we flew over and I knew they were gonna be upset over this. But they cooled down after about a week and many a story was told about that incident!

I remember hearin' one of 'em them tellin' how he looked up and seen that plane comin' at him, and he didn't know whether it was gonna go under his horse or over it! He said it was some mess! They only got about half of them cattle back and they had to wait 'til the next year to get the rest of them out.   ፐ

Searching for Louise

$$\mathcal{F}$$

The Rescue

The year was 1947. I was seventeen years old and things were looking good for me. I'd gotten through some pretty perilous years still in one piece, and I had some money that I'd earned from extracting venom from the snakes. I'd been doing other jobs too, and still hustling with my pool shooting. I won a billiard championship and when I went up to get the trophy the guy asked if I'd rather have money than the trophy, and I said "yes." He said he'd use the trophy for the next year.

I was no longer in school, for ten reasons or more. I couldn't finish up and I didn't really care 'cause I had me a car, a 1941 flathead Ford. I'd been watching some of the guys that had hopped up their cars into what we called hot rods in those days. I bought some of those parts to make mine run a little faster and I was starting to enjoy life a little bit.

Well, I was out doing something in town and I thought I might as well go in and see if I couldn't get a pool game going with some of the local boys. I'd been putting them on a weight reduction program – lightening their wallets. They enjoyed shooting and so did I.

As I came into town, I parked in the same place I always did, across the street by the railroad tracks by a pole where there was always a night light on. I went over to go into the pool hall and I met Val comin' out. Val owned the barber shop, the Lucky Horseshoe Bar and the pool hall. Probably owned more than that, and he was a friend of mine. Then there was the Horseshoe Cafe next door. He had something about horseshoes... I don't know what it was.

Well, he came up to me that day.

"Tom," he asked, "does the name Randall mean anything to ya?"

"No, I don't think so, don't think I've heard that name at all before. How come?"

"There was a man and a woman here by that name lookin' for you," he said. "I think he works for the railroad from the way he looked."

Val said he had on railroad overalls, rolled up at the legs, was about fifty. He had his wife with him and they were looking for me.

"I don't know anybody by that name," I said. "They probably have me mistaken for somebody else."

"No, they knew exactly who you were and what they were after," he insisted. "They wouldn't talk to me much about it, but he said it had something to do with their daughter."

Well, that made me get to thinkin' really fast about this name Randall, but I still didn't recognize the name.

"I don't know the name," I said. "Did they seem upset?"

"Not upset, Tom, but they seemed serious and real concerned about something. The woman could hardly hold back her tears."

"And you're sure they're looking for me?"

"Yeah."

"What do you make of this?" I asked. "What do you think I oughta do?"

"I don't know, Tom," he said, "you know you're a little prone to get in trouble from time to time."

"I don't even know who they are," I said, "there's been no shootout or nothin' lately."

"Well, they're coming back here at the cafe between six and seven tonight to see ya. They've been hangin' around here most of the day waitin'."

It was then about three o'clock in the afternoon.

"Well, I guess it won't hurt to meet with 'em," I said. "I'll come back a little early in case you find out who they are. I don't want to go in there not knowing anything."

"I don't think they're gonna do you any harm."

"All right," I said. I trusted Val. He'd done me right many times in the past. Later, when I went back into town around half past five, I looked up Val to see what he'd learned. I parked around behind the cafe and went through the back door. Val said they were there and that he didn't know anything more about them. They just sat down at a table and neither one never said a word. They just waited. The woman sat there fidgeting with a package in her hands.

I went into the cafe and stood there for a few minutes looking around and saw two people sitting over in the booth. They immediately looked at me and I looked right back at them. Then I looked off. I wasn't sure I liked the situation. I learned a long time ago locking gazes with somebody sometimes puts you at a disadvantage under some circumstances. So I looked away and went over and sat down for a minute to think things over. I could tell from the corner of my eye they were still watching me. But they weren't sure who I was 'cause they'd never seen me before. Of course I'd never seen them either.

I could look up into the mirror behind the ice cream parlor and see that they were talking to each other and then looking at me. I don't think they knew I was watching them in the mirror.

The man was gray haired, with his glasses tucked in a shirt pocket of his big overalls. She had her hair done up in the back, rolled up real tight like they did at that time. She had on a pink dress with a little lace around the edge. She sat there watching me.

Finally, the cook came up asked me what I wanted to eat. I told him I was waitin' for some people.

"You won't have long to wait," he said, "they're sitting right over there. They've been askin' everybody in town what you looked like, so I'm pretty sure they got an idea who you are."

I told the cook I'd buy them something to eat as well as for myself. That was really something big for me 'cause I mostly never had enough money to buy anybody anything to eat. But I thought I was really coming up in the world at that time.

Then I stepped over to them and asked, "Is your name Randall?" He didn't say nothing, he just looked at me. She said, "Yes, it is. Are you Mr. Fisk?"

"Well, ma'am I ain't never been called Mr. Fisk," I explained. "I'm just plain Tom Fisk. So, are you lookin' for me? I ain't never seen you before, have I?"

"No," she said.

"And I don't think I've ever seen your daughter before. I'd sure like to get that established right now if there's any problem with that. You know there's several other guys around here. You could be thinkin' of one of them." I was already starting to explain myself out of this thing because I still had no idea what was going on.

"If you'll sit a little while, I'll tell you what we want," she said in a soft and gentle voice.

"Can I buy you something to eat?" I asked.

"We're not very hungry," she answered.

"Would you mind if I ate something 'cause I haven't ate all day."

"Please do that," she said.

So I ordered a cup of joe and a roast beef sandwich. I sat down with them but the man across from me still hadn't said nothin'. He was looking at me all the time and I was watching him and wonderin' what he was thinkin'. So I decided to put my hand out to shake his hand.

"I'm pleased to know you," I said, and he shook my hand but still didn't say nothin'.

"Well," I said, "tell me what's wrong. Why do you need to see me?"

"You're the man who's been catching those German prisoners coming down the San Pedro River, aren't you?"

"I've caught a few," I admitted. "I made some money on it, bringing in four or five of them."

"Well, we want to hire you for a job," she said.

"You want to hire me to catch some German prisoners?"

"No, not quite that," she said.

"Okay," I was really curious now, "what do you want me to do?"

Well, my food came about that time and they watched me eat for a few minutes. Didn't say anything. Made me a little nervous. They finally ordered a cup of coffee and that made me feel a little more at ease.

Then she began to explain what was goin' on. Three, going on four days earlier, down in Hereford where they lived, their daughter, Louise, went down to a little town called Palominas. Palominas was just about four of five miles from the Mexican border. Louise had driven the family pickup down there to a ranch. She had just gotten her license. She went to a party and was due back home that night about eleven o'clock or midnight, but never returned home.

The next morning they found the pickup truck parked on the outskirts of Palominas, but Louise wasn't in it.

"Have you talked to the law about this?" I interrupted.

"Yes," she said, "of course we did."

"What does the law say?" I asked.

"We talked to the sheriff down there," she explained. "He went down, looked around and asked if anybody'd seen her. He didn't find out anything. But we know where she is."

"Well, if you know where she's gone, you don't need me to get her. Just go get her."

By now I'd pushed my food back out of the way. The roast beef sandwich was either getting cold or I was getting where I didn't want any part of this. And that guy still had not said a word.

Mrs. Randall continued, "We thought she might have struck out afoot from the pickup, cut across to town or something, but there were no tracks like that. It looked like she just pulled over. The sheriff asked if she had a boyfriend and we told them she had two boyfriends and wasn't serious with either one of them. But one of them was kind of rowdy and had run away from home a couple of times and we knew he'd been gone from home about three weeks.

"My daughter would never ever run off with him, I just know it. She'd never run off with anybody." She was so sure.

"So what does the sheriff think about this?" I asked.

"He thinks that the kid came back for her and the two of them have run off together."

"Well, ma'am," I explained in my wisdom, "I'm going to tell you right now, I don't think she's gonna come home until she gets tired of her boyfriend or runs out of money. Then she'll call you from somewhere and she'll be ready to come home."

But the mother refused to budge or listen to me at all. The more I talked to her about it, the more I knew she wasn't going to change her mind on this. There had to be something more to the story.

"If the law can't find her, I don't see how I can do it," I said.

"The law can't go after her," she said.

"Where do you think she is?" I finally asked.

"She's in Mexico," she stated firmly.

"Ma'am, wait a minute," I said. "Do you have any idea how big Mexico is?" I asked her. "It's a lot bigger than Arizona."

"I know that," she said, "but we think we know where she's been taken."

She fiddled around, turned to her husband and asked him for something. He unsnapped his overalls, pulled out a piece of paper and laid it on the table. The first thing he ever said to me was where he lived on that map.

"And that's where she went to the party," he pointed. "We think she's been taken down into Mexico from there."

I didn't know that part of the country that well, but on the other side of that range, I knew Naco, right on the border, real well. That's where I rode for the Morales brothers along the east side.

"That's terribly rough country in there," I said. "There's no road across the border where your daughter left her pickup."

I explained that if you go around the Bisbee Mountains, past the Bisbee Mine, into the town of Bisbee, you could get into Mexico. But they would have to go through an inspection station. I knew better than to go askin' questions at an inspection station.

Then Mrs. Randall brought out this rolled-up old envelope tied in the middle with a string in a knot. She held it in her hands, then put it on the table with her arms folded over the top of it. I thought well, here comes another map.

It was starting to be pretty clear that the idea was for me to go into Mexico to find this girl. I didn't know what she looked like. I had no idea where she was or who took her in the first place. I knew there were not a lot towns around there and the few there are hard to get to because of the road situation. I was thinking that this wasn't something I wanted to get involved with. But to be polite, I talked with them and figured we'd work our way through it, and then I'd get out of there. I'd pretty much made up my mind already.

But she kept holding on to that little package, lookin' at me.

"Why don't you go down there with a picture of her and ask around?" I suggested.

"I do have a picture of her," she said. Then she reached in her purse, pulled stuff out of it, and brought out a picture that was wrapped in some kind of paper folded over it. She opened it and just as gentle as she could, turned it around, and said they called her "Lou."

"How old is this girl?" I asked.

"In this picture she's nine years old."

"She's nine years old and she's driving a pickup truck?"

"No, no," she said, "this picture was taken when she was nine. It's the only picture we got of her."

"Ma'am, you want me to go look for a sixteen-year-old girl with a nine-year-old picture?"

My idea of going down to that inspection station with a picture didn't seem so good either. "Why're you so sure she's down in Mexico anyway?" I asked. I knew the country well enough to know that in order for her to get into Mexico she had to cross at one of two places: at Naco or at Lochiel, below the Washington Mining Camp. I had crossed at Lochiel a couple of times, taking dudes in there hunting, and I knew it was rugged. It could be done in a high car with sixteen-inch tires, which could go just about anywhere.

There wasn't really an inspection station there. Just a Mexican sitting there, and if he's not asleep you go through and he'd get up and ask you where your papers were or you could just give him ten dollars, and he wouldn't care if you had papers or not. Mrs. Randall insisted they had to have crossed at Lochiel. Apparently, the rains had recently washed out the road to the crossing between Palominas and Bisbee.

Then she picked up the little package with this string on it, laid it down on the table and put both her hands in front of it and pushed it across the table right in front of me.

"I want my daughter back," she said. "This is the money we got together to hire you to go and bring her back."

"Well, ma'am," I said, "I've never been in Mexico hunting for captives or anything like that. There's the Federales down there and the Mexican police, and neither one of them are any good to me. Then there's bandidos all over the place. And the Mexican people alone aren't going to take kindly to me poking around in their towns."

"That money's yours," she pointed at the package, "if you'll bring her back."

"How much is in that package?" I asked.

"One thousand dollars," she said.

"Well, ma'am," I said while I pushed it back to her a little bit, "that's a lot of money but I can't take it. I wouldn't even know where to start to look down there. You need to go to the law about this."

"They can't go in there," she said shaking her head.

I already knew that, but I wanted out of there, out that door and into my car.

"Please just think it over," she was pleading with me.

Then Mr. Randall said, "Mr. Fisk, she's all we got."

Mrs. Randall gently wiped away her tears and tried to keep herself together. Then she gently pushed that money toward me again.

"I know you caught them prisoners and brought them back," she said.

"I'll tell you what," I said. "I think she's with her boyfriend, and if you want me to drive down around there and ask a few questions I'll do it."

"That's already been done by the officers," she was still shaking her head. "They've been very nice. They went and asked about her at all the places that they might have stopped."

"Did you check any places where they could've stayed overnight?" I asked.

That old boy across from me started to wince when I said that! I thought, man, I've done said something wrong here. He stiffened up, straightened up in his chair and I thought he might just hit me so I apologized for that right off. I was tip-toeing, trying to get out of that real quick.

He finally backed off and I said, "Okay, I'll tell you what. I'll think this over. Is there someplace where I can call you?"

Then I saw her eyes go down to the floor. I knew right then and there she wasn't believing me from there on out – and I wasn't either. I wasn't telling the truth. But I didn't want to get any further involved. I assured her I would call her in the morning.

Then Mr. Randall stood up and said to her, "Come on, we need to go home now."

So we all got up and I paid for the food and opened the door for them. They both went outside and stood there talking quietly to one another.

"I got your number," I said, "I'll give you a call."

I went around back, got in my car, pulled around the side and onto the main street. They were still standing there. I pulled over to the side of the curb about fifty yards from them and stopped. He was standing there, looking off across the railroad tracks and there was a big old steam engine coming in. She was still clutching that package in her hands. I sat there for a few minutes in the car and then got out and went around behind the car. I have no idea what I went around there for, I just wandered around there for a minute. Then I knew they saw me. I walked toward the gas station and looked back and she was looking right at me. Mr. Randall was looking off towards that track again. I went back to the car and I remember standing there and putting my hands on top of the car and putting my head in my hands, looking down, thinking about what I should do.

I remembered Sam once told me if I had to think long and hard about doing something and it looked real bad, chances were that it would be every bit as bad as I thought it was gonna be.

With this runnin' through my mind I said, "God damn it," and looked back at them again.

He'd started off to their pickup but she was still standing there, clutching that little package.

"What am I gonna do?" I said to myself. I started back up towards the service station again, thinkin' that I wasn't in school, nobody's around here to worry about me. No one cared about me too much anyway. But I never liked the idea of ending up with a damn Mexican bullet in me.

So here's this woman standing down there, lost everything she had, and I thought to myself, "I can relate to that. I know what it's like to be alone with nothing and nobody to love you." So that's when I decided I'd do it. I'd go down there and look for that girl.

I crossed the street and I saw her head come up; by the time I got there she had a smile on her face. She knew I was gonna do it. I will never forget that little joyful smile.

It would, in days to come, strengthen me along the trail.

She tried to give me the money but I told her to hang on to it.

"Ain't no way or place for me to spend it down there," I said. "I've got enough to get where I'm going." Even though I didn't have the slightest idea what I was doing or where I was going. But here was this little woman clutching that envelope in the middle of the street, needing me.

"I'll come by your place in Hereford tomorrow," I said. "I've got to go down and talk to a friend of mine, find out what I can do down there."

When Mr. Randall came back he grabbed my hand, shook it hard, sayin' he knew I was gonna find her. I thought the only thing I was gonna get was a damn bullet from somebody sure as hell.

I just said, "All right."

Then we went back in the restaurant, over to where the stools were, and she wrote out their address and phone number in nice, neat handwriting.

"Is there anything we can get to help you?" she asked me.

"Find me six or eight little bells about the size of an egg, and make them dark with some lamp soot or boot polish or something."

She never asked me why I wanted them or what they were for. Then I started to leave and she reached over and stuck the money down my shirt.

"Now, ma'am," I said, "there's going to have to be an understanding between you and me about this. If I'm going to do this for you, you're going to have to listen to some of the things that I need to say."

"I'm listening," she said.

"Then you take this money and you hold on to it. And when I come back, we'll talk about it."

She said okay.

When I headed out she grabbed me and gave me a hug and a kiss while she was standing there, tears comin' out her eyes, sayin', "You can do it, I know you can."

Then they finally left me standing in the middle of the street, looking at the ground. I looked over at the cafe and saw the waitress and the cook with their faces right up against the window, lookin' at me. The cook was shaking his head like, boy, you just bought the farm. So I started back to my car and I went to talk to Val.

ADVICE FROM VAL

I explained to Val what was going on.

"You're going down there, aren't you Tom?"

"Yeah, I said I would," I admitted.

"What do think you're going to do down there?" he asked.

"I've been there before," I said, tryin' to sound like I knew what I was doing.

"I heard tell about some of that," he said, not too impressed.

"I'm going to talk to Sam," I said, "you know he's spent a lot of time down there."

"I know another man near there who can help," Val offered. "I'll see if I can get in touch with him and tell him you're coming."

"Who you talkin' about?" I asked.

"John Slaughter of the Slaughter Ranch," he told me. "His place is right around the tip of the Bisbee Mountains. Come back through here tomorrow on your way down to Hereford. I'll tell you whether I reached him or not."

With that, I headed along the river up to where Sam's place was, the Buzzard X. I hadn't seen him for quite a while, but he was about as close to a father as I'd ever had.

ADVICE FROM SAM

I came up to the gate, hollered at the house, and Sam yelled, "Come on in, Kid," from inside the house.

It was about 8:30 in the evening and I could tell he'd already been in bed. He was wearing his old, red, long underwear with big white buttons. His socks went up just below his knees. I used to see him down at Carmella's dressed like that. I often thought them girls had to be pretty imaginative to see him in a romantic light.

He rolled a cigarette and got to coughing a little bit. He was probably one of the homeliest men Heavenly Father ever put on this earth. He had teeth on him that a javelina would have been proud to own. One rancher referred to them as "snags," which kind of fit.

"Kid, you're running from the law, aren't you?" he asked right out.

"No," I said.

"What about the Bill Jones thing?"

"That's all over," I said.

"Kid, you never lied to me, that I know of."

"I ain't lying to you now, Sam."

"How come you're down here in the middle of the night?" he asked suspiciously. "You look like you just seen a ghost or something," he said, knowin' something was up. "What've you gotten into this time?"

Then I figured I was gonna to have to straighten out this Deputy Bill Jones thing first.

"How'd you come to find out about this Bill Jones thing?" I asked.

"The Sheriff of Benson came out here looking for you," he explained, "about ten days ago. You gonna tell me about it?"

So I sat down and explained how I'd never seemed to get along with Bill. Sam agreed with me that not many people did. But somebody'd robbed the drugstore in town and someone said they saw me in town parked close to the drugstore. They figured I was the one that robbed it and told Bill about it.

"I've never known you to ever even pick up a biscuit laying there without askin'," he said.

"Well, I didn't do it," I told him. I was in town that day but I didn't know what had happened or anything about it. My car was there, yeah, but I was in the pool hall with a game going at the time. I was still playing pool when Bill walked in, took the cue stick right out of my hands and there he stood.

He was about six foot four, taller than I was, rangy with big hands. He always carried his damn German Luger pistol, the only one I'd ever seen like that. We used to call him Luger Bill because of that pistol.

"I know you're the one that robbed that drug store," he accused me. I thought he was going to hit me with the cue stick.

"I don't know what you're talking about," I said with a smart mouth.

"I got witnesses who saw you come out of the drug store."

"Who saw me come out of the drug store?" I demanded.

"I don't need to tell you that. I'm placing you under arrest."

"I haven't robbed any drugstore," I insisted coolly, "I've been here playing this pool game, and I don't take kindly to bein' accused of something I didn't do. I work for whatever I get."

"You've been in trouble ever since I've known you as a kid," he said.

"I've been in a scrap or two," I admitted.

"A lot more than a scrap or two," he was getting mad. "You got a mean part to you."

"No, I don't," I said, "I just don't like being trapped, and you're trapping me right now, and I don't like it."

"You come with me now, kid. I'm taking you to jail for this one," he yelled at me while he grabbed me good. Then we paraded out of the pool room, past the barber shop, Val's place and the show house, with three or four guys that were shooting pool with me following us. Two of them still had their cue sticks in their hands.

"You tell those guys if they use the cue sticks on me, I'll shoot them."

"You tell them," I said, "you got the gun."

He had a hold of me tight by the shirt, and he wasn't turning loose of it either. I just figured I was going to jail and there was nothing much could be done about it right at that moment. But when we got near the restaurant there must have been ten people in there, eating. Bill walked up, draggin' me with him, opened that door and shoved me right inside. I almost fell into the counter. There I stood looking around and everybody in there just stopped and looked at me and Bill. Some people had food in their mouths, just frozen, watching, wonderin' what was going on.

Well, Bill shoved me and told me to get up on that stool right there, sit and don't move. Then he announced to everyone that he finally caught me, that I robbed a drugstore and he was gonna put me in jail this time.

"But before I do," he said to everyone, "I'm going to have me something to eat and drink. You're going to sit right there and watch me eat," he said to me, actin' kind of cocky. "Then I'm going to lock you up for the night."

I sat down and he got on the other side of me and he said, "Kid, there's the door. Why don't you try to break for it?"

"You'd probably shoot me in the back with that damn old Luger," I said.

"That's exactly what I'd do and that's what you deserve."

Two or three people got up and left. One little boy I knew came up and said he'd known me most of his life and he didn't think I did what Bill Jones said.

"I don't care what you think," Bill said, "I'm the law here, and I got my prisoner."

Two or three more people came in and he was braggin' about catchin' me. It got to the point where I'd had as much of this as I could take, so I turned to him and asked him why didn't he just take me in and lock me up right then. "I don't need to hear your mouth going off," I said.

Then he slapped me good, back-handed me right in the mouth. Bloodied my mouth.

"Shut up," he yelled at me, "when I want you to talk, I'll tell you to talk."

The waitress came over, dipped a cloth in some water and wiped the blood off my mouth.

"That's no way to treat a boy," she said to Bill.

"He ain't no boy," Bill told her. "He's been riding with a rough string around here for years."

I just kept takin' in his remarks while he finished up eating. Then he said he wanted some ice cream. They had an ice cream freezer thing where they kept these large, open cartons of ice cream down in there right in front. Some of it was melted and it looked like they were cleaning it out or something.

The waitress said, "I'll tell you what, you son of a bitch, you want your ice cream, get it yourself." Then she turned around and walked off. I thought, boy, I hope that don't get me slapped again.

But he said, "I'll do just that." Then he reached over and he got a coffee cup and reached down in there scooping his ice cream out. That's when I reached over and grabbed the back of his hair with one hand and his belt with the other. I turned him end over end into that ice cream thing and then I headed out of that place.

I saw him start to reach for his Luger but he fell back down into that ice cream thing again. I left him down in there just blubbering and yelling.

He'd taken my car keys away but I always kept an extra key in my boot. I ran out the back door as he was just fightin' and flailin'. He couldn't get out of there. I went right to my car, got in and took off for Tucson.

They told me later that when they finally dug him out of there, his Luger was plumb full of ice cream and he had ice cream all over him. He was yelling that he was going to kill me. They said he looked half-painted with white ice cream on his face. They said he wiped it off his eyes so he could see, turned around, went off the wrong way, then fumbled out the door and got into his police car.

Eventually, they got the cars going after me and the Highway Patrol got into it. They chased after me that day and into the night. I went all the way back down through the southern part of Arizona and they kept after me. I ran two road blocks, dropped back around and went up into the old horse camp in the mountains where Joe Kitchen was holing up. I pulled in there, and I told Joe the law was after me and I needed a place to hole up. He knew me well enough to know I didn't do what they said I did. So he put my car in the barn with a tarp over it. We brushed them tracks out to the main road and ran several horses over it. Then he said I could stay there with him until this was over with.

The next day he went into town to find out what was happening. He heard they burnt out two patrol cars trying to catch me. I'd just fixed up my car and it was quite a hot-rod at the time. I outran them, all right.

Joe was gone a whole day and about 11:00 that night he came back. I was hid out because I'd seen the car lights coming. But I came up to the house when I saw who it was.

"They caught the man who did it," he announced to me.

"You mean I can go back into town?" I asked.

"I'd wait a day or two," he advised. "If Bill sees you he says he's gonna kill you. They're calling him 'Ice Cream Bill.'"

While I was tellin' all of this, Sam was just sittin' there listening.

"So it's over with," he said, "then why are you here?"

I explained to him everything about the Randalls.

"Kid, is that money worth that much to you?"

"I didn't take it."

"Why not?" he asked me, like I was stupid or something.

"That woman was crying like she lost the only thing in life that meant anything to her, and I just couldn't take the money knowing I probably wouldn't ever find her daughter anyway."

"I never seen you have too many weak moments," he said, "but you had one there. Do you know where you're going and what you're going to do?"

"I have no idea," I admitted, "that's why I'm here. You know Mexico better than anybody I know."

"All right," he said, "I'll help you out. You going down in a car?"

"No," I said, "goin' horseback, and I'm gonna cross between Palominas and Lochiel. I figure I can ride and make good time."

"Stay out of the sides of the river banks, stay out of the salt cedars, and if the water's up, be careful riding the trail across that border. What are you going to ride?"

"Not sure," I admitted, "I got my doggin' horse."

"You know, Kid, you ain't going to find her."

"You go tell that woman that," I said, "'cause I couldn't."

"You need a good set of horses."

"Well, Val knows John Slaughter," I explained, "and he's setting me up to talk to him about that. Do you know him? I thought I'd rent the horses from him."

"Yeah, I know him, and you better buy them 'cause there's a good chance you ain't comin' back."

"I'll get back out of there," I insisted.

"Take some candy bars and try to keep them out of the heat so they don't all melt together. Be respectful of the Mexican people – it's their country, you know. You know what to drink and what not to drink, right? If you come across a bunch of unfriendly Mexicans you just take your Winchester and hold it across your lap as they come up to you. If they come up near you, just rifle one of them across the brow, kick the other in the face with your foot and then bail your horses right out through the middle of them. About the time they get them machetes out, you're already gone. You got that? But try not to shoot one. They do get a little excited when you shoot one – he's always somebody's brother or uncle. But you've learned well. We've been through some tough things together haven't we, Kid?

"The next group you're going to run into is the bandidos. You may or may not see them coming. But there's ways you can tell, like I taught you before. They usually run five to eight in a bunch on horseback and they usually hide out in the hills and hit the miners and rob them of horses or money or gold dust.

"Then there's the policia in the towns. They hate the bandidos almost as much as gringos. But the worst group is gonna be them Mexican Federales. If they get on to you for something it becomes a hunting game for them. Huntin' a gringo is a sport to them. They'd rather do that than go after the bandidos.

"The biggest thing is getting outfitted right, so when you go see John Slaughter, you tell John that I said to fit you with the best. Because should

you find this girl and bring her out, you'll probably have to outrun somebody. They won't just give her up easy. You tell John to fit you with something that's long and tall and not afraid of rifle fire.

"Kid, where are all your belongings?" he asked me out of the blue.

"Up at the house I'm staying at," I told him, wonderin' why he wanted
to know about that.

"Well, why don't you give me a paper that says whatever you got left I
can have?" he said.

"Why in the hell do you want somethin' like that?" I asked.

"It's just something I can show the sheriff when I load it up."

"Why would you be loading my stuff up?"

"Kid," he said seriously, "I really don't think you're coming back."

"You're just trying to scare me."

"Is it working?"

"Yes, and I didn't come down here for you to scare me out of it. I came
down here so you'd tell me where to go."

"Okay," he said, "John Slaughter knows the country better than I do.
You talk to him about that. You takin' that new rifle you just got?"

"Yeah," I said. I was pretty proud of that new rifle.

"You're the only one around this country that's got one like that."

Then he started getting dressed and said we were goin' out to the barn
to get a pack saddle. He said if I looked too good, like I was on some kind of
a special breed of horse they ain't ever seen before, I'd be a marked man. I had
my own saddle, but I needed another one for the pack horse and he had an
old, light, relay saddle.

Then he said, "Now if you're going to share that $1,000 with me..."

"I didn't say a damn thing about sharing that $1,000 with you! You're
tryin' to scare me, get all my stuff and the money! I'm startin' to wonder why
I came out here at all."

"I'm helping you," he said. "You can't go in there askin' about a white
girl with a saddle horse with you. They'd have her stashed somewhere and
you'd never find her. You got to go in there like you're looking for work."

That sounded right.

"You're going to have to go to Cananea," he said. "Do you know why?"

"No, but you're gonna tell me, right?"

"Later. Let's get this pack saddle right."

So we fixed the pack saddle on top of the relay saddle. We put a britching
around the butt of the packhorse to secure each side of the pack saddle. This
kept the supplies from sliding forward on the horse in rough country. The
breast collar was fitted around the chest of the packhorse just below the neck

and attached on each side of the pack saddle to prevent the saddle from slipping back during a climb or chase. We put on two ore bags so it would look like I'd been haulin' ore out of the mountains. There was no way anyone could tell there was a saddle underneath there. If I found her I would pull everything off except the saddle and she could ride on that saddle to get out. There was no way to get us both out of there on one horse.

Sam pulled out his special saddle boot for my rifle, and he showed me how to put it on. He told me to put my bed roll stuff in a certain spot a little bit behind me. If it got pretty heavy I might want it there to take a bullet and keep it out of my back.

"I ain't going to go anywhere where I'm gonna get shot," I said.

He told me how to slip my big Springfield in there on the right-hand side of my pack saddle with my slicker draped over it, keeping the rifle out of sight.

"If you find her, you think they're just going to say here she is, she's yours? It ain't going to work that way, Tom. You could get the both of you killed." Then he said, "You're all set up. I'm going to let you have the saddle and this rigging, and I'll deduct it from my share if I don't see it again."

"Damn you," I said, "you don't got a share."

"Yeah, I do," he insisted. But it was getting late by then, so I dropped it.

He gave me some stuff to camp and cook with and some canned food. He warned me about the water down there, how it was contaminated from the mining.

I thought I was in pretty good shape, so I spent the night and planned to head out early in the morning. He cooked me up some biscuits to take with me. I had some money and a bed roll with a tarp to go over it. I had my six-shooter and plenty of cartridges and I was planning to wear it strapped on. Sam thought that was stupid 'cause somebody would see through the miner cover if I was wearin' my pistol. So he took an old pair of saddle bags and slit a little hand pocket on the side. Then he cut a hole in the center to go over the horn of the saddle. He told me to put my pistol right inside that little slit pocket with some food and stuff, and put the cartridges on the other side the same way. I could reach down in there and no one would pay much attention to it until it was too late. Sam told me where I could pick up some nitro sticks and fuse and to stow them in the saddle bags. I thought I was about ready.

"Is there anything more I got to learn before I try to sleep tonight?" I asked him.

"You ain't going to sleep tonight," he said. He had me up at 4:00 a.m. and he had my stuff all fixed up. I was amazed at how efficient he was, and it

202 ✦ THE GRINGO KID

was runnin' through my mind that he'd done this before a few times. I thought I'd just ask him, but I didn't.

"Kid, I hope you find her," he said as we parted. "And if you do, she may not be in too good a shape, you know."

"You gonna tell me why you think she's in Cananea, Sam?" I asked him.

"I think they probably crossed the border at Lochiel and if they had a pickup, they probably went all the way to Las Cruces, then down into Miguel Hidalgo, then to Cananea."

"How do you know this stuff, Sam?" I asked.

"If she's sixteen and some Mexicans kidnapped her and she's pretty, I know where she's at," he said.

I reached in my pocket and showed him the picture. He started laughing when I told him she was only nine years old in the picture and that was all I had to go on.

"Well, if she's pretty, she'll be at Cananea," he said. "They'll take her to one of the whorehouses where the gringo miners go. They'll probably beat her up some first. So you be ready for that."

I headed out of there not quite sure what I was doing, but sure I was doing it anyway.

THE RANDALL PLACE

From Sam's place I headed toward Hereford to meet with the Randalls. On the way, I went through Benson to look up Val and see what he had to say about John Slaughter.

"Did you talk to John?" I asked Val.

"It wasn't easy, but I did get in touch with him," he said. "He says he knows who you are, Kid. He said he heard about that thing with the Morales brothers down there."

"Does that mean he dislikes me?"

"Oh, no, no," he said, "it just means he heard that no one should mess with ya. He's going to fit you up with some horses."

"And just what are they gonna cost me?" I asked.

"Nothin'," he said, "I told him what was going on and he said, 'Hell, if I was twenty years younger, I'd go with you.' So why don't you strike out of here and head towards your meeting with the Randalls? You should get down to the Slaughter place this afternoon. John said he'd come out to the ranch and work things out with you. He's got some directions and information for you."

I asked Val if I could take an old pair of handcuffs that were up hanging on his wall. He said sure and gave me the key, too. Never even asked me why

I wanted them. Good thing, 'cause I didn't know why. They just looked like they might come in handy.

I bought some chocolate candy bars like Sam said and some American cigarettes, Lucky Strikes they were called. I had about everything I could think of. So I got myself a change of clothes. I didn't want to carry too much.

I took off from Benson with my stuff all together stashed in my car. I had my saddle and my guns, dynamite, and everything. While I was driving I got to thinkin' back to where I'd spent most of my time as a kid in these river bottoms. It was around there where I'd learned to rope calves. I stopped at Trestle Crossing where the railroad crossed over the San Pedro River, got out, walked around there lookin' down in the river bed and recalled how Midge and me used to go down in there when I was just thirteen. I was thinkin' maybe I was leaving this country forever.

I got back in my car and drove half way to Fairbanks, goin' along pretty good and not thinkin' much about my speed 'cause I didn't have a good speedometer. It'd been stuck on the 100 mark since I ran from the cops. I was going along there and around the corner was a highway patrolman sitting in his car. I noticed it looked like a brand new car. I just kind of glanced over at him as I passed and I could see he was reading a book. He looked up at me and I knew he recognized me. Then sure enough, he came after me. I thought, well, I better slow down or I'd get a ticket. I didn't want to be explaining anything to him.

He fell in behind me and was running about two car lengths back. I was riding along pretending like I didn't even see him. When I looked up in the mirror I could see he was really set in the face, but I didn't recognize him. Then he started closing the gap on me. He came right up about a car length behind me – no siren on or nothing. I just kept driving and thinking maybe he'd tire of this after a while.

The next thing I knew was when I looked in the mirror, I could see the full expression on his face. I could see the lines in his face and this big mean looking grin. He wasn't no more than three feet from my back bumper and he stayed right there.

I must have gone another mile like this, with me still acting like I hadn't seen him at all. But then I looked at him in the mirror and he was looking right at me. We went a mile or two further and then I saw him back off a little. But then he came up and just rammed me right in the back of my car. I set my mind not to let him provoke me into doing something wrong, but he hadn't asked me to stop.

I didn't know what he wanted, but he laid back a little bit and then he hit me again. After a third time he finally backed off, and then he pulled up beside me. Well, there was no more hide and seek by this time. I knew he was there. He knew that I knew he was there. He made a hand signal and I thought maybe he wanted me to slow down, but he meant for me to roll my window down, so I did. He reached over and rolled his down. And all this while we were going' fifty or sixty miles an hour down the road. If anybody'd come, it would have been bad news.

He looked over at me with one finger sticking up, sayin', "One more time, just one more time."

I didn't have any idea what he meant by that. Then it dawned on me that he was probably one of the cops that ruined his car when he was chasing me. My '41 Ford was sure easy to recognize because some Mexicans put a big old red "X" on four of my fenders, so I had painted all the fenders red to cover them up.

He finally backed off a little. I kept going and went on into Fairbanks, stopping there to eat. He pulled over to the side of the road, just sat there and watched me.

I thought if I left there and headed for Hereford, he'd be right behind me and this problem would be on again. I had more pressing things to deal with, so I wasn't sure what I was gonna do. Fortunately, he got tired of waiting for me and didn't follow me when I took off for Hereford.

When I finally pulled into Hereford, I had to figure out where the Randalls lived. It was running about 10:00 or 11:00 in the morning. Someone told me where they lived, so I went right over there. Their home was just a small, modest house on a couple acres of land. I saw her out in the yard and she came up to the fence and opened the gate for me. She was smiling and I didn't see Mr. Randall anywhere.

She told me to go on in. She said she had fixed me up some food to take with me. There was so much, I wouldn't have any room for anything else if I took it. I could tell that she was still locked into the idea that she knew I was going to find her daughter. She had a package about the size of a regular shopping bag tied up with string. It seemed like everything she had was tied in string. She said it was a set of clothes for Lou, 'cause she knew she'd need them on the way home. She had some medical stuff in there too, just in case. She also had the bells that I'd asked for, eight or ten little bells, all dark. They were in a little package tied up with string.

I was feeling pretty much on the spot. "I don't know where I'm going," I said, "and I don't really know what Lou looks like. But I'm willing to go in there and spend a reasonable amount of time looking for her."

"How long is that?" she asked. "Days? Weeks?"

"I don't know," I said evasively, but I wasn't thinkin' weeks, that's for sure. "I'll wire you if I find out anything."

"I'll pray for you," she said.

That was okay. I knew what prayer was, so I figured I could use the help. I loaded up and was ready to go.

"I know you're going to find her," she insisted. Then she tried to give me the money again, still wrapped up in its own little package with string.

"I've got enough," I told her, pushing it back to her. "You slip it under your mattress or whatever."

Then she started crying and I looked back at the house as Mr. Randall came out on the porch and waved at me. I could tell he didn't want to get too close to all this. I don't think he was as confident about me as his wife was. But I waved back at him and off down the road I went, headed to John's place.

THE JOHN SLAUGHTER RANCH

When I finally found the ranch, I pulled in near the barn. There were some stables and stalls with a ranch house off to the left. I got out and walked around a little bit. I saw several head of horses and some cattle at the water trough. As I looked across between two buildings up about fifty or sixty yards, I saw a ranch hand walk across there and he just glanced towards me. I looked at him but neither one of us said anything. I figured John would show up eventually.

I decided to start trying to get some of the stuff organized a little bit, so I unloaded it out of the car. As I was doing it, I heard somebody walk up behind me and I kind of looked over my shoulder. I saw this gal standing there lookin' at me.

"You Tom?" she asked.

"Yes," I said.

"I'm Kate."

"Pleased to meet you, Kate." I was bein' polite.

I climbed out of my car enough to reach over and shake her hand. And shakin' Kate's hand was an experience in itself. It was like puttin' my hand between a buckboard and the barn. She cranked down on my hand and I thought I was gonna have to ride down to Mexico with a broken hand.

"John had to haul cake to the east pasture," she explained.

"All right," I said as I was recovering from the handshake. Cake is food fed to the cattle at certain times of the year. It has molasses and some other stuff in it.

"He'll be back soon," she said. "He told me to take care of you."

"All right," I said again. I didn't ask her whether she was his daughter or anything. She kept calling him John so I didn't know who she was at this point.

"First thing we need to do is get you some horses. My dad tells me you're the gringo kid that rode for the Morales brothers on the other side of the mountains over there. I heard about that."

"Oh, yeah?" I said.

"How old are you?" she asked. It seemed like everywhere I went somebody was always asking me how old I was.

"I turned seventeen last August 12th," I answered truthfully about my age for a change.

"You're older than I am," she said. "You want to pick your horses?"

"No," I said.

"Good, 'cause we already picked them for you."

One was a big, sorrel-colored, Thoroughbred-Morgan cross. He stood a little under sixteen hands and she said you can do just about anything on him. "I broke him and trained him myself," she said proudly.

I was watching her pretty close now. "How come you're looking at me like you are?" she bluntly asked me.

"Well, I'm just trying . . ." I stuttered.

"Haven't you ever seen a flat-chested girl before?" she blurted out.

"Well, yeah – I guess," I was still stuttering.

"Have you or haven't you?" she demanded.

"I think I have," I insisted.

"You better be a lot more decisive down in Mexico," she said. "How many have you seen?" she kept at me.

"Hell, I didn't count them," I said.

"I just noticed you were looking," she said.

"I didn't mean to be staring," I apologized. Apparently I was staring, but this girl had absolutely nothing there. I got caught staring down the wrong road and she sure brought that to my attention.

We finally went to get the horses.

"You can shoot off of him, or anywhere around him and he'll do whatever you ask him to do. John'll explain why we picked him."

I still thought it was kind of unusual for her to call her father by his name. I never met a girl that did that. She still hadn't really told me who she was.

She caught the horse up and came over to me.

"You think you're going to find her?" she asked me.

"I don't know," I answered. I wasn't much on the social graces that day.

"How far you goin' to go in?" she continued to grill me.

"I don't know that either," I answered, keenly aware that I was sounding pretty stupid by then.

"Well, if you do find her what are you going to do with her?" she went on.

"I'm not sure," was all I could say.

"Boy, you sure have trouble making up your mind."

"You aren't helping me asking me all these questions. You sure do talk a lot."

"That's part of my job here," she said.

I was wonderin' just what her job really was. She brought down the other horse.

"You got your own saddle?" she asked.

"Yeah, I do," I said, thinking I had that right anyway.

"Well, drag it out and let's see what it looks like," she ordered me.

I thought, gosh darn, now I got to show her what my saddle is like. But I got it out, we got the blankets in place and put the saddle on. We put it on the big sorrel.

"I'd like to get out of here before too late," I said. "You figure John'll be back soon? I'd like to make maybe ten miles before I make camp."

"You think I'm too tall?" she asked me out of the blue.

"No, I don't," I said, not sure what was the right thing to say.

"Why don't you think I'm too tall?" she asked. "Most people do."

"I think you're just right," I said, hoping that would end this line of questions.

"Just right for what?" she asked.

"How come you're askin' me all these questions?" I turned one on her.

"I notice you're looking," she said.

"I ain't looking," I insisted. "Maybe I was, but I ain't no more. You broke me from that about ten minutes ago. I'm not looking!"

"You can go ahead and look if you want," she said.

I figured I better get my mind set on how to get my rigging and gear out of there as soon as possible. At least she thought that my saddle set pretty good on the sorrel. We started to put the gear on the other horse. I asked her to get on him and spin him around a couple of times.

"You afraid he's going to buck out?" she asked me.

"No," I answered, "I just want to see what he can do with you ridin' him. You know him and I don't."

She accepted that, so she got on him, moved him around, brought him back up, walked over and picked up something that was laying there. He seemed pretty gentle. She told me he could really run and she figured I might need that where I was goin'. She could tell I was pretty well fitted out for the trip.

"I'm figurin' I should go with you," she stated firmly.

"What?" I babbled back at her.

"I should go with you, that's all," she insisted.

"You're not going with me," I said flat out.

"Why not?" she asked.

"I got enough problems keeping me alive down there," I explained. "I don't need anyone else along doublin' my problems."

"You don't think I can cowboy that country?"

"No, that's not it," I answered, but I knew I was in trouble here.

"You're worried about me being a girl, aren't you?" she said. "I can dress like a boy. I know you noticed that, didn't you?"

"Damn it, Kate," I said, "I'm trying to get loaded up here, and you're distractin' me."

"How are you going to tell who she is?" she continued on my case. "She's a friend of mine and I know what she looks like. Now do you think maybe I ought to go with you?" she asked again.

"No, no, I don't want you to come with me," I said, "and I don't want to hear any more about it."

So we loaded the rest of the gear up on the bay mare I was gonna use for a pack horse.

"How far down to Mexico have you been?" I asked her. I was thinkin' that John wasn't going to show up.

"You're thinking about taking me, aren't you?" she said.

"No, I'm not," I said, still tryin' to be polite but losin' it a little.

Then she explained that these two horses were raised together and while on the trail I could unsnap the bay from the bull rope and she'd follow the sorrel anywhere.

"You know," she said, "if I go I could help carry the load with another pack horse."

"Lady, you're not going with me," I said again.

"Well, we'll see about that," she said.

I was getting anxious to get goin' by then. Everything was pretty much loaded up. She'd done a lot of the packing and I could tell she knew what she was doing.

When she was standing across me she said, "Tomás . . ."

"Why are you calling me Tomás?" I reluctantly asked her.

"That's your name in Spanish, isn't it?" she said.

"It's Tom wherever I go, even down in Mexico," I insisted.

"You like me, don't you, Tomás?" she said.

"What in the hell ever made you think I liked you?" I finally gave up on the politeness. "I haven't known you an hour and you're goin' at me with all these questions."

"I can tell you like me, that's all," she stated.

"Just help me load the rest of the stuff!" I gave up.

I was putting stuff in one saddle bag and here she comes carrying about eight sticks of dynamite, fast fuse and everything.

"What're you going to blow up, a bank or a railroad?" she asked.

"You're going to blow us both up carrying that stuff like that!" I said, "Kate, put that down!"

"I know how to handle it," she insisted. "We blow up stumps all the time."

"Just let me pack that," I said as I took it from her.

"I still want to go with you." She wouldn't give it up.

"You can't."

We got it all loaded up and I was ready to head out of there when she said, "Would you like me better if I had big tits?"

"You're gonna to get us in trouble. This is not a proper way for you to be talking here."

"It's the truth, ain't it?" she said.

"Now don't say nothing like that again." I'd had enough.

"I could go down there with you and help keep you warm at night. I could tell John that's what you'd like me to do."

"Don't you dare even say anything like that," I was getting desperate.

She went into the house and came back with something behind her back, but I wasn't really payin' any attention to it.

"Come here, Tomás," she said. "I want you to stand right here, put your hand on the side of the horn, and close your eyes."

"What are you doing?" I said. "I haven't got time for this."

I was thinkin' she was about fifteen years old and began thinkin' real fast about the situation. I even had the thought that it might be nice to have her along. You know, she was good at puttin' on a diamond hitch on the pack and everything else, and she knew the country, and knew who the girl was.

I stood still, closed my eyes and took a chance. Then she held my face with both her hands, and she told me to open my mouth a little bit. I was thinkin' this was getting out of hand but I stood there with my mouth open like she asked. All kinds of thoughts were going through my mind. Then she stuck an oatmeal cookie in my mouth and said, "Isn't that the best thing you ever had?"

I opened up my eyes up and said, "Yeah, it sure is." No better way to get a cookie than that! She packed me some more to take with me, and I gotta admit they sure came in handy over the next few days.

About then I looked down below the fence and John was coming up leading two pack horses. When he pulled in, he got off and came right up to me and said, "You must be Tom and I see you already met Kate."

"Did she run up on you?" he asked me.

"Yes," I said. "She's got a real unique way of doing that, doesn't she?"

"She's a good hand," he said in a proud way. "And it looks like she's got you packed up pretty good here."

"Let me show you where I think you should head," he got down to business. "I'll make you a map."

Using the map, he showed me where I should head and told me about the country.

"How much do I owe you for the horses?" I asked. "I don't have very much money right this minute."

"No money," he said, "if I was younger, I'd be goin' with you."

He told me the horses were top of the line and I told him I could tell that. Then we went over who I might run into down there and what I should do about it if I did. He told me more about the Mexican people, the bandidos, Mexican police and the Federales. It was not a pretty picture.

"What guns did you bring?" he asked me.

I showed him the 45/70. Then I pulled out my new rifle with the scope. He thought it was quite a rifle with that telescope on it. I ordered it out of a catalog and no one else around there had one like it.

INTO MEXICO

I finally took off from the ranch, leaving Kate and John behind. I crossed into Mexico that afternoon, following John's instructions. That evening I went through a town called San Pedro and then into Palominas which was part on the American side and part on the Mexican side. I followed the San Pedro River for a couple of miles, then cut across and hit the railroad tracks. I turned right at the fork of the river and picked up the railroad.

Soon I unsnapped the rope to the bay, like Kate told me I could, and from there on, that bay mare was always following, all by herself. I never worried about her from that time on.

There weren't many towns. I stopped at a place or two and the town people wanted to know why I was going down into the interior. I just told them I was going down to work in the mines. I camped out on that first night about ten miles inside of Mexico. The country was pretty and so far it had been easy to ride down in the bottoms.

I hadn't gone too far the next day when that sorrel I was riding just stopped still. I looked down to see if there was a rattlesnake on the trail or something, but there wasn't anything. I urged him on, but he wouldn't move. I thought, well, we got a problem here, and I didn't know what it is. Instinctively, I reached down and got my six-shooter handy and put my hand on it. I sat there for a little bit and I nudged him a time or two. But the bay mare behind us didn't pay any attention to what was going on.

I'd learned over the years to listen when a horse is trying to tell me something. Something was there, so I nudged him a little further and I saw him look off in the brush. Then I saw them – four Mexicans, kneeling down together out in the open. I didn't see any guns or anything. Two of them had their hats off, which bothered me 'cause they were holding them in front of them between their knees.

Sam told me anytime you see them come into camp and sit down in a squat to talk to you, you're okay unless one of their hands comes off their sombrero. If it comes off and goes in behind the sombrero, Sam said to shoot the son of bitch on the spot. He was serious, so I was a little worried about these boys. I was hopin' these boys held tight to their hats 'cause I didn't know exactly what I was gonna do if one of them hands disappeared.

Well, they sat there and watched me, nodded their heads, and asked me where I was goin'. I told them a story. I asked them the same thing and they said they were going north to work. They were friendly and they seemed more scared of me.

I saw a lot of people usin' the railroad tracks between little towns. They'd walk in the middle of the tracks to get from town to town. It was too hard on the horses up there and the berm of the railroad tracks fell off pretty steep on either side. John told me to avoid the towns if possible and to keep the horses out of sight. He said they'll kill for horses like these, and for the rifles. He agreed with Sam that I should keep everything hidden. That day I made pretty good time.

Seemed like I had everything I needed to keep me going if a horse lamed up on me. I'd be in big trouble if that happened so I was prepared just in case. I also brought along grain for four or five days.

After a while I stopped in at a little place called Casa Blanca. It's a little town with nothing there, no services or nothing. I talked with some folks and they invited me in for a rest. They had little corrals for the sheep and the goats. Everything was handmade. A lot of cooking was done outside on an open oven.

I couldn't speak Spanish as well as I needed to. Mixing English and

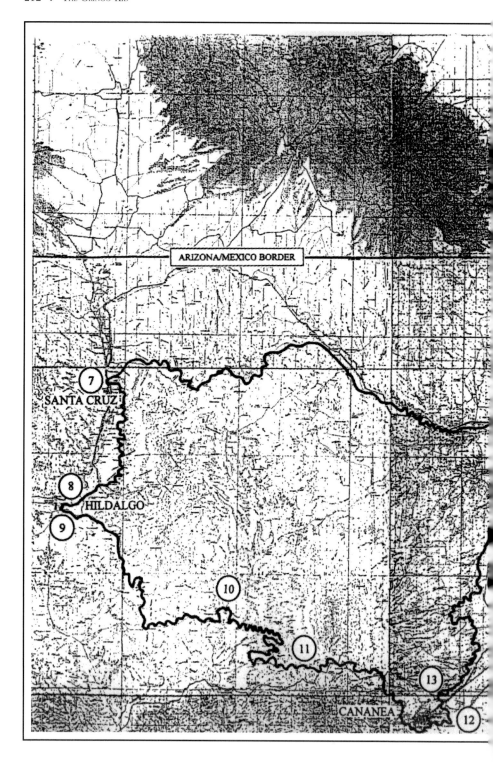

ARIZONA/MEXICO BORDER

SANTA CRUZ

HILDALGO

CANANEA

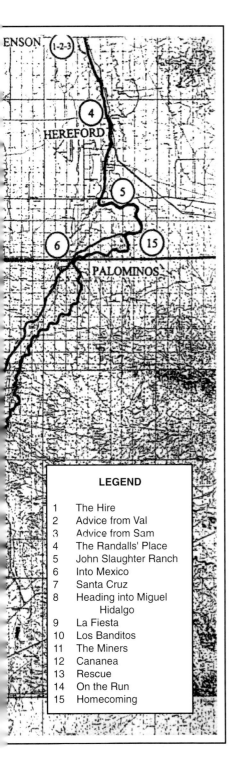

LEGEND

1	The Hire
2	Advice from Val
3	Advice from Sam
4	The Randalls' Place
5	John Slaughter Ranch
6	Into Mexico
7	Santa Cruz
8	Heading into Miguel Hidalgo
9	La Fiesta
10	Los Banditos
11	The Miners
12	Cananea
13	Rescue
14	On the Run
15	Homecoming

Spanish, I got my meaning through all right, though. There were some pretty girls there. Two or three especially pretty, very shy and very polite to me. I'd catch their eye once in a while and I wasn't against smiling at them. That was polite, I thought. But no time for romance here – I had a job to do.

So I didn't stay there long. I had supper and slept a ways out from that little town. I figured I'd bypass Las Cruces and make it all the way into Santa Cruz the next day. I hadn't had any problems so far, so I was feeling pretty good at this point.

The night was a little cool and I was thinkin' Kate was right about me wanting her around. I would have liked to have Katie there with me. I was getting lonely. So in the morning I was glad to see some Mexicans on the trail and for a while I followed them while they were hauling wood. I met them along the way and we talked a little bit. I was pretty relaxed ridin' along with them. Soon the road turned along with the railroad, not really a road there, just a trail following the railroad. No road signs anywhere and I had no idea where I was. I didn't have a map. I didn't want to ask too many questions, since I was in there without any papers. I would be subject to questioning and probably be arrested if someone got too interested in me.

I decided to turn off and go to the south a little. That put me into some fairly rugged country, but nothing I couldn't pass through if I was careful. Soon I picked up an old vaquero trail. I saw some peasants farming along there while I was going due west. I kept in the bottoms to keep out of the mountains so I wouldn't labor the horses. Along the way I stopped a couple of times and ate with some people, trading canned goods for fresh food. My candy bars came in good with the kids.

Finally, I made my way on into the town of Santa Cruz.

SANTA CRUZ — FIRST CLUE

Santa Cruz was another small town on that well-worn road down into the interior of Mexico. There were about fifteen buildings that I could see in town, but I didn't ride all the way in. I was afraid to take my horses in there. I found some people who were nice enough to let me tie up just outside of town. I pulled my gear off, which was something I didn't want to do more than I had to, hid my guns and told them I'd be back in three or four hours. I felt pretty confident everything would be all right there so I went on into town.

I took a look at the town and there was a little cantina there. They were serving food and it had been two or three days since I'd had much to eat. So I went in just dressed in my dirty jeans and denim shirt. I pulled my spurs off and had my Stetson hat on. I thought I'd fit in, but I stood out a little bit because most of the people there were peasants that came in off the farms or rancheros. A lot of them carried six-shooters dropped down in holsters. I saw some other Americans that looked like tourist types.

After I finished eating I went from door to door, one store to another, looked around and asked a few questions here and there. The more questions I asked, the more interested people got into who I was and what I was doing.

I went across the street into a dry goods store where they had some mining equipment, big bags of flour and lots of things hanging everywhere. I looked around lookin' for somebody to talk to and decided there wasn't anyone. When I started to go out, I looked over and heard somebody putting some cans on a shelves. She was a young girl, her hair was brown and she looked 5'5", 5'6". As she raised up her hands to put the cans up I saw that her arms were white. Definitely white.

My heart started racing so I waited for a little while and messed around like I was trying to buy something. When I turned around again she was looking at me. She smiled and I smiled back and then she went back to doing what she was doing for a minute or two. I thought for a second she could fit the description of Lou. Wouldn't it be something if I just lucked into her like this? But my brain was tellin' me she wouldn't be here at a store like this, smiling at me.

I remembered Lou had sandy-colored hair, blonde and brown mixed together. But I was watching this girl and wanted to make sure about her, so I asked her something in English. She shook her head no and I said something else. She got a puzzled look on her face and said in very heavy accented English that she didn't have what I asked for. That was all I needed to know. The minute she spoke to me I knew it wasn't Lou, so I left and went back out on the street again to check more stores for someone to talk to.

I saw two gas stations in town. One on each end of the town. I went up to one station and spoke to someone for a bit, askin' about people fillin' up with gas in the past few days. He didn't have any news for me. But he told me to walk down the end of the street and talk to the men at the other gas station. He said anybody coming through town would have to fill up with gas there. Especially if they were coming down from Lochiel, Miguel Hildalgo, or going down into Cananea.

So I walked down to the other station at the other end of the town and spoke to the guy running it. But he said he hadn't seen anybody like I was askin' about. There was an old man sitting near there and he was carving on a piece of wood, making a whistle or something. The old man apparently overheard me 'cause he raised his head and told me to come over there.

"You, gringo," he called at me, "come over a minute."

"Bueno," I answered.

"Who you looking for?" he went on, in Spanish of course, since he didn't know much English.

I told him what I was looking for and he said about five or six days ago he saw a car come by there with two Mexicans and a young white girl in the back seat. She looked kind of drunk. He said he looked in the car as it went by and she just looked up and rolled her head. He was sure she was white and her hair was the color of palomino, which is a yellow or golden brown.

I figured I'd found some good information there. Then the old man told me I should go down to Miguel Hidalgo where they were having a big fiesta for the next two days, that maybe they'd be there. He said I could ride there in one day so I decided that's exactly what I'd do.

HEADING TO MIGUEL HIDALGO

I went back to my horses and got my trappings up. I felt good about what the old man had told me so I was anxious to move on. The old man told me to stay on the east side, away from the main road. So I went down and it was good traveling. I went through lots of little farms, none of them fenced.

When I finally got into Miguel Hidalgo I found a town about the size of Santa Cruz. But I could tell the fiesta was going on. Kids were running here and there. I stopped along the way and talked to two or three people. The people were friendly and helpful. Finally, I decided to do the same thing I'd done in Santa Cruz. But first I had to find a place to put the horses and gear.

I found a little house away from town. They had a couple kids, one of them about ten and the other about eight. I asked them if they'd look after my horses and they agreed in exchange for some candy bars.

When I got to town I walked around the new part of town, but didn't see or find out anything interesting. Nobody knew anything. So I went back to my horses and planned on heading on to Cananea. But after I started out I thought I'd ride on through the old part of town. There were a lot of people there on horseback. I felt it might be useful to ask the way to Cananea.

Two or three Mexicans gave me about the same directions, so I was feeling more confident about where I was headed. The old part of town was only three or four blocks long and as I started going out of town an old man got up and asked me where I was going.

I told him I was probably going to Cananea to work in the mines – this story was working pretty good by now.

Then he asked me to come and sit with him. There was a hitching rail there and I checked around for Federale troop vehicles. I sat and talked to him for a while and then he said, "I don't think you go to Cananea to work in the mines."

I tried to insist I was, but he knew I was lying.

"No, gringo," he said, "I don't think so. You got the look of a hunter." He spoke English pretty good.

"Yeah," I said, still trying to cover myself, "I hunt deer."

"No," he said, "You've come a long ways and those are very fine horses you're riding. The best I've ever seen around here."

"Yes," I agreed on that.

"Don't go in any other part of town with them," he warned.

"I won't," I said, "I'm heading out. You speak pretty good English."

"You speak pretty poor Spanish," he laughed at me. "You should stay tonight for the fiesta."

Then he told me that there was a young girl from Spain who was born there and returns each year to celebrate her birthday. This year was her 17th and the whole town was in the middle of celebrating her birthday.

Finally we talked enough to where I felt relaxed in speaking a bit more to him. He kept askin' if I was looking for someone.

"Yes, I am," I gave up lying to him.

"Is it your woman?" he asked.

"No," I answered, "I don't have a woman."

"Who is it that you look for?" he insisted.

"My sister," I told him firmly.

"Why would she be down here?"

"I think two Mexicans went up on the American side and brought her down here." I told him I didn't know the word for kidnapped in Spanish. But I explained that she did not want to come with them.

"Where do you think she is?" he asked.

I told him what the man at the gas station in Las Cruces had said that they may have taken her to Cananea because of the whorehouses there. "How far is it to Cananea?" I asked.

He told me it was probably forty-five to fifty miles in a straight line but I got the feeling he really didn't know. So I told him I thought I'd rest up and head out in the morning. Then he invited me to go with him to meet his wife. He said he had a place to put my horses and I could have some food and water.

It took us a while to get to this old man's place. It was a pretty typical little house with a little porch on it. Lots of things were outside and the inside had a dirt floor. But they had windows and his wife, Teresa, kept the house as clean as possible. Everything had its place and was hung up here and there.

I washed up and Teresa got some food cooking. Those tortillas were made from the dough that she'd rolled in her hands. She spun it around in her hands and then laid them out on the top of the wood stove. I was fascinated watching her.

"You're going to leave tomorrow?" the old man asked me.

"I've got three or four hours of riding time left tonight and I could camp out there," I said.

"You're taking a big chance where you're going," he warned me. "Nobody rides alone in those mountains. You get up high, you'll be in trouble. Stay down low, but don't go down in the flats. You got papers?" he asked.

"No," I admitted.

"If you run into the Federales they'll steal your horses for sure and probably kill you. Why don't you stay here tonight and you can go to the big fiesta. There's gonna be a big dance with lots of young, pretty girls there."

"I don't think so," I said.

"There might be some gringos there. I will take you there," he insisted. "A lot of people have come from a long ways for this fiesta. People have come from Cananea."

I had danced many times in Naco and Agua Prieta.

"You got some more clothes?" he asked. He could tell I was thinkin' about goin'.

La Fiesta

I cleaned up, put on some clean clothes and went to the dance. On the way there I saw people running by with little banners and the kids had all kinds of things. They were playing with their hands up like horns. One would have a cape and they'd be acting like they were riding a horse. I enjoyed watching them. I heard some firecrackers goin' off and they had a big wheel on the side of the building and it was spinning around with fireworks on it. I started to relax and didn't see any harm in enjoying myself for a while.

When we got to the dance area, I took a look around and saw a big table with lots of food on it. They had cooked a whole pig and fish was layin' out there on the table.

As I entered the dance floor, I noticed a lot of girls. The girls were on one side and all the boys were on the other side. The older people were sitting at tables and some were milling around. The music was live and really great. There was some dancing goin' on and the boys would go across the floor to ask the girls to dance.

The old man started to go off on his own and I asked him if he was gonna stay with me.

"No, Gringo," he said laughing, "I can't dance, I'm too old and too ugly. But you're not."

"I'll just stand out of the way and watch," I said.

I did watch for a while and more and more people came and lots were dancing. Every once in a while when a dance was over I'd look across the floor to watch a girl sitting in a chair. Beside her was an older man and an older woman. I also noticed standing behind her were two of the biggest Mexicans I had ever seen. They had on their pistols and they wore very, very nice clothes; beautiful Spanish dress clothes with gold lacing, ties and a vest on each one. They had their big hats thrown back on the backs of their necks.

I noticed that none of the boys who were close to me had gone up to ask this one young girl to dance. So this one guy came by me and told me to ask his sister to dance. I went over and asked her and we danced a couple of dances. She liked to dance and she wanted to know who I was and where I was from. But I was just having trouble communicating with her so I went back to my post against the wall.

Then I asked one of the muchachos about the girl from Spain. He told me her name and it was a long Spanish name. I couldn't even pronounce it, let alone understand it. I asked if she was allowed to dance and he explained that she only dances once with each boy during the evening but most were afraid to ask her.

I asked about the pistoleros and was told they made sure no one got more than one dance. Kind of a joke, but it wasn't a joke to me. I take pistols pretty seriously. Then a couple of the muchachos got on me to ask the señorita to dance. One said he would dance with her and ask her if she'd ever danced with a gringo.

I was thinkin' it was about time to go soon. So I went over and got myself something to eat off the table. While I was eating I saw that muchacho go over and ask that girl to dance. I saw him talking to her and then she looked over at me. She could dance really well and she held herself differently than the others, very smooth and light.

They danced by me as they were going around in a circle and he pointed straight at me. She was watching me all right. I just nodded my head, and I got a little smile from her, that was all. It was just a courtesy to say hello, you know, because I didn't want to get involved in anything around here. But after the dance that boy came over to me and told me I could ask her to dance, that she said it would be okay.

I felt brave and said I'd like that. All my fears evaporated. I knew some dances and I could dance pretty good. So I started across there and the music had just started. I remember that I paused for a moment and thought, what in the hell was I doing? Why didn't I turn and go out that door right then? But I went over to her. Her mother was making something with some thread. Her father had his arms crossed and he was definitely looking at me, with no change of expression. I just kept going. I figured what the hell, I'd been in trouble before.

I boldly walked up and asked her as politely as I could if she'd like to dance. I never even looked at the pistoleros. She accepted in a pure sweet voice and she got up. I took her in my arms, held her out a very nice, respectable distance. I thought, okay, I can do this, and we danced one turn around the floor. I had to look down to see if her feet were on the floor. She really was a feather in my arms. She just glided and turned so easily. This was pretty exciting to me. I had never danced with anyone like that. She was so gentle and her hand felt like a piece of silk in my hand.

As I danced I looked around, and saw that all eyes were looking at us. She started talking to me really good English. She said she had gone to a Catholic school in Spain and had learned English, French and of course she knew Spanish. She asked me if I was nervous. I told her I was a little. She said not to worry and she told me she wouldn't break. So I held her a little firmer as we finished out the dance.

"Would you like to dance with me again?" she asked when we were done.

"They told me only one time," I said.

"I'm not telling you one time. I'll tell my bodyguards not to shoot you."

I thought that'd be a good idea. So we danced three or four more dances.

Then she asked me to teach her how to dance the American dances. She stopped in the middle of the dance and walked across the floor, towing me behind her, over to the mariachis. She talked to them in Spanish, asking them to play American tunes. Apparently they knew a few because they were from Nogales. They started playing an American tune and I showed her how to do a waltz kind of dance that I was pretty good at.

Everybody was watching and soon others were trying to do it. When she told me I was the best dancer she'd ever danced with, I was in heaven. Then I noticed as we were going around and around that there was nobody else on the floor. They'd all quit dancing. We just kept going for the next three dances. I showed her the two-step, the waltz and the jitterbug. When we got done, everyone was clapping for us.

Here I was trying to keep a low profile and I was out in the middle of this dance floor, making a scene with this pretty girl. After the dancing was done, she asked me to sit over by her. The muchachos were razzin' me. When the dance was over she told me I had to speak to her father before I left. I was wonderin' if I'd held her too tight or something.

So I went over and introduced myself to both of her parents. Her father asked me to sit down for a minute.

"My daughter tells me you have no mother or father."

"Really?" I said back.

"Where do you work?" he asked.

"Wherever," I answered.

"Why are you here?"

"I'm just looking for someone," I said.

"Gringo, you ever been to Spain?"

"No."

That señorita then said something in Spanish to her father and they talked back and forth for a few minutes. I couldn't understand them at all.

"Tomorrow we leave for Spain just before noon," he explained. "I'm inviting you to work at my ranchero in Spain. If you do not come, we will understand. If you come, we will understand."

I looked at her and she looked at me with a smile that was pretty irresistible.

"If I decide to come I will be here," I said.

Then I went over, took her hand, raised it and kissed her right on the top of her hand. I turned and walked out of there, thinking I was in a different world. I turned around and looked back, and she was smiling and nodding her head.

I went back to the old man's house and he was waiting for me.

"Gringo," he said, "news travels fast here. I understand you danced many times with Padrino's daughter."

"Yes, I did," I said with a smile on my face. "She's beautiful."

"What are you going to do now?" he asked.

I told him what they offered me.

"You going to go with them?"

"Part of me says yes, and the other part of me says no."

"What part of you says no?" he laughed. "Is there another girl?"

"There is one girl who I've liked since I was around fourteen," I explained. "I'm just hopin' some day she'll like me back."

He paused, then said, "I talked to a friend named Ramon, a relative of mine who lives in Cananea. We drank tequila and limes for a couple of hours and he said the girl you seek is in Cananea."

"What?" I said.

"She's probably the one you want," he continued, "and she's hurt. He told me she's new there and they're using her as a whore."

I was listening for more.

"She stays with two Mexicans on the outside of town. I knew you were a hunter. You have the look of a hunter. You got a choice to make," he said. "You can sleep in that room there, but you know something gringo, I don't think you're going to sleep very well tonight."

I washed up and a few minutes later Teresa brought out the clothes that she had washed for me and she took my sweaty ones to clean. I told her she didn't need to clean them, but she took the clothes and washed them that night.

It was late when we all finally went to bed. I went into that little room and a bed was made up for me. I laid down there, amazed at how nice these people were being to me. Lots of thoughts were racing through my mind. Finally, I slept.

I heard this voice in the morning when it was still dark. There was no electricity. Teresa called me to come in and have some breakfast. The smell of food was sneaking into the room where I was, and I was hungry. So I got up and felt around for my clothes and boots. I was polite about having some of that coffee but I had to grimace once in a while.

"I told my husband not to call you Gringo," she said apologetically. "We had a son named Tomás and you are Tomás, so he is supposed to call you Tomás. I told my husband that you would not go to Spain."

With that said, we ate the breakfast and then I went outside to load up my trappings.

But before I went outside I took two $10 bills, wadded them together and put them in the jar that Teresa called her little bank. I didn't want her to know I left it there because she wouldn't take anything from me. It felt good to leave that there for them. The old man came out to help and he was pretty interested in my guns so I showed him the scope and how it worked.

"There will be those who will want to steal this from you," he said. "Some would kill you for it."

After most of the gear was loaded, Teresa came out and handed me a little sack with a drawstring on it. It had two metal tins in it. I thought they probably contained food.

Then she opened it up and laid it on the table and showed me the tobacco. It smelled and felt like really fine tobacco. I told her I didn't smoke but she explained it wasn't for me. She thought it might be good for trading in a tight spot. I knew she'd taken her hard-earned money and bought that expensive tobacco specially for me. I thanked her and stuffed it in one of the saddle bags. I shook hands with each of them and Teresa gave me a little hug.

"Be careful. Remember, don't go straight up into the upper country," the old man warned.

I had no map but I knew the direction to head. I'd been lost, but never too lost. I knew how to follow the trails.

Cliff Diving

I was ready to go so I just swung aboard. I looked up and the morning rays of light were just starting to come through a blue haze. It was still a little chilly. The saddle was cold and creaky and I sat there for a minute. I told my hosts I was thankful for all they'd done for me. I looked up again and saw some really rough mountains ahead of me. Now I felt like I knew where I was going and there was a purpose. If that girl was there, I'd find her; if not, it was the best that I could do and I could do no more.

If I didn't find her I sure hated the idea of going home to tell Mrs. Randall I'd failed her. So I nudged that sorrel along and we made good time 'cause it was good trail. I stayed down in the bottoms and just kept pushing on. It seemed like the canyons flew by.

I covered a lot of ground and kept him at a good pace until I pulled him up and gave him a chance to blow. I got off to check my cinches and saw my pack was riding good. The bay mare was right there, following along as usual. She was always eating when we stopped.

I picked up a good trail, but it was rugged. Lots of fingers had started to swing around, keeping inside of where I was trying to go and yet I didn't want to drop off too far in the bottoms – the Federales were there. I was feeling pretty good. Maybe a tad cocky. The day was nice and I was following this pretty good wash. I followed this trail about ten or twelve miles. Then I dropped down into a little place where there were quite a few tracks, some cattle but mostly bighorn sheep and deer, javelina and maybe a wolf or coyote track. The game came through there 'cause there was water back in there.

Tracks in this one little spot showed that there had been some horses coming up headed north. There were some horses running shod and some unshod. I followed them for a while and I noticed that they never stopped to graze and pull off to the side. These horses were going somewhere with somebody. It made me a little bit nervous about what I might be riding into. I got down and took a look at the trail closer. Tracks on a good day without a wind won't crust on the track until it's maybe two to four hours old. You can push it off to the side and get a good idea how old they are. If there's a wind up, that can drop down to an hour or two. The more I looked at these tracks the more I didn't think they were fresh so I didn't think there was much of a problem. But I pulled out my Winchester anyway.

As I started on down this long narrow stretch of the trail I started seeing some fresh tracks, some deer and javelina. These tracks in the sand told me they were traveling pretty fast, like something was chasing them. I was curious but didn't worry about it. The canyon was starting to get a little steep on the right and on the left. I was sitting there just for a minute thinking about whether this trail was gonna take me toward where I wanted to go. Then I heard some rocks roll. The canyons echo so it's hard to tell exactly where sounds are coming from. Then I moved on out and then I heard it again. This time it was pretty clear. So I pulled out my binoculars and looked up there and saw a big horned sheep and a couple of ewes. He was making good time up there but I couldn't understand why he seemed in such a hurry. I noticed the ewe in the back kicking with her hind feet, swinging her head around to the side and back. They were all heading down toward where I was on the bottom trail. I was thinkin' maybe something was chasing from above but I didn't see anything. I headed on and hadn't gone fifty yards when I heard some rustling in the brush and some thrashing around. Something was moving through the brush in a hurry.

My sorrel was getting pretty jumpy and I spurred him on a little bit and said "come on, let's see what it is." Both his ears were forward. So I got him up a little further on the trail and this noise was getting louder and we both knew something was coming our way. I nudged him a little bit further but he wouldn't move. I could tell there was more than just one animal but I didn't know what kind. My sorrel snorted a couple of times and was leaning back. I eased him over to the side trying to get him up close to the rock ledge on the right. If he whirled to turn and get out of there he'd have to go to the left and as I was ready to handle him and keep the Winchester in my right. I was a little concerned about what was going to happen because he was so nervous.

The first thing that broke into the trail ahead of me was a doe and she was running fast with three more right in behind her. They all had their tongues out and that meant they'd been running a long way. They hardly glanced at me as they passed and went on. Then there was silence. I watched them go up the rocky trail and disappear. Not long after a second bunch of deer came through in the same scared manner, a forked-horn that looked like he'd hurt his foot and was kind of limping, a big doe was bloody on her flanks and neck. Still, I didn't know what was causin' them to run like that. I figured something was yet to come down that trail.

Then I saw something that I had only heard about once before, a swarm of Mexican deer flies. They're about the size of a bumble bee, usually two shades of black. This swarm was like bees would be, up about four to six feet off the ground and six or eight feet wide. They's move fast and then just stop for a second or two, then move on. I was sitting there watching them and not knowing what to do and not having a lot of choices. I felt my sorrel flinch and pull his shoulder a bit to the side and I looked down and there was one of those deer flies that lit right on him. I reached down with my hand, slapped it and then turned my hand and saw the blood. Another one landed on the neck and I reached over and flatted him too. Then another one landed, then two. Then I knew I had a problem.

I decided it was time to ease around and try to go back out the way we came in. I turned around and started out at just a trot, looking back over my shoulder at that swarm. My Winchester wasn't gonna do me no good with this problem so I put it back in my saddle boot.

Then the bay started kicking and when I looked back I knew that swarm was definitely headed our way. I put him into a slow lope and figured I would just have to be as careful as I could. Then I felt one land on my arm and bite, so I took off knowing they were after us. I reached down and pulled my bandana up over my face. A lot of them were keepin' up with me so I knew we really had a problem. We were getting more of them on us biting and my sorrel was starting to swing his head because they were trying to get to his ears. I was trying to knock them off and ride at the same time. I could hear them and I could see them all around me.

I saw ahead of me that same big wash that had led from north to south where I'd seen all the tracks so I headed down in there. The walls were high and there was a little brush there. I noticed that the water had come down through there really heavy 'cause up on the sides there was a lot of driftwood piled around. We were still traveling pretty good in through this sandy wash. But it didn't seem to matter, there were still too many of them landing on us. I was fightin' them off with everything I could. But I knew the horses were getting bit.

The canyon started to narrow and I didn't know where we were headed, didn't care much at the time either. We were starting to drop pretty fast. I went around a bend and looked up ahead and it looked all right to keep on going. I was still afraid to slow down. When we came to another bend I slowed a little, but then I saw that we were really in serious trouble. My sorrel knew too, and he tried to stop and I started hollering at him, whoa, and tried to pull him up. He did everything he could to stop and then he slipped. We'd gone out of the sand onto smooth granite rock. As we slipped on down to a lower ledge and he just couldn't get his footing. I could see we were up on a steep cliff where the water had dropped off with nowhere to go.

I supposed my sorrel knew what was best to do. I sure couldn't see below me and all I could see above was sky. He bunched up and I'll be damned if he didn't jump. He jumped straight out in the air – literally out in the air. I remember bein' thrown back so far the back of my head hit him right in the butt. I'd lost my right stirrup my feet were were up with his neck. I thought this was it for me, that I was gonna die in this canyon and the coyotes were gonna have the damnest meal they'd ever had.

I hadn't seen the water but luckily we were over a pool of water. I didn't know how deep it was, but there was no time to think about that. We were on our way down. I knew the bay was somewhere right behind me and she'd probably land right on top of me. The sorrel went in head first all the way down under the water takin' me with him. When his head came back up I hit the pole right above my right eye in the eyebrow. It knocked me completely over him and off of him, going into the water about eight feet in front of him. Then I didn't know where I was. I was totally disoriented.

When I came up out of the water my hat tie-down was choking me bad. My hat had come back off my head and caught full of water. I couldn't get my hands to it while I was trying to swim and getting dizzy. The sorrel was swimming to shore and I saw him coming by me. About that time the bay hit the water, she lit within about two or three feet of me and the force of the water drove me back down under. This time I felt the bottom and came back up quick as I could. I reached out and grabbed at anything. I felt the stirrup of the sorrel and held on for my life.

He was draggin' me through the water and I think I kinda blanked out. When I felt the ground under me, he kept goin' ahead, lunging and pullin' me right up on the bank. I couldn't see out of one eye and I kept wiping it off.

I got my hat off while I was still laying there hanging on to the stirrup. That sorrel just stood right there beside me, didn't move. I noticed the bay had come out and was standing there too. She busted her britching when she hit the water, and her pack had slipped up on her shoulders. But these two horses had been trained to stand still and wait for orders. The bay was shaking with her head down, trembling. Finally, I thought I had to do something. So I started talking to the horses. I tried to get up but gave it up and put both my arms around the stirrup and hung there for a minute more. The sorrel turned his head to look at me and I noticed blood dripping where he'd been bit pretty bad. He was blinking and moving his head. Other than that I thought he didn't look too bad though.

Finally I decided that I had to get up so I pulled up and got a hold of the saddle horn and looked around. When I let go of the saddle horn I was so disoriented I began falling backwards trying to catch myself but after a few wobbly steps I fell flat on my back and there I laid. I'm laying there in the middle of no where, looking up seeing these big high mountains on both sides. Then I looked up and saw where we'd come off the cliff. I was in denial tellin' myself, "no, we didn't come off there; no, we came off somewhere else." Well, I laid there for a while and as I started to get up again my head was screaming. The whole canyon was tilting this way and then the other way. I'd dropped into a hole that I knew I wasn't goin' out the way I came in.

When my head settled a bit I started pulling off the pack saddle but all I wanted to do was lay back down and go to sleep. While working the rodeo they'd always told me if I got knocked off and my head hit something not to lay down and go to sleep. So even though I felt drowsy I knew to try to stay up and awake. My legs were staggerin' around while I worked on getting the gear off my horses.

My Winchester was still there in the saddle boot, but when I checked for my six-shooter it was stuck around almost to the back of my butt. I pulled it back around in place and I was startin' to feel more like myself.

The bay didn't seem to be hurt. She was standing on all fours which indicated to me that her legs were alright. If she'd hurt a leg anywhere, she'd been putting one up and one down and shifting her weight. It crossed my mind that John Slaughter really wouldn't want his horses jumping off cliffs into little pools of water. Anyway, I got them both stripped, took them down into the water to clean 'em up a bit. They both had bites from those deer flies that were still bleeding.

The sorrel wasn't gonna let me lead him into that water again so after fussin' around with him for a while I got a board and she went out just about hock high but wouldn't go no further. Then after about three or four minutes of unsuccessful coaxing my teeth started chattering and we both got out of that water.

After the horses were tended to with mud packs over the bites I began to go through my stuff. Luckily, I kept my stuff mostly in metal canisters, just in case it rained or somethin'. The shadows were getting longer and the sun was starting to hide over to the left. This canyon was no more than thirty or forty yards wide and built itself out after playing along a little flat spot with some brush. I really couldn't see how far it went after about two hundred yards.

It looked like the smartest thing to do was spend the night right there and recover a bit so I got a fire built up against this rock. Then I kicked it out a little ways and hung my blankets over those warm rocks to dry. Everything was wet. I knew it was going to be a miserable night. The horses went grazing while I got me some wood to keep that fire going. I was hopin' to get me some coffee going. Things were drying up faster than I expected and things began to look a little better for night so I rustled me up something to eat.

My boots were off and stuck on two wooden limbs near the fire. I checked on the horses one more time, came back and settled in for the evening. Before I really settled in I checked my Winchester and my six-shooter thoroughly, cleaned them and had them loaded and handy. Finally, a couple of the blankets were dry enough to where I could wrap them around me. So I laid down there between a rock and the fire. I was plannin' to keep that fire going all night long. I recall laying there watching the shadows from the fire on the rocks wonderin' about evil spirits and such. It was eerie quiet in that canyon, seemed as if even the birds had stopped chirpin.' I could hear the water trickling down those steep canyon walls. It was a long cold night.

At daylight I got my achin' body up and fixed myself something to eat. The horses were both laying down still sleepin' and I left them alone. I needed to think this through about gettin' out of there. My boots were still wet, my socks were ice cold and even though it was daylight there was no sun yet.

I started off down the east side along the canyon wall lookin' for some kind of trail. After a while it seemed that every side went straight up. Then I noticed there were some signs of wildlife comin' down on the southwest corner where there was a little meadow. So I found this trail and started following it. Soon it was clear that this trail was made by deer, javelina and sheep comin' down to water at the pool. It would be tough going to fit me and my horses up that trail.

After hikin' a ways up there and gettin' all scratched up I went back to my camp, got my pistol, put it over my shoulder and grabbed my machete to clear the brush out of the way. I hacked my way up that trail, pushed a few rocks out of the way, and was knocking branches off so I could get the pack saddles through. This wasn't gonna be easy but nothin' I do seems to be easy. One broken leg on one of my horses would be the end of me. Usually a trail up this steep an incline will have switchbacks, but this one didn't. I had to push a couple of big boulders out of the way and I finally dragged myself up to the top of this ridge and looked around. Anywhere I looked from up there was straight down. "And this was my way out with those horses?" I thought.

After checking around some more I found a little spot on this ridge with some heavy brush. When I cut out as much brush as I could, I saw to the north the way I wanted to go to get back to the original trail I was on earlier. I made my decision that this was the best I could do. We were all comin' up that steep trail and not stoppin' 'til we reached the top.

So with a determined mind I went back down, saddled them up, checked the shoes, hung my six-shooter belt on my saddle and we started up that trail, me in the lead with the lead rope. Immediately I was in trouble. The sorrel wanted to go faster than I could go. He knew where he had to go to get to another foothold and stoppin' would make it harder. Whenever he'd move, he'd lunge or jump a little bit and I couldn't keep out of his way. I popped him in the nose two or three times and got his attention to where he would quit running up on me. We worked that trail pretty hard until we got to the top of that narrow ridge. At the top I wanted the bay to hold up so I tried to stop her and get the saddle bags off. But she came right on by and I swear the saddle bags caught something, scraped along the rock and pushed her all the way over the ridge. Rocks were falling, I was trying not to get trampled as she was trying to get her footing and she finally got back up on top. From there on out, we followed the top which was a little better trail.

After a ways I got up and rode. I was tired but I knew then that we were on the way back to the original trail where all the trouble started. Soon I could see my tracks where I was in a heck of a hurry. I was not in the mood to see any deer flies.

When the sun started heading down I got off, went down and found a good place to camp, and turned the horses loose to graze. Built a good fire that night and got something to eat. I was thinkin' that I'd probably gotten through the worst part of this trip. Soon after I learned this wasn't exactly true.

LOS BANDIDOS

In the morning I pushed on, heading in what I thought was the right direction. But soon I was traveling among those rough and gnarled fingers. I saw some tracks of wild burros and horses, so I decided to follow them for a while up this canyon and on up onto a ridge. After a while I stopped and checked the tracks again. These horses had riders. Someone had crossed here and I wondered who they were – the Federales troops or the bandidos I'd been warned about.

At that point I became very apprehensive. I untied the diamond hitch, took the tarp off and reached in for the sticks of dynamite. I brought them up front and took two of them and put real short fuses in with caps on them and stuck them in my saddle bags where they'd be handy. I took out my Winchester 45/70, tied my diamond hitch back on and rode holdin' my Winchester fully loaded and ready to go.

I kept pushing and pushing and came to a place where the trail divided. I chose to go to the left. Then I went to the top of a ridge and looked way off to see where I was at. I'd been told that the Federales troops would be down in the flats and that would be big trouble for me. So I decided to stay up in the hills for now.

I'd been in there three or four miles and saw a good trail leading off on the right hand side of this canyon, so I picked it up and started off. It started winding up the side of the canyon with really severe switchbacks. This was tough country and sometimes the horses would lose their footing a little bit. I decided to ride it as best I could, and had gone three or four miles up and got right on top of the ridge. As I kept going up, I let the horses blow more and more. I stopped and got off and got something to drink and eat.

As I walked around to the right hand side of my horse to get myself something to eat out of a little bag, I caught a glimpse of a flash of something on the other side of the canyon, maybe 500 to 700 yards across from me. I looked over there but couldn't see anything, so I got myself a drink – then my horse's head came up sharp. He turned and repositioned himself, almost stepping on my feet.

At that point I saw something coming down the other side of the canyon that sent a chill through me. At first I just saw two men walking. Then I counted five more men on horseback. My first thought was that they could be a group of miners packing out their gold. That'd be all right, I thought. But they were definitely dressed in white Mexican clothing. I dug out my binoculars and mounted my horse. Then I knew for sure they were not miners and they were not Federale troops. They had bandoliers on them and I could see at least three carrying rifles. These guys were bandidos, no question in my mind about it. As they worked their way down the hillside, I stood as quiet as I could, still sitting on my horse. They were a long ways away, but I figured if I moved, they would surely see me.

Well, I'd forgotten about the bay mare wandering around and she decided she wanted to step up on the ridge to get some more grass. There was no way I could get to her to hold her still. I called out to her – whoa, whoa – but I noticed the men had stopped. I could see that one of them in the back got off his horse and walked around to the two in the front. I could see him pointing over at me. I knew then that I had been seen, but still I felt with the entire canyon between us I shouldn't worry too much about them.

I put my canteen away, got my rifle up and rested it on my legs so they could see that I had a rifle with me. I admit I was feeling a little vulnerable out there by myself. I just started pushing right up the mountain and acted like I didn't see them. I'd look over at them a little as I went but they hadn't moved yet. I could tell they were watching me.

I probably went five hundred yards, working up that trail off the ridge. I didn't like being in plain open sight. I felt like I was naked out there. Then I saw the one in the back walk around and get back on his horse, and they headed down. I just kept going at a reasonable pace, not really knowing where I was headed. They were working their way down that ridge towards the bottom. I knew then that they were coming across after me.

If I pushed my horses too hard, one of them could get hurt because that trail was so rough. So I kept going at a slow but steady pace. I figured they were probably at least two or three hours behind me. But I realized they were making good time across the canyon.

The two in front would trot and didn't seem to tire. I was getting concerned about the whole situation and the only thing I could think to do was keep on pushing ahead.

Finally, I reached a point in the trail where the climb petered out and the trail started rimming around this huge mountain. I started making better time and it was taking me more towards the direction I wanted to go. Soon I lost sight of them. Periodically I would stop and look back, but they weren't where I could see them anymore. By afternoon, the trail took me back up on top and out in the open again. And there they were, still comin' after me.

The ones running out ahead were making better time than the ones on the horses. Only one rider had his rifle out where I could see it. Then I saw the ones out in front stop, so I stopped and looked right at them. They looked at me and then sat down and continued to watch me. I thought they were waiting for the horsemen to catch up. I was figuring at this rate they would catch me pretty soon. So I started thinking about what I could do to stop them. I'd never been in a position like this before.

I started looking for a good place to stop and get ready for them.

I picked a place and changed rifles. The new rifle handled five cartridges in the magazine and one in the chamber and I got it ready to go. I put the safety on and thought about what to do. I thought if I had to shoot, the best I could do is get one and then the rest would hide. Then they'd wait me out until dark. I did have that scope and they didn't know about it. Maybe I could get two. But there were seven of them. I knew I had better horses but I couldn't outride the foot soldiers on these steep trails.

So I laid my rifle down on a rock and from that position I could see those guys sitting down there watching me. Then they got up and walked a little ways and they were standing out in the open when I saw the first horse-back rider come over the ridge. I put the scope on him but it was about 500 yards – still too far to shoot. My plan was to try to take out as many of them as I could.

I slipped the safety off, and cradled the rifle in a small swell in the rock. I tried to breathe as slow and easy as I could. My heart was pounding like a sledgehammer. I picked the largest one standing in the front of the rest. I put the crosshairs in the scope on his head and figured the distance to be about 500 yards. They were standing there looking and pointing at me. I raised it up a little bit and noticed the rifle was shaking. I couldn't hold the scope steady. I was scared, there was no question about that.

If I shoot, I thought, they'd scatter, so I didn't do it. I thought that they might back off.

So I got back on, still carrying my long rifle. Then I saw that the two walkers again headed after me with the horsemen about 100 yards behind them. I proceeded on up the trail and got into a really rough place with all kinds of rock ledges with no way to climb up or down, but I thought I had to keep following this trail.

Soon I pulled up and stopped, and saw that they had closed the gap now to about 300 yards. They were gaining on me pretty fast now. Down in the flats I could have smoked them with my better mounts. But up there I decided to bail off and take a stand. I tied up my horse so he wouldn't run off and left the bay loose.

I positioned myself down next to a tree, carefully setting my rifle in the crotch. I picked the Mexican that was closest to the horseman. If I overshot the standing Mexican, I might get the rider on the horse. Then I put the crosshairs in the scope on the top of his sombrero, held my breath and squeezed off a shot. Almost immediately I saw his knees buckle and he lurched to the side and went down on his face. I knew I had hit him good. The horsemen whirled their horses around and spurred them down the ridge out of the line of fire.

One man ran up the side of the hill. I was firing at them as they ran. I shot again and missed him. At that distance it was difficult to hit a moving target. I shot again as he ran, but nothing hit. This Mexican had nine lives, but I thought maybe I had bought some time and some respect for my long rifle. I had the feeling they'd never seen a rifle that could shoot that far 'cause they trotted out there again and I let go again. This time another one was down. I think I must have hit him in the arm or the hand because I saw him grab his arm, spin around and go down. From that point on, they all hid. I think they now knew they couldn't just walk up there and take everything I had away from me.

I stepped aboard again and rode to the next ridge. There were some really big outcroppings of rock above me and below me, and I was getting an idea about how to keep those Mexicans from coming after me up there. I could see they hadn't given up and were going to dog me and track me until sundown.

When I reached the top of this rocky ridge I was thinking five to one was not a fair game and I knew I had a problem with daylight. It was a matter of time and they could play the waiting game better than I could. They were raised in these mountains.

I wasn't going to let them ride up on me any closer. I'd been warned about not trying to negotiate with them. I'd been in shootouts and standoffs with people who had guns, but I'd never been in anything like this. I was the one being tracked and hunted. Something had to be done soon on that mountain. They were only moving when I moved, keeping at least 500 yards between us. Time was on their side. I knew I couldn't work that trail during the night.

I looked around at the country as I sat there on my horse. I could see the long ridges coming down from the higher mountains in the northeast. There was a valley spreading about 600 yards across below me. It was strewn with a lot of heavy brush and rocks that had tumbled down from the rock ledges above me. I was on the only trail around. It looked like I might have two hours of daylight to go at most, and I already knew I couldn't outride them on that trail.

I waited, and then I saw them come down the other side, two on foot ahead of the horses, and they were movin' good. Then they waited for the others to catch up. I could tell they knew the trail well. Everything would change when it got dark. I didn't have any good plan yet so I moved on, making sure that I didn't go too fast so my horse didn't get hurt.

There were five of them coming after me, and I knew there had once been seven. Everytime I'd stop and look back at them, they'd stop and sit there with their hands crossed across the big horns on their Mexican saddles. I looked at them through my binoculars and I could make them out real clear.

As I went over the next ridge, I saw another one almost identical. The area was a mess of rocks and huge boulders. I crossed through the next little valley, which was a little more confined. Then I headed up the next ridge on the other side. It was coming on dark and I had no time to wait for them to do something. Things were starting to look bad for me and I didn't know whether I was going to get out of there or not.

This part of the trail was pretty good and as I rode I looked back over my shoulder, watching and watching, but saw nobody. I began to think they'd probably send one rider ahead a different way around me. The sun was just starting to set over the mountains. Soon the light would get bad and even the scope wouldn't help much.

I pushed on and decided this couldn't continue. I looked up to the left of me and here was this big pile of rocks. I thought maybe I could hide in there. But no, they'd wait me out until the morning or until I fell asleep. I had to do something. There was not gonna be a standoff. I remember takin' off my hat, bowing my head and saying something to the Lord, hopin' He had a few minutes for me. Told Him I needed a little help here. I figured it was the best effort this young cowboy could do at that point.

Then I made up my mind what I had to do up there on that ridge. Put my hat back on and looked up at that rock pile again. I had about an hour of light left. I looked back and there was one of the riders stopped, lookin' at me, waitin'. Then they bunched the horses together and started moving ahead walking behind the horses. It was the perfect way to close the distance with the horses protecting them. Then I saw one of them slip off to the right and I saw that he had a rifle as he went out of my sight. Now I had to deal with four or five of them behind me while one of them was going to show up in front of me.

I was thinking I'd never hear the shot that killed me. So it was time to act. I'd come in there with eight sticks of dynamite and with that I could blow out some rocks underneath that ledge and it just might fill that whole valley and anyone down there too. When I was younger and worked as a powder monkey in the mines, I had learned how to drop a mountainside by blowing the base rocks away. So I got off my horse and tied both of them in the brush where they could see them. I took the Winchester with me, pulled my hat off and laid it right smack where they could see it stickin' out there. I saw one of them go over and squat down to wait. Pretty soon, two or three were there, sitting and waiting.

I pulled my spurs off, ripped my chaps off as quick as I could. I knew where I had to go and I had to move fast. I went over to the pack, reached in and got the caps, my pocket knife, and a roll of slow fuse. I gathered the fuse up as much as I could. I unbuttoned my shirt and stuck six of the dynamite sticks inside my shirt.

My pursuers hadn't moved. So I headed up the right-hand side of that ridge out of their sight. They could occasionally see me go up but they wouldn't know what I was doing.

I went as fast as I could. Two or three times I kind of slipped a little, but that didn't bother me. The canyon wall was falling off fast, sometimes straight down 200 to 300 feet. The shale rocks moved when I stepped on them. I kept looking back and they were still sitting down there, watching me. I had to keep going. Finally, I slipped across the top and found what I wanted.

After looking over the situation I picked out a place underneath the biggest ledge of rocks. If I could blow the rocks from the bottom of those giant cliffs, I figured a good rock slide would keep them from following me on the trail. I grabbed three sticks, pulled them out, wrapped a leather thong around them real tight. Then I did the same with the other three sticks and put the longest fuse on them I could.

I had to get back around under the bluff, move across, set the next charge below on half the fuse or at least two-thirds of the fuse. They had to blow within two or three minutes of each other. I thought I had a good plan – if it worked. It was important to have the base dynamite charge blow before the top charge.

The shadows were getting long. Sweat was dripping down and off my face. My clothes were wet and I was hurrying the best I could. I got a kitchen match, pulled it up on the side of my Levi's and struck it. I just stood there and looked at it for a second, thinkin' this was the craziest damn thing I'd ever done in my life. Then I lit that fuse, reached over, and swung it so the bundle of dynamite would drop right down under this great big rock ledge.

It missed the ledge I wanted it to go on, and bounced and tumbled down out of sight. I just knew the force of the rock hitting the caps as it tumbled would prematurely set off the dynamite. I put both hands to my ears 'cause I thought it was goin' to blow right then and there.

I snapped out of it and headed down around the side with the second bundle in my hand. I kept going and probably passed in open sight of them Mexicans down there. Then I reached the second spot and I lit the fuse, swung it around and let it go right under the biggest rock I could find there.

Then out of there I went. I got up and on the ridge and headed back across as fast as I could go and then I went down the ridge over toward my horses. I had gone maybe 100 yards out in plain sight when I heard the first bullet go by me, just like a bee buzz. And then – I heard the shot go "VABOOM!" Then again, the same thing. They were shooting way short and way long and I just kept going. I got about halfway to the horses, all the time thinkin' it was going to blow any second. Then I went down. I fell on my left side and the pain was sharp as I rumbled over a boulder, bounced and then hit the ground again, still on the same side, trying to get my footing so I could keep going.

For a second I thought maybe I'd been shot. I was having trouble moving on the left side. I'd hurt myself and had a little bit of a limp with about one hundred yards left to go. I reached over and grabbed a tree stump and held onto it to catch myself, wiped off my face and looked over at them. They'd moved right out in the open below me and they were lined up like a firing squad. I could see the powder fly from their rifles as they shot at me. I could hear the bullets hit and chip on the rocks. I rested for just a second and the pain was really starting to go down my leg, but I knew I could make that next hundred yards, and I did.

When I got there I grabbed my hat and put it on and grabbed my rifle. My chaps were already strung across the saddle, my spurs were already in the saddle bags. So I started to climb aboard, but I couldn't make it up. My leg wouldn't bend and my hip wouldn't work good enough. I kind of slid back down and then tried again. When I looked back I saw they were scrambling up after me. That gave me the extra energy I needed to get up into the saddle and I took off.

Then all I was wonderin' was when was it going to go off or was it gonna go off. I didn't know anything except to keep moving. Off to the left there was a place where I could get up against some rocks where I thought I'd be safe for a few minutes. That was the only thing I could do at that point. I was out of ideas. My saddle slipped so I got off, reached up to pull the cinch strap up, and I heard this "WHAMMM!!" It shook the ground and rumbled for some time. I thought, she's off, I've touched her off!

I wanted to ride back and look but I couldn't do it. So I scrambled back up on my saddle and rode on a little ways, lookin' for a place to hold up for the night. I looked back over the top of the ridge and I saw a big cloud of dust starting to roll down the side of the mountain. More movement was going on with the dust curling up into the air.

I got off again and put both my hands on the ground to try to feel any rumbling. Then I heard the second "BOOM!" Not like the first one, kinda muffled. It was like I'd heard before in the mines when everything was packed in tight with mud. I waited there with my hands on the ground. Nothing. I waited some more and then I felt something begin to rumble. It got louder and louder. Something was going down on the other side of that mountain. Then I smelled it. There's a distinct smell after a blast unlike any other smell.

It's happens when rocks violently rub against each other. It's not like dynamite or black powder. I knew that there were a lot of boulders and rocks
moving. I'd done something. Hopefully, I blocked the trail between those
Mexicans and me. At least enough to slow them down some.

I got up and rode into this brushy place to bush up for the night. It was
dark and useless to ride any further. The brush was heavy, real heavy. As I
went in, it was all I could do to hold myself up and keep the brush out of my
face. The horses had their ears laid back with their heads down and they
didn't like this at all. We broke through there and cleared a place to hole up.
There was a little water seep and some open room for the horses. It was an
ideal place.

I could still smell that odor over the top drifting right in there. Then I
saw a little bit of the dust cloud coming down off over the side of the ridge. I
pulled my gear off trying to get things settled before dark. I knew this was a
pretty good spot. They couldn't come in above me, and if they came in on
either side, I would be able to see or hear them before they got to me – if I got
lucky.

I took my saddle and pack bags and made a make-shift barricade. Then
I backed in there, and there I laid. I immediately started to stiffen up. The
place on my hip was starting to hurt bad. I didn't know how bad I was hurt –
I hadn't had time to think about it. I reached over and pulled my britches
down and looked at it. It looked like a bad wound four or five inches long
and four inches wide. I had really dug in and there was a hole in my jeans.
But it didn't seem like anything was broken. I was just stiff and cold. I scooted
myself back into there, took the 45/70 Winchester, set it up laid over the top
of my saddle. I took out my handgun, laid it there, got a handful of cartridges
handy. If I had to, this was where I was going to make a stand. Couldn't think
of nothin' else I could do.

After a while I got up for my canteen and realized I was hungry but I
didn't care. I drank as much water as I could then I settled back to wait.

Then it was dark. If anything moved, I thought it had to be one of
those Mexicans coming up from the side. But nothing came. I waited and
waited and then I slipped off to sleep. Then one of the horses moved and I
immediately woke up and pulled back the hammer on the Winchester. I put
it back down again when nothing happened. I figured they were waiting
until daylight, so I needed to try to get some sleep. I started to get cold and to
shake. I pulled the blanket around me but it wasn't enough, so I put another
one down around me and there I laid. I don't know how long I slept. I had no
idea of the time. But it was cold.

Then I noticed my right boot was damp with blood. While I pulled off my boot and bloody sock I was thinkin', 'how'd that blood get there from my hip?" I lit up a little so I could see and got to feeling around to see if I could find where the blood was coming from. I found that there was a messy hole in my leg about the size of my little finger. I knew I was hurting just about all over but I didn't know I'd been shot.

It was obvious that the bullet was still in there and I knew it had to come out so it wouldn't get infected and kill me. I stuck my finger down in there and could feel the bottom of the bullet with my nail scraping over it. It was in there maybe three-quarters of an inch.

"How was I going to get it out? I was askin' myself over and over.

This was going to be a problem. Putting my finger down in there got it hurtin' quite a bit. I got a pair of fencing pliers from my saddle bags. I knew the round ball part of the bullet was into my leg muscle but it hadn't hit a bone. So I took my pocket knife out and the leather punch. I took my pliers and grabbed a hold of the end of that little punch blade and held it over the flame.

While it was heating up I sat there watching, listening, hearing things. The horses were moving around and the slightest shadow looked like a Mexican coming over the ridge to get me. I drew my weapons close with the Winchester on my lap and the pistol laying next to me. Boy, I tell you, I was a sad sight at that moment with my leg propped up over the side of my saddle where I could hold it and see it by the light of the candle sitting in the crotch of the saddle.

I finally got the blade to where it was hot enough to bend just a little bit and it didn't break. Then I got it hot again and bent it a little more and it still didn't break. By then I had a little bitty hook on the end of it that might work. I reached into my bag and got some mescal that I had to clean the wound with. My leg was still propped up there while I tied a knot around the back of my leg with some of that white material Mrs. Randall had given me. Then I got a thin little limb and put it under that material a¡nd turned it to make a tight tourniquet. The more I turned it the more it pulled the flesh of my leg down to where I was getting closer to the exposing the bullet.

Well, every time I turned that thing I couldn't believe the pain. When I got down as far as I could stand it without hollerin' I could feel the bullet easy. I stuck that hook down in there and caught on the ridge that bullet and pulled but the damn thing didn't move. I tried on the other side and went down. By then it was bleeding all over pretty heavy. Then I clamped down hard on my leg and stuck that hook down in there to dig this thing out even if it killed me.

You know I got that hook under there and felt it grab and the bullet moved a little. All I wanted was to get it out of there before I passed out. I pulled the hook out and stuck it in on the other side, and it moved again. Now blood was everywhere. Then I put some of that mescal over it and that's when I figured it wasn't the infection I should be worryin' about that mescal was gonna kill me right there on the spot. Tears were rolling down the side of my face. I was desperate and running out of time so I stuck that hook back in and out getting that thing loose. I was starting to get a little bit nauseated and dizzy while I was doing this and when that bullet finally came out I was thinkin' I'd rather fight the bandidos than do that again. That was the worst pain I ever had. After I recovered a bit I dressed up the wound and put a pack on it. Don't think I slept at all that night.

Soon daylight would be coming and with the daylight they would be coming. Many things went through my mind. What was I doing up there anyway? At dawn it was the coldest and I was shivering and shaking. No way was I going to build a fire. I just laid there, feeling confused.

Every sound was deafening, even a bird. Then I heard movement below on the trail, and it wasn't a bird. Bells were ringing. I had tied those little darkened bells together about three feet apart and stretched them about six or eight inches above the ground across the trail. If anything came up the trail it would hit that line of bells and I'd hear them. Those bells told me right where they were, about thirty yards from me. Then I heard another movement, and knew it was a horse. I had to crawl underneath the brush down pretty low so I could see underneath it, but I still couldn't see them. As I tried to get in a little better position, I heard the bells go off again.

Sam had told me many times if a man was coming in on you, just wait him out. But I was getting mad. These guys were chasing me up this damn mountain, shooting at me, and I hadn't done anything to them. I was getting damn tired of this. So I tried to stand up to get my leg going, but I could hardly move I was so stiff. I hobbled across this little clearing and laid down to watch that trail. I had my Winchester with me in my left hand, and in my right hand I had the six-shooter. I thought it was too brushy in there for the Winchester, so I put it down.

Now I was down to a six-shooter. I thought I would just move in on him no matter what. I knew it was the wrong thing to do, but I was scared and tired. I knew I had to get in the first shot so I should lay and wait for him, but I was lettin' my temper get away from me. I was definitely ready to take him on. I was down on my belly moving toward the trail even though I still couldn't see anything. Then I heard movement on the trail again, closer.

I saw something move and got down as low on my face as I could. Everytime I breathed, the dust would puff out of my face where my nostrils were. My head was so low I could see the black fetlock of a horse. There was starting to be enough light so I could see pretty good and that horse was coming my way, no more than thirty feet from me. Then he stopped. I figured they were moving in a little bit at a time to find me. I thought, fine, I'll wait him out. I got ahold of myself and held my temper.

I just bit my lip and held still. He took another couple of steps. My heart was pounding so hard that I thought it was going to jump out of my shirt. I thought, why don't you come? Come on! He took another couple of steps closer. I kind of withdrew back a little to the right. I could see both front feet of the horse pretty well. He was an unshod horse, but I knew it wasn't a stray mustang. This was a saddle horse. I could hear the saddle scraping the brush as he moved through it.

I laid back, pulled the hammer back on my .45, and kept my finger off of the trigger. Then the horse took another step and was no more than fifteen feet from me, and I could see his legs clear. I wanted to jump up and start shooting at anything. I started trembling and both hands were shaking. Then he just came right by me and stopped. That horse looked right down at me and I saw his face and he saw me, eye to eye, no more than eight feet away.

He snorted a little bit and then went on. I just watched and waited. I noticed there was some blood running down the side of his leg, quite a bit of blood. Looked like a little bit dried and some fresh blood with it. As he went by me my horses nickered at him and he called back. I got up a little and saw that the saddle was empty. There was nobody in the saddle. Damn them! They sent that horse in there to draw my fire. So I figured they'd be right behind.

I pulled back and got back to where I could watch down the trail. Time went by, maybe fifteen to thirty minutes. Nothing. Nobody was coming. I scooted back, grabbed the Winchester and crawled out of the brush to where I could stand up. I looked all around and there was nothing. No sounds, no Mexicans, nothing. Nobody showed.

I thought it was a good time to get out of there. I went back to my gear and loaded up as fast as I could. The whole time I was loading up here's this black, sad-looking gelding. I didn't know where the rider was but I could guess he wasn't in great shape.

I pulled his saddle and bridle off and threw them out of the way. Out of there I rode, Winchester in my hand, breaking brush as I went through to the trail. I didn't stop for anything.

The next hour I rode steady. I'd stop a little bit, and look back. There were three of us going off that mountain. The black gelding was following us, dogging along, just like he would with the rest of them. That didn't really bother me and there was nothing I could do about it anyway. I rode for two to three hours with nothing else coming behind me.

I had to get off that mountain back to the main trail. Everytime my sorrel stepped down in the trail, the jolt shot a bad pain through my side and leg. Finally, I made it back to the bottom trail. It seemed like I'd gone a long distance the wrong way but I was headed back the right way then. Hadn't seen anybody. Didn't know what had happened after the rock slide. Didn't want to know. Just knew that I'd made it out of there.

I finally stopped, got off, and that gelding came right up to me and stood there. I got some smear out of my saddle bags and doctored up both his knees where he was hurt. I shooed him off, told him to git and ran him down the trail a little ways. Then I got back on and headed along the trail. I felt tired and weak. After a while I stopped in the middle of the trail. I was eating with one hand and holding the rifle with the other hand, watching everything.

THE MINERS

I continued on down that trail until I found a place that had some feed that looked good for the horses. It was time to check cinches and let the horses graze for a minute and see if I couldn't doctor my hip. I was sore and stiff and I used a little flask of tequila to clean out the bullet wound. I rubbed that on there and, boy oh boy, did that smart! I wanted to put my chaps back on but they rode too much on the place I skinned up.

When I figured everything was in pretty good shape, I started down the trail again, heading for Cananea. At least I thought that was where I was heading. Believe me, there were no road signs. In fact, I was pretty much lost.

What I really wanted to do was build a fire and have a good hot cup of coffee, but I didn't think it would be wise, even though I really didn't think anybody was behind me anymore. What I was really after was to make a lot of distance between me and what had happened up there. I think I was half asleep while riding that afternoon.

I heard someone laughing, loud. Then I heard horses and we were coming around a sharp bend with me coming up one direction and whoever was laughing coming up the other way. I pulled over to the side, started to get off, thought no, I didn't want to be afoot. So I swung my horse to the right, pulled the clicks back on the hammer of the Winchester and waited for them to come around the bend.

After a few minutes, three riders came around with two pack animals following them. The man in front was probably the most impressive sight I saw on the entire trip. This guy had a hat on with long flowing red hair coming out from underneath, and a long bright red beard. My eyes just riveted right on that red beard. I couldn't believe it. He was a big man and he was riding a big saddle mule. That mule was enormous – it had to be to carry that guy.

Of course, when he came around that bend he looked up, saw me, and they all stopped. The second rider was probably Chinese. The third rider was a Mexican. I also noticed they each had 30/30 carbines – saddle guns. The big red man stood there for a minute and then smiled at me.

"Laddie," he said with a heavy accent, "what be ya doin' in this part of the country?"

I was kind of glad to see this guy. He definitely wasn't a Mexican bandido.

"I'm not sure what I'm doing here," I answered.

Then he rode on up to me and stopped close by.

"You're a long way from home," he said. "Where's home?"

"North," I said.

We talked friendly for a few minutes, with him asking most of the questions. He did tell me his name, something Irish. I couldn't hardly say it the way he did and I didn't want to embarrass him by trying.

I told him I was headed for Cananea, but didn't know if I was on the right trail.

"You're on the right trail," he said and I was sure glad to hear that. "You shouldn't be out here on your own, laddie, you're taking a big chance."

He said they were heading to Hildalgo, so I told him I'd just come from there.

"You know the hills up there are bad territory," he said. "Where'd you pick up that black gelding? You been in those hills?"

"Yeah," I admitted, "didn't mean to though. I saw some bandidos up there."

"I guess they didn't see you, laddie," he laughed, "or you wouldn't be here." They all laughed.

I let it ride. I didn't want to talk about it. By then that black horse was up right in amongst us, standing around, looking dumb. I just told them he found me and started to follow on his own.

"He's not a wild horse," Red probed.

"I know that," I said.

"And he's hurt," he continued.

"I've been doctoring him," I said.

"That's why he loves you," they all laughed again. "You're his doctor."

"You don't know where he came from?" he said, not believing me at all.

"No, I don't," I insisted. I was trying to be friendly, but I didn't want to say anything more. I didn't know who these three guys were, friendly or not.

"Where'd you stay last night?" he asked.

"Up on the mountain," I answered.

"We heard a big slide," he said. "Did you?"

"Yeah, I did," I answered. "Didn't see it, though."

Then he told me how to get to Cananea and they started to ride off. Red turned back to me and said, "You haven't told me everything, have ya?" Then he asked me, "Laddie, what can I expect in the next few miles as I head for Hidalgo?"

I told him to ride with his Winchester loaded and close by 'cause there could be trouble. I didn't say anything more as I watched them ride off. I smiled and waved. Then I put my horse in a long walk and, whenever I could, I put him in a trot. I never saw anyone else along that trail and I was just as happy about that.

I was eating as I rode and finally got to a point where I could look down and see what I thought was Cananea down in a flat area with a big body of water off to the right.

Cananea

I thought I'd go down to the bottom side of town and look around a little. There were lots of little buildings and huts so I tried to avoid them. I did run into some Mexicans and talked to them. They wanted to know where I was going so I told them I was just passing through. They were very friendly and offered me something to eat, but I could see most all of them were poor around there.

I had an idea and asked them if they'd like to have a horse. I told them I had an extra one and pointed to the black gelding, although I had become accustomed to him being right with us wherever we went. The Mexican could see that he was hurt. But I said he wasn't hurt that bad. I left him with this little bottle of stuff that had a cotton dabber on it and I showed him how to doctor him with it. His wife ran and got a rope and came out to help bring him in. They were pleased and I think the black horse was, too. I could tell they had never owned a horse and I knew they could use him for transportation, plowing the garden, and probably as a good babysitter for the kids.

Then I went out of town and tied up in the brush, got my spurs off and dusted myself off a little bit. I walked maybe a mile into town. My hip and leg injuries were still very sore. I could tell the hip injury was trying to heal, but the leg wound wasn't. I felt pretty good where the horses were. I didn't think anybody'd seen me go up in there. So far I didn't feel there were any problems.

There were maybe about ten buildings in the whole town and the town was laid out kind of funny. It didn't appear to be on the north, south, east, west basis, but it didn't matter. I walked into town and quietly looked around. I moved around pretty good and then I finally got to where I could see this cantina, the one I was told about earlier.

There wasn't anything going on there that I could see, so I decided not to enter just yet. It looked like one or two people were in there. Everybody I'd seen so far was Mexican. I saw what might have been one gringo but his back was to me and he was walking away from me, going into another building.

Right across from the cantina they'd had a fire and part of the burned building had collapsed down against the brick chimney on the other side. First I went into a store, just lookin' around. The man in there looked at me a little strange and I felt uneasy. But I knew where the cantina was now, and that was important to me.

Then I went to the other end of town, went into a combination food and dry goods store and got myself something to eat. I needed it. The waitress talked to me for a few minutes and could see I didn't want to talk very much and left me alone. I didn't ask her any questions. I just ate and left.

As I went back out of town again, I looked and saw where the cantina was again. Then I started back up to the horses. I was tired and sleepy. I dug out some blankets, pulled off my pack and trappings, ground staked the horses, fed them and bedded myself down.

Next morning, I was up before dawn. I had bought some balm salve at the dry goods store and hoped it would ease the pain and dryness of my bullet wound. I applied the balm and changed the bandage on my leg. I fed the horses and made sure the ground stake was in a good place to hold them there. I didn't want them to move around too much. Then I went to the east side of town. This time I had my pistol with me stuck in my belt on the right side of my hip with my shirt pulled over to conceal it. I had stuffed my shirt pockets with jerky.

When I reached the burned out building I crawled inside by a leaning wall, pretty well hidden. First I checked for rattlesnakes or anything else I might not care to be around. I laid on a board where I could look right across the street and watch the cantina. I'd been told maybe this girl would be brought into that cantina at some point during the day. I laid there and watched and nothing went on through the morning. Two or three people came and went. A couple of gringos showed up about noon. It was pretty comfortable there and even though some people walked by pretty close they didn't see me. I even fell asleep for a while.

Then all of a sudden I heard this animal sound and I was even afraid to open my eyes 'cause I could feel whatever it was no more than four or five inches from my face. I could smell the breath and it was bad. It was hot and it was growling. When I finally opened my eyes and looked, I looked into the eyes of one of the town dogs. He'd set down with both front feet out and was growling in my face. I couldn't get to my knife stuck in my boot and I couldn't get to my six-shooter without disturbing him. So I was just laid there thinking about what to do. He laid there looking and growling at me. Then I got an idea. I remembered the jerky, so I reached in my shirt pocket and took a piece of jerky and flung it at him. He picked it up, chewed on it for a minute and I thought it was going to work. I went back for another piece and lifted it toward him. He was a scroungy looking mutt, half starved, with scars on his face and legs from doing battle with other dogs. He picked that one up in his mouth and got up and left, just like that.

It wasn't but a few minutes after that dog left that a big convertible touring car with wooden spoke wheels and two headlights the size of medium washtubs pulled up carrying several Federales with hats, belts, pistols, and khaki brown uniforms. The driver jumped out and went around and opened the other door. He had a little broom-type thing to brush the officer off. This Mexican had braided insignias on his collar and had to be someone important. Maybe he was El Presidente for all I knew.

He was wearing what looked like old flyer's goggles. He pulled those off, straightened his uniform up and then went in the cantina. Now I was really interested in what was going on in there because these were the first Federale troops I'd seen. He stayed in there about an hour while the other soldier sat on the boarded sidewalk in front of the cantina swapping stories and guarding the touring car. At least one or more times they glanced across the street directly my way but showed no indication they saw me. I laid very low, very quiet, hoping the town mongrel didn't come back for more jerky. Soon the General appeared and the soldier sprang to attention, opening the car door, and then they drove out of town.

I started thinking that maybe the Randall girl would be brought to a back entrance. So I crawled out of my hiding place and went around to the back of the cantina to watch for a while. There were outhouses back there where I could partially hide but I would sooner or later be spotted and I would be in trouble.

I stayed there for a little while, watching the back of the cantina and then decided to take a look around at the other buildings so I could still see the back door of the cantina and watch anyone coming on the side road. I found one and peered inside. It looked abandoned so I went inside and saw cracks in the walls. There was a big knot hole in one wall and I pushed on it 'til it fell right out.

While I was doing this I heard somebody coming before I saw them. I looked out back and saw two Mexicans coming with a young girl between them. One of them had ahold of her hand and she was a sandy-haired white girl if I'd ever seen one. She had on a red and white dress, pretty low cut in the front with fringes on the side, around the waist and some on the bottom. She was walking like she was hurt. I watched from my hiding place as they went up these stairs into one of the buildings.

My heart was pounding hard and I was thinking fast about what I needed to do. I was trying to get this girl out of there without a shootout. By this time I was pretty sure she was the girl I was after.

Well, I stayed there for a while and it was getting dark. I decided I'd have to come back the next day after I had a plan. Then just as I was getting ready to leave, they came back out again dragging her between them. The looks on their faces told me that they were mad at her and might be taking her back to where they were keeping her. So I followed them.

They went down another road and then up a little trail between some large trees. I got in behind them, keeping back a ways so they couldn't see me. They finally went into a frame house, not an adobe house. It was built up to get out of the water, I guess. They went up the stairs and onto a porch where there was an old swing, and then they disappeared into the house.

RESCUE

I knew this was where they were keeping her so I decided I'd come back next morning with a plan. I slept near the house that night. Early in the morning I went and packed up my horses and got them situated hidden away from that house. The house itself was facing east and west and had two windows on one side, and the gable of the house went up in the center allowing an attic window to overlook my position. There were no fences around it. The back porch was squared off with a lot of screens. It was a pretty old weather-beaten place. There was a wood pile next to the path about twenty yards from the house with an outhouse over to the right of the wood pile. The trail behind the house was well worn, leading up to a well, maybe seventy-five yards from the house.

The well was a typical, hand-dug circular hole about five feet across and probably twenty feet deep. An adobe block retaining wall about three feet high surrounded the well to keep out the children and varmints. Two large, forked, cedar posts had been buried in the ground just outside the retaining wall and a round timber with a crank had been placed in the crotches of both cedar posts. A rope was attached to the pole and when turned, a wooden bucket could be lowered into the well to retrieve water.

I'd decided if this was the right girl, and I was pretty sure it was, everything was going to happen right here and it wouldn't take much time when things got started. The horses were tied where I could see them from near the well. The brush was heavy down there so I thought no one would be wandering around them. I took the pack and pack bags off of my pack saddle and off of my saddle. I fixed up the relay saddle, put the reins looped long enough to be over the saddle horn and left her there ready to ride. My horse was already saddled up and ready for me.

I pulled out my Winchester from my saddle scabbard and tried to figure out how I could slip up to the well. There wasn't much cover for me, but I figured I could get in there if I moved fast. I crawled for quite a ways until I got almost all the way up to the well and heard some noise back to the side of me. There were some horses down in a pen raising a lot of commotion for a few moments. So I backed out and went back down in the canyon where I had both horses tied up.

If I was lucky enough to get her away from the house and mounted on the bay mare, we would make a run for it and I figured they would surely try to follow us. On foot they would never catch us, but on horseback they might get within rifle range. So I slipped down into the arroyo and crawled up to the pen where the horses were acting up because of my presence. While lying on my side, I took my rifle barrel and with the tip of it I slipped the wire ring from the top of the gate. I eased open the gate and moved over to the side of the corral while still laying down. Then I started pitching small pebbles against the legs of the horses. They became irritated and were trying to get away from the rocks. When they spotted the open gate, they disappeared down the canyon away from me.

I felt this gave us an advantage. By the time they rounded up their stock, we would be miles away.

After things seemed to settle down some, I went back up near the well, worked myself up next to it, got under it a little and laid there, waiting. A cedar windless post about eight inches in diameter was across the top so I could raise my head up behind it and look off toward the house. Some noise was coming from the house but I couldn't think of anything else to do but wait there where I was. I knew somebody would have to come and get some water sooner or later. My problem was that I had no idea who would be comin'. If I laid up close to the adobe retaining wall opposite the house, I thought I might not be seen. The pain in my hip was keeping me alert, but I wasn't feeling too great about my plan just then. I couldn't get any closer to the house without being out in the open so I stayed put.

Tom Fisk in 1947 in Palominos, Mexico on his rescue journey.
This photograph was taken by Henry Palmer, Louise's uncle.

I had decided against trying to get her while they were taking her down to the middle of town. I'd been there about half an hour trying to figure out what I could do, when I heard the screen door open and close. Somebody was coming down the stairs and I thought I'd better have a look to see who it was. I slowly eased my head up and what I saw was really pleasing. It was that young girl. She was coming out carrying this big bucket and I could see that she was barefooted. I figured they made her leave her shoes behind so she couldn't run off because of the rocky ground.

She worked her way up to the well and put the bucket on the side while she reached over to attach the rope. I raised up my head and put my finger on my lips to tell her to keep quiet and she went, "Ah!"

"Just look down in the well," I said.

She looked in the well and then she looked right back at me.

"Please, don't look at me. Keep lookin' in the well," I pleaded. "Hook the bucket on the rope."

She did what I said, but she was looking worried about the whole idea.

"Who are you?" I asked her. I could see her lip was cut badly and had swelled up some.

"My name's Louise," she said.

"Damn!" I thought, "I found her!" I traveled all that way and had gone through so much hell and now I'd really found her. "Hot diggidy damn!" I thought.

"Are you Louise Randall?" I asked just to make sure. I was still in shock.

"Yes," she answered, "and who are you?"

"That's not important," I told her, "please keep looking in the well. I'm here to take you home. Your mother and father sent me."

She moved around to where she could get to the crank to bring up the water. She told me there were two men in the house and one had been drinking heavy. Apparently she was getting water to fill the bath, and they were heating the water on the stove. She said it would take about four trips to get enough water.

"They'll kill us if they catch us," she said in a worried voice.

"No one is going to kill us," I assured her. "I'm going to take you home. Just do what I tell you."

"Okay," she agreed.

"Now, don't change anything you're doing, don't smile, don't look happy and don't cry. Do you understand me?"

"Yes."

"Can you ride a horse?" I asked, and she said she could.

So she left carrying the full bucket, changing it from hand to hand, then with both hands in front as she went up the stairs.

The second time she came back out I heard the door slam. At least I hoped it was her. So I peeked around and it was. This time I asked if they had guns in there. She said there was one rifle near the stove and another one with two barrels somewhere in the room.

She let the bucket down into the well and asked if anyone else was there to help. I told her, no. When she filled the bucket she struggled back up to the house with it. It was no time at all that she was back out for the third one and she said there would be one more trip.

"When you come out for the next one, put your shoes in the bucket and make sure they don't see you. When you get out here, slip your shoes on and don't look back at the house. I'll be watching it."

I explained where the horses were tied up and how she was to run to the horses, counting to fifty real slow. I had her take a couple of minutes and practice counting real slow. She was to untie the sorrel and get on the bay, still counting.

"If the stirrups are too long, stick your toes in between the leather straps above the stirrups and be ready to ride. When you get to fifty, if I'm not there, ride up the canyon straight north."

"What about you?" she asked.

"You just go for a couple of hours and then stop and wait one hour for me. If I can get there, I will come. If I don't, then ride another hour, stop and wait again."

She said she was really scared and started to cry.

"Don't do that," I begged her.

I could see she was badly beat up and I was worried if she could pull this off. I could see blood through her dress and she told me there had been a fight between two miners and one of them had bit her lip. Her side had been cut by one of them swinging a broken beer bottle. I told her we'd doctor her up once we got out of there.

When she came out that last time she quickly put her shoes on, and boy did that gal take off toward those horses. Her hands were flying. I watched the house and nothing happened. I knew that Louise was counting and time was running out. But I decided to watch a few seconds longer, just to make sure no one came out. I wasn't going to crawl out of there and I didn't want to be shot in the back. I was counting the same as she was counting, slowly, so I felt I had a little time left.

At about the count of twenty-five the door opened and out came this Mexican. He stood there for a minute on the porch looking around. Then he went back in the house. I could see him, but he couldn't see me. I saw him come back out with a big leather shaving strap, like what they used to hone a single blade shaver. He started yelling, "gringo bitch," and trotted down the steps. He slapped that strap on his legs a couple of times as he was moving towards the well and me. He was looking around. If he kept going he would be able to see the horses – and me.

When he was about halfway there, I stood up with my Winchester down low in my left hand. I heard him curse really bad as he walked over to the wood pile and picked up a machete. He started at a slow walk, then he went to a trot, coming straight at me.

There was nothing I could do, so I raised up the Winchester and shot from the hip. When that rifle went off, the recoil about busted my hand. I remember hitting that Mexican dead center. The machete went right up in the air, and he went right down and over backwards. He raised up, turned over, raised up again and then collapsed for good, down face first. I looked at the window of the house, saw nothing and started backing out.

Then I saw the other Mexican look out through the window. I raised up the Winchester and tried to get a shot through the window, but he'd moved out of the way. But he didn't come out the back door. I waited a little, but I knew I had to go – so I ran. When I got to where she could see me, I'd quit counting. Louise was already starting to leave.

On the Run

When I reached my horse, I slammed that rifle down in my saddle boot and we both took off. We hit a high lope and then I let the sorrel out. He laid his ears back. He and the bay mare were going home. I looked over my shoulder to see if Louise was okay. I could see that she had a death grip on the saddle horn and was gritting her teeth. Any minute I was expecting a rifle shot, but I never heard one. We must have run for an hour and the horses were labored and tired and breathing out.

I finally pulled up to rest, and Louise was crying and trembling bad. I got her off and held her for a few minutes. Then I told her she had to quit it 'cause we had a ways to go to get home and no time to spare. She asked about what happened back at the house, and I just told her there was one Mexican that would never bother her again. After we rested a little bit I knew we had to ride with the wind and cover as much distance as we could. All I knew was that we had to travel east by northeast. We were not going back the way I'd come, and country on the left side of me was really rough. There were big, tall mountains with lots of rugged bluffs running down into the flats. I knew there was a railroad on the right side somewhere.

As we mounted, I put her back in the saddle and asked her if she was all right. I could tell she was hurting and scared, but she was willing to go on. I told her to grab the saddle horn and hang on. I knew about horses and knew how to use them as much as I could, for as long as I could, and not kill them off.

I told Louise when she'd taken all she could to let me know. For a while she seemed to ride pretty good. I could tell she hadn't done a lot of riding, but she was hanging on, doing the best she could. The trail looked good. It had been traveled. The time was somewhere around noon. I figured we had thirty or forty miles to go to the border. I thought I might be able to wire the Randalls if we got near a small town. We had planned a little coded message to let them know I had her.

We dropped into a trot, then a long walk. The horses were holding up good, but I could tell they were ready to go home. I was hoping my horse knew where he was going 'cause I wasn't sure. I kept us away from the rough country and kept looking back over my shoulder to see if Lou was all right, and she would kind of nod her head to keep going. I noticed she had a little trickle of blood starting to come off the side of her mouth.

It was comin' down to be a race against three things: I didn't know if they were comin' after us, or how long Lou could keep riding, or exactly where we were goin'. After a while I turned and went up through a pretty rugged canyon and started to climb. We'd gone maybe three or four miles in this rough country when we crested out a little bit. I kept looking back and I noticed that Lou was looking back, too. I finally pulled up and had her come up beside me. I reached over and grabbed her reins. I could see she was getting scared. She was picking up signals from me so I stopped lookin' back.

As we went over the top of this little pass, I got a pretty good look at the country and what I saw looked good, not as rough as I expected it to be. I could see the trail below for quite a ways. I decided we needed to keep traveling and we did cover some ground. The horses seemed to be doing good. I listened to the breathing of the sorrel.

I wanted to put at least ten to fifteen miles between us and Cananea. But as I thought about it, it didn't make a whole lot of sense. Those Mexicans would not be able to find a lot of people to help them go after a girl they had kidnapped in the first place. I was starting to figure we were going to be okay.

After a while, when I looked back at Lou I could see she was starting to tire. She couldn't take the pace much longer. She was riding her horse off balance and that can really tire a horse. We covered another mile or two and I heard her gasp a couple of times, so I pulled up and stopped.

I got her something to drink and asked her if she wanted to get off and walk just a little bit. She looked at me as if she was holding me back, like she wasn't good enough. I just told her to let me worry about everything. I helped her off and she walked around a little.

I checked the cinch on her horse and I noticed some blood on the seat of the saddle.

I had no idea what to do, and I kept trying to think this could be that time of the month or she could have been hurt by some of the activities back there. When she came back over near me I told her I had a package that her mother had prepared for her, all wrapped up, tied with string. But she didn't want to stop. Then I offered her some mescal but she said she didn't drink that kind of stuff. I told her I didn't drink it either, but that I brought it to clean the wounds. She said her mouth was really dry so I reached down and picked up a pebble about the size of a pea and told her to put it in her mouth. I knew it would bring saliva to her mouth and would help. I'd done it many times.

Then we mounted up and headed out again. It wasn't too long before I could see it was really starting to get hard on her and we were starting to run out of daylight. So after about four more miles it was time to find a spot for the night. I stopped and told her to wait for me while I rode along a ridge looking for a good place to hold up. Lou looked worried about me riding off, so I told her I'd stay where she could see me. I pulled up on that ridge and looked back down the trail we'd come up. I could see two or three miles back, no dust, no motion, nothing.

Just to be safe, I figured we'd find a little canyon away from the trail, with some water in it. We found a good one and moved in there to check for water. Sure enough, there was enough water in there to suit us. I let the horses breathe a little bit and drink a little bit, but not too much.

Lou was helping with the horses, but she was getting too tired. Her hands were starting to shake. I had to find a good spot pretty quick. We ended up riding a mile or two up the canyon. There was water in that area and I knew it would be near impossible for anyone to follow us back there. But it was rough, so I got off and told Lou I needed to tie her into the saddle. I assured her we would go real slow up through the rocks.

We started up going really slow and I didn't want to leave any tracks scarring the rocks. We just took a few steps at a time. Well, we topped out and rimmed around and it wasn't too bad going. Then I picked up an old sheep or deer trail and moved around the side of the mountain. I dropped off into a little box canyon. There was a little meadow there with quite a bit of brush. I got off really quick and checked the air currents by letting a handful of dirt filter through my hand. Couldn't be any better. This was the place, so I got her off and let her go over to sit down. I pulled out two blankets and wrapped one around the top of her and one around her legs. As we settled down, I pulled all the trappings off the horses and set out to build a fire.

Our location inside that box canyon made it so I didn't have to worry about anyone seein' the smoke from the fire. I was talking about things to more or less tell myself and her that we were gonna be all right. She just nodded with her head kind of dropped down and her knees pulled up underneath her. I thought back to what happened at the well while I was gatherin' wood to build a fire. I was thinkin' I'd shoot him again if I had it to do over. I wouldn't hesitate to put another round in him.

Finally, I got a little fire going. Then I got my pocket knife out, opened up some canned chicken soup, and heated it up. I thought it was important to get something warm in her. I only had one cup so it was going to have to be a shared thing but that was okay.

While I was heating up the soup, I kept looking at Lou and talking to her. Then she started shaking, trembling all over. I wrapped her up again as good as I could. I didn't know anything about shock, but it just seemed right to try to get her warm. I tried holding her a couple of times, but she would get to trembling again after a while so I knew that wasn't going to work.

When the soup was warm I took it to her and held it up to her, but when she raised her head up I could see her eyes were blurred, out of focus. She blinked some and acted like she was wonderin' who I was. I told her it was me and put her hands around the cup. She nodded and gave me a half a smile, but she was shaking pretty hard still.

She couldn't get the soup down. So I went to look back down the trail and told her no Mexicans were coming after us. I didn't know that to be the truth for sure, but it sounded good to her. Then I found two big granite rocks with a little sandy spot in between them. I got as much wood as I could find and started a fire in the middle of those two rocks. I just started building it and building it and building it. I had it going pretty good and kept feeding it. It was starting to get a little dark and the moon was coming up full.

I went and got Lou over by the big fire and put her as close as possible to it. I could see that one side of her was warm and the other side was cold. The blankets didn't seem to be doing that much good. I didn't know what else to do and she was still shaking. She looked like she was ready to lay down, so I wrapped her up good and laid the other blanket over her and then grabbed my slicker off the saddle, rolled it up and put it under her head.

I ate a little bit of canned meat and it tasted good, but anything would have tasted good at that point. Lou had some meat too, and we ate together for a while. Pretty soon the fire had created a pretty good bed of coals between those big rocks. I had an idea.

I went in there and grabbed a big old, dead mesquite limb and scraped all the coals out of there and raked it out with my boot. Then I broke off a branch, folded it over on itself, and used it as a broom to brush everything out of there. Then I took the one blanket that I'd laid over the top of her and laid it down where the coals had been. I wrapped Lou really good in the other blanket and helped her lay down between the rocks on the other blanket.

She said it felt really warm, so that's where she stayed for the night. I fixed up my slicker underneath her head for a pillow and took the other blanket and wrapped it around me. I went down by where the other fire had been. I took the Winchester out, sat it right next to me, and just sat there watching her sleep.

The horses moved around a bit while they were grazing. I knew I needed sleep bad but it didn't come easy. I leaned up against the pack bag and the saddle with the Winchester cradled in between my arms, and laid my head down against the saddle bag.

I guess I must have slept two or three hours before I woke up suddenly with my heart beating really fast. I didn't know what had happened, but nothing was wrong. She'd turned over a little bit. Through the night I kept the fire up so come morning, when Lou woke up, I had some more food cooked up warm for her.

In the morning her lip had gone down a little bit and looked better. But she looked really bad with her hair matted and that dress was a mess. But it was cold and she was stiff, so she didn't want to change her clothes just yet. When she finally got up, I told her I wanted to take a look at her side where she was cut. Luckily it wasn't that bad; nothing had gone too deep. I could tell there was no infection setting in. Somebody had cleaned it up before. I opened up my bag and put a clean bandage on it.

Then I told her we had to get moving. It was still cold, so I took the big blanket and cut a slit down the center and dropped it over the top of her head. Then I cut two holes for her arms. It was kind of a poncho by the time I got done with it. I told her by sundown we'd be pretty close to the border. That sounded pretty good to her. She was aching all over and said so.

We started out with everything in place. We moved down into the flats and the trail was good. I knew if we stayed between the two mountain ranges, that the railroad had to show up somewhere down the line, so we just kept moving on north at a pretty good pace. Every once in a while I'd look back and see Lou gritting her teeth, so I knew she was hurting, and I'd back off the pace.

We finally dropped down into what turned out to be the San Pedro River. The riverbanks were high, but we could follow this lower trail pretty good. When we came to a natural dam I got off and checked the water and it was warm. I decided we'd tie up there and clean up. I noticed there wasn't any fresh blood on the saddle. I told her I had that package her mother gave to me for her. I told her I was going to go back up on the ridge where she could still see me, and for her to clean up and change, and for her to holler at me when she was done. I knew there were clean clothes, soap and a towel in there for her. I also told her to throw the other clothes away and that I wouldn't look at her. So I went up and sat down on that ridge with my new rifle, the one with the scope.

The sun was up and it was getting warm. It was a good day. I knew we were headed in the right direction. I think I dozed off once or twice. I could see back down the trail a mile or two and I saw nothing coming. Pretty soon I heard Lou call out to me and I went back down.

My goodness, Lou really looked good. She had changed, and had on jeans and a blouse. Her hair was washed and still wet. She said she felt much better. I was feeling like I looked pretty scroungy and felt dirty, but I didn't want to take the time to clean up just then. I wanted to get going.

From there on out we started riding hard. I could see a ways ahead of me what I thought looked like the railroad. When we crossed the railroad I knew we'd be no more than five to seven miles from Palominas. We were going to get there about sundown or before.

Sure enough, we came near a town at the crossing, so I left Lou hidden outside of town and I went on in to see if they had a wire service there. I figured they did because of the railroad being so close.

I was surprised to see three or four little buildings and an old station. When I asked about the wire service, a Mexican told me there was a telegrapho. I noticed the poles going through town. I dug the address out of my jeans and wired the message, "Mrs. Randall, the cargo shipment has been found. I'll deliver it..." I asked the Mexican what day it was but he didn't know either. So I put "tomorrow." That's all I could do. Then I told him I would check for a return message later.

I went back to Lou and told her the wire was sent and that we were going to camp there that night. She was starting to hold her own. We talked a while and I told her about bounty hunting for the Germans.

Lou asked me if her mom and dad had paid me to come down there. I told her they'd offered it to me, but I didn't take it. She said I'd earned it, every penny, and she never asked how much. We talked about a lot of things that afternoon.

Later I went back into town to check on any return message. The Mexican there said there was one and it read, "Want to verify cargo shipment. Coming now. Henry Palmer." I wondered who in hell was Henry Palmer! So I took the message and headed back to Lou.

"Who in the hell is Henry Palmer?" I asked her.

"Henry Palmer is my uncle," she answered. "He's a businessman over in Bisbee."

"He's coming down here," I said, a little perturbed. "He's only got maybe ten miles to get here." I told her she'd better stay put and I'd go wait for him to come into town. The road he was coming down from the border was good for nothing more than two cows walking side by side to water. I doubted any pickup could make it.

So I went into town again and waited. It was getting on evening when an old pickup with two guys showed up. I went up to them and told them who I was and asked why they'd come down there.

Lou's uncle said they were afraid I might not have the right girl and they didn't want to take a chance it was a mistake. They had an old box camera with them and he wanted to take her picture. I didn't like that idea and I wasn't pleased they were there at all. He said he'd come a long ways and he wanted to take her back with him.

"Like hell you will," I said. "I don't know who you are. You may be her uncle, but I'm taking her home like I said I would." I'd been through a lot of hell he'd never know about and I was getting in this guy's face.

"Well, let me go see her," he demanded. "Or bring her here."

"Don't tell me what to do," I said angrily. "Where the hell were you four days ago?" I yelled at him.

But I took them out to see Lou and she ran up to him, calling him Uncle Henry.

"Are you satisfied?" I asked.

"Yeah," he said, "and you're not going to let me take her with me, are you?"

"I'm the one that's taking her straight to Mrs. Randall and put her in her arms."

Before they left they took my picture with that old camera, me holding my gun and everything. Lou's uncle wanted us to ride along with them on the road, but that wasn't my plan.

I was only about eight to ten miles from finishing this journey. So Lou and I loaded up and got ready to head up to the ridge.

"Do you feel bad about not driving in with your uncle?" I asked Lou.

"I feel good about being with you," she said.

"Feeling better, aren't you?"

"You've been good to me and been looking after me," she said. "Can I give you something?"

"Like what?" I asked.

Then she gave me a big old kiss. I remember that, I do.

Homecoming

We picked up the trail and I could tell the horses were definitely going home. When we finally pulled into where we could see the old ranch corrals, there were a bunch of people looking like they were having a picnic down there. There were a lot of them. Lou was crying, with tears rolling down her

face. I could tell when they spotted us coming across there, and it was exciting. We just piled off that ridge right down in there among the people. I slid
off my saddle and helped Lou out of her saddle. Then everyone started hugging her and me and everyone, saying "bless you, bless you." Then her father
came up and grabbed ahold of me and hugged me. I thought he was going to
crush me.

"I knew you'd do it," he said. It was the first time I heard that from
him.

Mrs. Randall came up to me and asked me if I was hurt. I was walking
with a little bit of a limp, but I told her I was all right.

After a while I knew it was time for me to go, so I told Lou I'd come
down to see her after she'd seen a doctor and things got all straightened out.
She started to hug and kiss me and I got embarrassed, but she said she didn't
care. I held her for a while and she took my hat off and ran her hands through
my hair.

"You're what I prayed for and you came," she told me.

"I'm just glad you're home where you belong," I said. "But now I got to
get out of here." I still had to ride to the Slaughters and return the horses.

When I pulled in there I told them what had happened. John was really
surprised I ever made it back – and with the girl too!

"I rode a long way, John," I told him wearily.

He noticed I was favoring one leg and told me to go in and have his
wife doctor me up.

"It ain't that bad," I insisted. I was a little worried I'd run into Kate and
I didn't feel up to that right then.

I loaded my gear in the car and thanked John again, tried to pay him
but he wouldn't take it.

"You've earned your money," he said to me.

"I may not take that money," I said. "I might take enough to cover the
gear that I left down there – the saddlebags and a pack saddle. It don't seem
right to take the money after what that girl went through."

I saw Lou again a couple of weeks later. She ran up to me and jumped
in my arms. We were talking, hugging and kissing. Then she introduced me
to her friends while she held my hand. We went to a little restaurant in town
and the whole time she never let go of my hand. She was telling the story of
what happened.

The thought occurred to me that maybe Lou and I might go on to
something else from there, but I wasn't one to stay in one place too long and
I didn't really belong around there.

So I moved on . . . again.

Afterword

So what is the Tom Fisk of the 1990's like? Who did the "Gringo Kid" grow up to become?

Today Tom is a man who still works twelve-hour days on several business and family projects at once. He owns and manages a high-pressure medical equipment maintenance and design company. Keeping in touch with his past, he deals in western collectibles and still searches for gold and treasure whenever the call of the wild is too strong to resist. Perched on a mountain in Rescue, California, his ranch-style residence is called home by his gracious wife and frequent visitors, including their four children and a multitude of grandchildren. A respected man within his community, Tom draws upon his early survival experiences as he assists in planning emergency preparedness and services for the county. He's a religious man in his own way, with firm values about honesty, responsibility, marriage and family. A man who is grateful for his country and his God. A man who knows who he is.

The process of creating this book has enlightened Tom about why he is who he is. Recounting the experiences of his youth has helped to explain why he still demands to sit with his back to the wall facing the entrance of a restaurant; why he tells people up-front that he is not a person to be messed with; and, why he prefers dealing with a handshake rather than legal documents. It is evident that some of the more traumatic trials of his early years have left scars, physical and emotional. Getting these stories down in print has eased some of the pain that he has kept buried throughout all these years. Some healing and reconciliation has taken place.

With more adventures down the road, Tom continues to be the dynamic, and at times aggressive, personality revealed in his stories. The privilege of looking into his soul has been mine and the readers of this book.

Gunfighter's
Last Request

*(As told to Tom in the fall of '39
by one of the very best)*

"When I die I want to be skinned and

have my hide tanned and

used to cover an English saddle.

Then I want it placed

on top of a big shiny black horse.

Then put a beautiful woman aboard

and let her ride off into the sunset.

I'll be happy then,

sitting right between

the two things I love the most."

Glossary:
Tom's Cowboy Definitions

Adobe | Mexican style building bricks made of clay and straw.

Afoot | Referring to a cowboy in cattle country without his horse. A man afoot in cattle country was always eyed with suspicion. Also being afoot limited your working performance and quite often subjected the man to danger from cattle, natural elements, etc.

Angoras | Cowboy chaps made of a goat hide with the hair left on. Also known as "wooleys."

Arbuckle | A name given a green hand or rookie.

Arroyo | A small shallow depression in the desert floor.

Association | The Rodeo Association designed a bronc saddle that gave little saddle security to the rider and gave the bronc an advantage to unseat the rider.

Bandidos | Mexican bandits – big, ugly, mean and good at stealing.

Bandolier | One or two cartridge belts holding rifle or pistol bullets worn across the chest and over each shoulder.

Bat Wings | Bell bottom looking heavy leather chaps that were protection against brush, cactus and cold weather. Easy to get into and out of without removing your spurs.

Bear Trap | A term given a certain style of saddle that afforded the rider extra security while the horse bucked. Considered very dangerous for rider should the horse fall or roll over.

Bed Ground | An open space where the day cowboys bunched the cattle for the night. Usually away from draws or heavy brush to avoid strays from getting away or the herd being frightened by predators.

Bed Roll | A cowboy's bed, along with some personal items, usually 6'x18' made of heavy duck tarpaulin and waterproof.

Bell Mare	Gentle mare with a bell secured around her neck, making it easier to gather horses or alert wranglers to danger or problems.
Belly Gun	A small caliber weapon carried in the waistband, very popular with gamblers.
Big House	Often referred to as headquarters or the big alligator's homestead and was the home of the ranch owner.
Bit	A part of a bridle, a straight or curved metal bar that rests in the horse's mouth and used as a stopping device. There are many types of bits: single port, spade, snaffle, ring and roller, some of which when used wrongly were very severe on the horse. Many cowboys chose to use a bosal around the bridge of the nose or a hackamore located on each side of the horse's muzzle.
Boot	The centerpiece of a cowboy's wearing apparel. Usually a sloped high-heel. But some bull doggers like a straight doggin' heel to prevent a torn ankle. Either heel is designed to prevent the foot from slipping through the stirrup. The sole is top grain leather. The felt and tops are made of lightweight top value leather. A good quality boot is often recognized by its stitching — four to six rows of stitching help to prevent the top from collapsing on the bottom of the boot. Three designs of tops are popular – a "V" shape slit in front and aft; a full top called a stove pipe; and large leather side straps to pull on the boot that are showy and are called "Mule Ears." If a cowboy can afford it he will always choose tailor made boots (handmade) and will quickly avoid the cheap products. The toe of the boot is pointed to facilitate easy entry to the stirrup, especially on a rowdy horse. If you want to know whether a man is a cowboy, drugstore cowboy or a dude, look at the care and style of his boots and his hat. They will tell you who he is, what he's made of, and probably where he came from.
Bosal	Braided rawhide halter or leather band used on a green horse while training, looped around the bridge of the muzzle of the horse (no bit). Sometimes made of hemp or horse hair rope.
Bougered	A cowboy or horse that has been scared.
Brand	A mark of ownership placed on livestock using a hot iron, searing through the hair, leaving a permanent design in the

hide. Can be placed on either hip or shoulder. One cattle company places its "RO" brand on the left cheek of all its horses. Good brands are designed to minimize the crossing of vertical lines with horizontal lines. These junctures usually cause deep burns and sores. Blow flies lay their eggs in such places.

Brand Artist A "wide looper" or rustler who uses a "running iron" to alter or change an existing brand.

Brand Book A record of brands carried by a brand inspector and recorded in the cattle association records.

Bridle The leather or rawhide headgear of a horse consisting of a browband or far slot, curb chain, fiadore around the throat, and solid cheek pieces, through which the cowboy can run his rope while roping calves. This keeps the horse's head at attention while facing the calf.

Bronco A wild horse or "broomtail" that needs riding and gentling before putting him in the riding remuda.

Buckaroo A cowboy name commonly used in the West and used extensively to this day in Nevada.

Buckin' Rolls A rolled up slicker, a blanket rolled up, or a custom set of leather holders attached to the pommel of the saddle which helps position the cowboy on a rank horse.

Bull Dogger A cowboy that approaches a steer running wide open and departs his horse at the same time to catch the steer's head and twist the steer to the ground.

Cantle The rear raised portion of a saddle that holds the buttocks of the cowboy.

Canyon Portion of the ground between two ridges. Can also be called a valley.

Cantina Mexican dance hall.

Cartridge Rifle or pistol shell, with powder, bullet and primer.

Castilian Spaniards from Spain. These Spanish women have their features immortalized by Michelangelo.

Cat Wagon A name given to a wagon carrying "tainted doves" to the men on a cattle drive.

Catch Pen Place to hold livestock.

Cedar Break Change in the height of the cedars in the forest.

Cerveza	Mexican beer. Usually tastes like stud horse urine with the foam blown off.
Chaps	Leather leg covers, either "batwing" or "shotgun." Used over regular britches to prevent the cowboy from abrasions from gates, fences, brush, horse bites, cold and rain. When a cowboy is afoot, working batwings are cumbersome and shotguns are easier. When trail driving cattle, a quirt or rope makes a good herd-gathering noise when snapped against batwings.
Chapparal	A type of sagebrush.
Cheyenne Roll	A saddle candle (rear butt piece) radically designed; changed changed from high cantle to a low rolling flange extending back of the cantle. Affords easier mounting and dismounting.
Cienagas	A flat open meadow surrounded by timber brush or mountains.
Cinch Is Getting Frayed	You've worn out your welcome. It happened to me several times when I was young.
Cloud Watcher	Describes a horse that travels with his head too high and doesn't pay attention to what he's doing. Also called "stargazer."
Colici	Clay that has been hardened under heat and pressure.
Colt	The young of the mares.
Conchos	A flat metal disk usually made of Mexican coins or silver pieces used on belts or spurs by vaqueros and cowboys for ornamentation.
Cook House	The kitchen in the main ranch house.
Corral	A circular catch pen made of logs, posts, or ocotillo branches. Built in a circle so livestock cannot hide in a corner and kick your teeth out with the other end.
Cow	Four legs, a body, horns, and not an oversupply of smarts.
Cow Sense	Common sense. This nation was built with it but now seems to have misplaced it.
Coyotes	Looks like a cross between a dog and a wolf. Loves to eat sheep. Forty million coyotes cannot be wrong.
Cutting Horse	A horse trained to cut or remove cows from a herd. Probably the most prestigious horses in the cowboy horse industry.

Dally	When a rider catches a horse or steer by a rope he wraps the opposite end of the rope around the saddle horn with a half hitch. It can be dangerous and that's why so many cowboys are called "stubby."
Dead Man's Hand	A card player holding aces and eights is considered bad luck. Folklore says Wild Bill Hickok was killed with such a hand.
Derringer	A small "hide-away" gun of large caliber used to fire close distances with maximum punch.
Drive	To move a herd of cattle or horses from one place to another.
Dry Gulch	Ambush to kill.
Dude	A person other than a cowboy. Usually what cowboys call Easterners who come to the West for a cowboy life vacation.
Dun	A tan colored horse with or without a line down the back.
Ear Down	This is when you grab and twist a horse's ear until his mean attitude is distracted. Often cowboys bite the ear with their teeth. I remember seeing a wild horse running around with a set of false teeth attached to his ear.
Empty Saddle	A sure danger signal when spotted on the ranch. Best to backtrack to find the wreck.
Easy on the Eyes	A beautiful woman.
Fast water	Water that has been polluted by livestock. Blow hard and drink fast.
Federales	Mexican government troopers.
Fence Crawler	Livestock that will not stay inside a fence. Can be cured by a well placed shot.
Figure Eight	Vaqueros started this by throwing a loop that resembles a figure eight. The bottom half catches the front legs while the top half catches the neck.
Flats	That portion of the desert away from the valleys, ridges and mountains.
Forked Horn	A young male deer with fork of each antler three inches down from the top.
Fresno	A shovel-like scoop used to move dirt and pulled by a team of horses.
Gadsden	Was the most elegant hotel in all the southwest; located

in Douglas, Arizona.

Gelding	A castrated horse. Works good on rapists and child molest ers, too.
Gin Pole	A devise for lifting buckets of dirt from the bottom of a hole while digging.
Grass Rope	A cowboy's rope made of manilla or bear grass.
Greener	Rideable but had to be watched.
Greenhorn	A cowboy's name for a dude or a tenderfoot.
Greenier	A special make of a double barreled shot gun.
Gringo	Mexican description of a white man.
Grizzlies	A pair of chaps tanned from a grizzly hide with the hair left on.
Grulla	A horse that is colored a mixture of grey, yellow, orange and black.
Heeling	Roping the hind legs of livestock.
Henny	A cross between a stallion and a jenny burro.
Herd Broke	When cattle get used to traveling in a bunch and do what they're told to do. Forty years of marriage gets some of the same results too.
Hobbles	Leather straps with buckles, each fastened around both front feet to prevent a horse from running off.
Hogback	A small hill resembling the back of a hunched hog's back.
Honda	An eyelet formed of rawhide or metal on the loop end of the rope that allows the rope to slide through when thrown.
Indian Side of a Horse	White eyes mounts his horse from the left, Indian mounts from the right.
Iver Johnson	Manufacturer name of rifle.
Jenny Burro	Commonly known as an ass. Usual height 10 to 12 hands, weight approximately 400-700 pounds.
John B.	Referring to a cowboy's hat. Named after the famous hat maker, John B. Stetson. If you favor your life, don't mess with a cowboy's hat.
Larder	Food storage container.
Lariat	A rope consisting of animal hair, hemp or synthetic material.
Latigo	A long leather strap used to fasten the saddle to the horse

attached at each "D" ring.

Lead Steer	Usually very large. Likes to lead the herd and acts like he knows it all. Remind you of your mother-in-law?
Line Shack	A building far away in an inaccessible area designed to house cowboys overnight or extended periods while away from the main ranch.
Lobo	Spanish word for wolf.
Long Horn	A Texas breed of cattle noted for their long horns.
Mail Order Cowboy	All decked out in western cowboy gear but nothing fits and isn't worn right.
Makin's	The tobacco used by cowboys to be rolled into a thin paper and smoked. Bull Durham and Lucky Strikes came in small bags with a drawstring.
Mare	Usually defined as breeding stock.
Maverick	A cow that has no brand whose ownership is not established.
Mescal	110 proof hard Mexican liquor with a worm in each bottle.
Mesquite	A tree growing to 10-15 feet in height and excellent firewood.
Morale	A gunny or burlap feed bag that has been cut on both sides to make a holder for grain and is tied or slipped over the horse's muzzle and tied behind the ears.
The Morales	Brothers who owned a large Mexican land grant in Old Mexico near Douglas, Arizona.
Mule	A cross between a jackass stud and a mare horse.
Mustanger	A cowboy engaged in roping or trapping wild horses. Also not opposed to checking out a brother or two.
Naco	A town in Old Mexico along the Arizona/Mexico border.
Neck Tie Party	A hanging.
Night Hawk	A night rider who keeps watch over a cattle or horse herd during the night.
Ocotillo	A form of bush 3/4 inch in diameter, 8-10 feet in height with large spikes top to bottom. Good fence building material.
One Horse Outfit	A small ranch or spread; sometimes called the old ranch.
Pachuco	Mexicans banded together to form a gang.

Pack Saddle	Used to carry your trappings or supplies to the mountains or from ranch to ranch.
Paint	Not a favorite type or color of horse. Not an easy learner nor quick on its feet.
Palomino	A golden-dun colored horse with silver or flaxen mane and tail.
Peacemaker	Usually referred to as a .45 caliber six-shooter. Five of the cartridges in the chamber were the law, the sixth one was justice.
Pigging String	A 3/8 inch thick rope approximately four foot long used to tie the three feet of a calf while restraining him.
Pistol	Cowboy slang for a tenderfoot rider. Mexican bandits often called "pistoleros." Commonly known as a six-shooter, peacemaker, hogleg, or handgun.
Pommel	That forward portion of a saddle that ropes are tied to. Often called the saddle horn.
Proud Cut	A horse that has had one testicle removed. Quite often a troublemaker.
Pritchel	A large metal spike.
Quirt	A hand-braided leather whip approximately 18 inches in length with three pieces of leather loose on one end. Designed to get a horse's attention.
Rank Horse	A horse that was unbroken or remained half broke forever.
Remuda	A group of horses confined and ready to catch and ride.
Rawhide	A part of a cow's hide that was a working hand's staple. Used to lash or secure anything.
Rawhide Latigo	The sinew of a cow that has been tanned.
Recurve	Type of design of bow.
Reins	Two leather straps six foot in length, extended down each side of the horse's neck and attached to each side of the bridle bit in the horse's mouth. This is the cowboy's steering mechanism.
Reata	A braided rawhide catch rope usually 44 feet in length, often Mexican made.
Ride Out	A horse broken to a green stage.
Ridge	That portion of a mountain range that rises higher than the bottom of the valley.

Rifle	A long barreled pistol designed to reach targets farther than a pistol could shoot.
Rim	A term used to describe an path around a ridge passing the valleys and washes.
Rough String	A group of horses destined to be working cow horses and usually rented out for a dollar a saddle per day.
Running "W"	A device used to stop or manner a rank or barn-soured horse.
Running Iron	Usually a two piece iron rod curved on the end, portable and used by "wide loopers." Easily carried or concealed branding iron; illegal in some states.
Rustler	Someone borrowing your cattle without your permission.
Sabino	A horse with a pure white belly and pink to red all over.
Sacking Out	Tying all four legs of a horse and pulling blankets, and all manner of objects over him, until he gentles and has no fear.
Saddle	Pre-ordained to toughen a man's posterior beyond its intended limits.
Sky Pilot	A nickname affectionately given a preacher.
Snubbing Post	A very large post securely placed in the center of a corral to snub rowdy horses while breaking, saddling and gentling. Similar to a "lodge pole" in your house.
Sombrero	A unique Mexican styled hat with a large brim.
Spurs	A persuasive way to get a horse to take you from here to there faster than he wants to.
Stallion	Usually heavy jawed, stout and often bad-mannered and always looking everywhere for the ladies
Stampede	300 to 400 cattle bearing down on you with no intention of stopping or turning.
Stirrup	A boot holder for the rider, one on each side of the saddle.
Sunfisher	A bronc horse that can buck to the east while headed to the west.
Syveno	Matching or unmatching eyes on a horse that have the appearance of glass eyes.
Tack	A cowboy's saddle and gear.
Tapadero	Foot covers for your boots when they're in the stirrups.
Transite	Asbestos and cement mixture, used in construction of

Sheets	buildings.
Vaqueros	Mexican cowboys. Good horse handlers, poor fighters.
Waddy	A young cowboy.
War Bag	Bag containing personal things like clothes or a lock of hair from a pretty lady.
Wash	Usually an old river bed that lies in the bottom of a valley.
Wide Looping	Cattle rustling.
Widow Maker	A killer horse.
Winchester	A favorite rifle of mountain men, miners, cowboys, Indians and Cavalry.
Withers	That portion of a horse's back directly above the front shoulder.

About the author...

Karen D. Fisher resides in the Sierra foothills of Northern California with her husband and the youngest two of her eight children. She studied at the University of California at Berkeley, California State University at Sacramento, and earned her degree in history from The Union Institute.

In addition to writing personal histories, she works as an independent litigation paralegal, enjoys family activities and travels whenever possible. The first draft of "The Gringo Kid" earned her The Union Institute's Academic Excellence Award in 1996.

About Tom Fisk...

Known in his youth as the Gringo Kid, Tom Fisk now resides in El Dorado County, California. His compelling younger years belie his businessman life; today Tom owns and is CEO of a medical instrument company. Between the years of living on the plains of Arizona and Mexico and his life today, Tom fell in love with and married Gay McNeil, gave up his "Gringo Kid ways," graduated from college, taught farriery and blacksmithing, and raised four children.

Tom's memories reached a crescendo some 50 years after his Gringo Kid days when he then resolutely started telling his heretofore untold stories. Tom regales his audience with tales of bravery, youth, foolishness — all passages of a young boy growing up alone in an untamed West.